Movement and Mimesis
The idea of Dance in the Sanskritic Tradition

Movement and Mimesis

The Idea of Dance in the Sanskritic Tradition

by

Mandakranta Bose

PRINTWORLD

Publishers of Indian Traditions

Cataloging in Publication Data — DK
[Courtesy: D.K. Agencies (P) Ltd. <docinfo@dkagencies.com>]

Bose, Mandakranta, 1938- **author.**
Movement and mimesis : the idea of dance in the Sanskritic tradition / by Mandakranta Bose.
pages cm
Includes passages in Sanskrit; with English translation.
"Indian edition first published in 2007" – Title page verso.
Includes bibliographical references and index.
ISBN 9788124604212

1. Dance – India – History. 2. Sanskrit language – Texts.
I. Title.

LCC GV1693.B595 2022 | DDC 793.31954 23

ISBN 978-81-246-0421-2
Indian edition first published in 2007
Second impression 2022

Reprint from the English language edition: Movement and Mimesis
By Mandakranta Bose

Printed and published by:
D.K. Printworld (P) Ltd.
Regd. office : "Vedaśrī", F-395, Sudarshan Park
(Metro Station : ESI Hospital) New Delhi – 110015
Phones : (011) 25453975; 25466019
e-mail: indology@dkprintworld.com
Web: www.dkprintworld.com

To my mother

Bina Roy Choudhury

CONTENTS

ACKNOWLEDGEMENTS

My first guide to the study of literature on dancing was Professor Thomas Burrow whose kindness and guidance has always been my inspiration and under whom I began to explore this field at Oxford twenty-five years ago. The first fruit of this was my B. Litt. dissertation, which later led to a guide-book to the technical terms used in the Sanskrit literature on dancing. Following upon that beginning, through the last two decades I gathered material to write this history of the evolution of concepts of dancing as recorded in the Sanskritic tradition.

It is a pleasure to record my thanks to my friends and colleagues. During my research at Oxford the critical advice of Alexis Sanderson and Jonathan Katz was invaluable. To Professor Bimal Matilal I am indebted for both moral and scholarly support. Professors Richard Gombrich and Samjukta Gupta have helped me with many details as has Professor G.C. Tripathi of Allahabad. I am grateful to Professor Ken Bryant of the University of British Columbia for the use of computer typography designed by him. One of my deepest debts is to Professor Arindam Chakravarti for suggesting the title of this book.

The Spalding Trust has placed me under a debt of gratitude by awarding me a Trustee's grant. I am also grateful to the Social Sciences and Humanities Research Council of Canada for a fellowship. To the Department of Asian Studies, University of British Columbia I owe thanks for the use of computer facilities.

My greatest debt is to my husband Tirthankar, whose criticism and help sustained me through the period of writing. My daughter and my son, Sarika and Pablo, have patiently borne my frequent absences. Without the support of my family I could not have completed this book.

ABBREVIATIONS

Abh.Dar.	*Abhinaya Darpaṇa*
A.B.	*Abhinavabhāratī*
Ad. Lib.	*Adyar Library*
AP	*Agni Purāṇa*
A. Soc. MS.	*Asiatic Society Manuscript*
DR.	*Daśarūpaka*
G.O.S.	*Gaekwad Oriental Series*
KĀ	*Kāvyādarśa*
KAnu.H.	*Kāvyānuśāsana of Hemacandra*
KAnu.V.	*Kāvyānuśāsana of Vāgbhaṭṭa*
KAlam.	*Kāvyālaṁkāra*
KS	*Kāmasūtra*
NN.	*Nartananirṇaya*
NLRK	*Nāṭakalakṣaṇaratnakośa*
N.D.	*Nāṭyadarpaṇa*
NŚ.	*Nāṭyaśāstra*
NR.	*Nṛtyaratnāvalī*
NRK.	*Nṛtyaratnakośa*
Nṛ. Adh.	*Nṛtyādhyāya*
Bh. Ar.	*Bharatārṇava*
Bh.P.	*Bḥāvaprakāśana*
Mā.	*Mālavikāgnimitra*
Mānas.	*Mānasollāsa*
RK.	*Rasakaumudī*
VDP.	*Viṣṇudharmottara Purāṇa*
ŚTR.	*Śivatattvaratnātakara*
Śṛ.P.	*Śṛṅgāraprakāśa*

SKA.	*Sarasvatīkaṇṭhābharaṇa*
SadC.	*Sadrāgacandrodaya*
SUS.	*Saṅgītopaniṣatsāroddhāra*
SC.	*Saṅgīta Candra*
SN.	*Saṅgītanārāyaṇa*
SDar.	*Saṅgīta Darpaṇa*
SDām.	*Saṅgīta Dāmodara*
SMak.	*Saṅgīta Makaranda*
SMak.V	*Saṅgīta Makaranda of Vedasūri*
SR.	*Saṅgīta Ratnākara*
SSam.	*Saṅgīta Samayasāra*
SSār.	*Saṅgītasārasaṁgraha*
S.D.	*Sāhitya Darpaṇa*
HM.	*Hastamuktāvalī*
HR.	*Hastaratnāvalī*

PREFACE

The most comprehensive view of the evolution of dancing in India is one that is derived from Sanskrit textual sources. These texts are the basic material that students of the dance in India must examine in order to uncover its past. Since the rebirth of informed interest in dancing in early twentieth century, its antiquity has been acknowledged but precisely what the art was in antiquity remains unclear. Discovering the oldest forms of dancing in India requires, as do other historical quests, a reconstruction of the past and, again as in other historical investigations, the primary sources of knowledge are records from the past. In this case the records are treatises and manuals in Sanskrit that discuss and describe dancing. These are the sources that the present work sets out to mine.

These texts taken collectively are more than records of a particular state of the art. They testify to the growth of the theory and practice of the art and thus establish it as an evolving rather than a fixed art form that changed as much in response to its own expanding aesthetic boundaries as to parallel or complementary forms of dance, drama and music that impinged upon it as India's social and political situation changed. When we place the Sanskrit treatises in chronological sequence it becomes clear that the understanding of the art has changed through time, in its infancy as well as in maturer periods. Following these changes through the treatises is essential to an historical investigation because not only do theoretical discussions in the texts reflect dancing as it was but the practice of dancing in turn seems sometimes to have followed the precepts laid down in the texts correlating dancing with other performing arts and setting its aesthetic objectives.

These texts are part of a tradition of discourse in the arts that was at once scholarly and practical. The earliest extant example of this tradition is the *Nāṭyaśāstra* of Bharata Muni, in which all the performing arts of the time are discussed and in which dancing is regarded as a technique for adding the beauty of bodily motion to dramatic performances. An ancillary to drama rather than an independent art, dancing carried no meaning and elicited no emotional response. In the works of later writers, however, its autonomy was recognized as also its ability to express thoughts and feelings and it began to be discussed fully in works devoted particularly to it rather than in works on drama or poetics–a clear sign of its growing importance in India's cultural life.

Bharata's work, however, remained of seminal importance. His description of the body movements in dancing and their interrelationship not only provided the taxonomy for all subsequent authors on dancing but much of the information on its actual technique. But Bharata described only what he considered to be artistically the most cultivated of all the existing dance styles, leaving out regional and popular varieties. These styles, similar in their basic technique to Bharata's style but comprising new types of movements and methods of composition, began to be included in later studies. These later works, most notably the *Saṅgītaratnākara* of Śārṅgadeva and the *Nartananirṇaya* of Puṇḍarīka Viṭṭhala, indicate a shift of emphasis towards previously neglected styles whereby the art of dancing underwent substantial structural and aesthetic changes. By the 16th century the newer styles came to occupy the central position in the accounts of contemporary dancing and coalesced into a distinct tradition that has remained essentially unchanged to the present time. This is the tradition, the present study argues, from which the present-day dance styles of India are directly derived, for modern styles, such as Kathak and Odissi, show striking parallels to techniques found only in the treatises of the later tradition, not in works of the earlier tradition of Bharata.

Necessarily, this study rests on an understanding of the technical terms of dancing, to facilitate which a glossary is appended at the end of the book.[1]

This study begins by setting out the broad periods into which the texts fall. Next, chapter 2 offers a chronological review of all the extant and available Sanskrit works on dancing, including works that discuss dancing as part of a larger interest in the performing arts in general. In doing so, the dating and interrelationship of some of the texts are considered This is followed in chapter 3 by a close examination of Bharata's views on dancing, including its legendary origin, its purpose and function, its types, and its relationship to drama and acting. Chapter 4 deals with lāsya, a type of performance basic to Bharata's understanding of the dramatic arts, which has caused much confusion because of the attempt of later authors to categorize it as dancing. In chapter 5 we turn to nṛtya and uparūpaka, which became major elements of the conception of dancing after Bharata but, like lāsya, were variously understood. Chapter 6 discusses a new method of categorizing dance forms that was devised in the early seventeenth century: the categories were bandha and anibandha, which seem to have been adapted from the literature of music to indicate two distinct systems, the formulaic and the non-formulaic, of structuring dance performances. These terms manifest an altogether new approach to dancing that signalled a widening of the dancer's technical and aesthetic horizons and one that corresponded with the growing strength of new forms. These forms, broadly classified under the rubric deśī, coalesced into a distinct tradition that assimilated older forms; this later tradition is the subject of chapter 7. Chapter 8 concludes the study by summarizing the historical process of the development of dancing in India as found in the texts examined here and arguing that this process was one of building upon rather than imitating the past. The process, therefore, was a flexible one

---

[1]For fuller explanations of these terms, see my *Classical Indian Dancing: A Glossary* (Calcutta: General Printers, 1970).

that permitted the assimilation of new forms and techniques and the redefinition of its purpose, function and aesthetic scope. This flexibility explains why the dance in India has not merely survived but has continued to develop, even though sometimes at an uneven pace, through centuries of social and political turmoil.

Chapter 1

INTRODUCTION

The literature of dance in India is vast, with a wealth of manuals and theoretical treatises in Sanskrit dating back to the early Christian era. Although the majority of these works have been available for a long time, systematic research on them is a comparatively recent development. As a result, these works have not been exhaustively mined for material relating to the evolution of dancing. A number of authors in the early part of this century briefly noticed dancing in course of discussing various aspects of drama and music, as for example, D. R. Mankad in his *The Types of Sanskrit Drama* or Ananda Coomaraswamy in *The Mirror of Gesture,* [1] but it did not receive the same degree of scholarly treatment that music and drama enjoyed. Some attempts were indeed made to classify and describe the major types of classical dancing in works such as those by Kay Ambrose, Faubion Bowers and Beryl de Zoete.[2] But rigorous research into the art and its history came later with the work of scholars such as V. Raghavan, K.M. Varma and Kapila Vatsyayan. A highly analytical study of the basic concepts of the dance drawn from such texts was that of K. M. Varma.[3] In a number of articles on *saṅgīta* literature and in his editions of the *Śṛṅgāraprakāśa* and the *Nṛttaratnāvalī,* V. Raghavan has shed light upon aspects of dance as described in Sanskrit sources.[4]

---

1 Mankad,1936; Coomaraswamy,1917.

2 Ambrose,1950; Bowers,1953; Zoete,1953.

3 Varma,1957.

4 Raghavan,1956; 1957; 1960; 1961; 1965; 1978.

The most extensive study so far of the non-specialist literature of dancing is that of Kapila Vatsyayan who has examined the Vedas, Brāhmaṇas, Upaniṣads, epics, purāṇas, grammatical literature, lexicons, gṛhyasūtra, dharmasūtra, the Arthaśāstra, the Kāmasūtra, Buddhist and Jaina texts and kāvya literature.[5] On the basis of this extensive search Vatsyayan presents a view of classical Indian dancing that is as analytical as it is informative. But essential as her work is to the understanding of the place of dance in Indian cultural history, her book does not offer a comprehensive survey of the Sanskrit manuals on dancing, concentrating rather on works from the earliest till the thirteenth century and selectively highlighting texts from the seventeenth and eighteenth centuries to show the continuation of the *Nāṭyaśāstra*'s tradition. Surprisingly, she leaves out Abhinavagupta's commentary on the *Nāṭyaśāstra.* Nevertheless, her survey of the vast body of early non-specialist literature forms a necessary complement to the account of specialist dance manuals attempted in the present study.

A systematic and exhaustive study of all the available Sanskrit treatises with a view to tracing the evolution of classical Indian dance concepts has not been undertaken so far. Yet in their detailed descriptions and careful commentaries these treatises offer us the fullest range of materials to reconstruct the body of dance theory and technique from the earliest times. Further, because these works span at least fifteen hundred years, they also mark the stages in the growth of the art-form. They thus form the primary source of the view presented here of classical Indian dancing.

References to dancing and dancers appear in the earliest literature of India even before the dance became a subject of study in its own right. First mentioned in the Vedas, dancing is referred to in a wide range of works, including the purāṇas and works in such varied disciplines as

---

[5] Vatsyayan,1968; see also Bose,1970

arthaśāstra, smṛtiśāstra, alaṁkāraśāstra,[6] and in seminal works such as Pāṇini's writings and the *Kāmasūtra*.[7] Technical terms of dancing occur in many works that are not specifically on dance or music, [8] suggesting that dancing was a well-known and developed art in early Hindu society. That there were also manuals of dancing in this early period is evident from Pāṇini's reference to the naṭasūtras, or guidelines for naṭas, by Śilālin and Kṛśāśva.[9] However, these are merely passing references and offer no clear view of the nature of the dancing of the time.

The earliest extant textual source for dancing is the *Nāṭyaśāstra* of Bharata Muni, which deals with dancing within the general area of the dramatic arts. While it is possible that works on dancing existed before Bharata's time, none has survived, possibly because Bharata's authoritative account made previous ones redundant. The authority that the *Nāṭyaśāstra* has exerted over all subsequent works on dancing is due not only to its chronological priority but also to the range of subjects it covers, from stage architecture to body movements. Scholarly opinion differs as to the date of the work, generally placing it between the 2nd century B.C. and the 2nd century A.D.[10] Whether it was the inspiration provided by

---

6 *Arthaśāstra*. 2. 27. 25; *Manusmṛti*. 4. 64, 12.45; dancing is discussed in a number of works on poetics, starting with the *Daśarūpaka* in the tenth century, down to the *Sāhityadarpaṇa* in the fourteenth.

7 *Kāmasūtra*. 1. 6.

8 *Vidhurapaṇḍita Jātaka*. (according to Varadapande, 1975, pp. 29-34); *Rājapraśnīya Sūtra*. 1. 23.; *Kuṭṭanīmatam*, pp. 220-29; *Karpūramañjarī*. Act I. 6, Act III. 14, Act IV. 9,10; *Mālavikāgnimitram*. Act I. prose passage following the prastāvanā; prose following verse 19; *Ratnāvalī*. Act I. prose passage following verse 5, 12, 16; *Nāgānanda*. Act. I. prose passage following verse 3.

9 Pāṇini, *Aṣṭādhyāyī*. 4.3.110-11.

10 Kane, 1961, p. 47; Krishnamachariar, 1974, p.852. It is difficult to determine the date of the *Nāṭyaśāstra* with any certainty. But it is likely that it was written before the chapters on dance in the *Viṣṇudharmottarapurāṇa*, since the latter–like all texts subsequent to the *NŚ*– understands the term lāsya to mean a form of dance, whereas

Bharata's scholarship or the heightened popularity of dancing that inspired interest in dancing as a subject cannot be known but the Nāṭyaśāstra was followed by a considerable body of literature on the subject. Sanskrit literature of the early Christian era has a great many references to works that evidently described dance techniques. Most of these works are lost but extensive quotations from many of them found in other works indicate the wealth of the material.[11]

In discussing dancing Bharata's concern was with a style that he evidently considered as one that formed the central and dominant tradition of the art in his time.[12] In describing it he established a framework of classification and description that all subsequent writers followed in principle, although in the details of the actual body movements they sometimes differed. This tradition of scholarship survived till the nineteenth century, after which no original work in Sanskrit is known to have been written, and the works that have come down since the eighteenth century are mostly in the vernaculars of the regions in which dancing flourished. Most of the Sanskrit works now extant were written between the eleventh and the seventeenth centuries, and these, while they follow the *Nāṭyaśāstra* in the main in their accounts, often attempt to fit into Bharata's framework altogether new types of body movements representing regional variations. One of the most important contributions

---

Bharata considered it to be a dramatic presentation. The portion on dance in the *VDP.* is believed to have been written around the fifth century A.D.

11 Almost all the manuals on dancing as well as the commentaries on the manuals quote from earlier authorities. Abhinavagupta, Śārṅgadeva, Kallinātha, Mahārāṇā Kumbhā, Vedasūri are some of the authors who quote extensively from earlier authors. One of the most often quoted sources is the lost work by Kohala.

12 *NŚ.* 9. 163-4; 25.116; 119, 123. Sculptural evidence from different regions of India dating from the first century A. D. gives us a good idea of how extensively the art had spread throughout India. Among these the dance figures at the gates of the Sāñchī Stupas,in the caves of Udayagiri or in Amarāvatī are early representatives of the tradition found in the *Nāṭyaśāstra*. See Vatsyayan,1968, pp. 262-332.

to the discussion of regional styles is that of the *Saṅgītaratnākara.* The texts that followed it from the sixteenth to the eighteenth century drew heavily upon it, although with their own variations. Evidently, the example of the *Saṅgītaratnākara* encouraged interest in regional varieties, for its successors began more and more to incorporate regional terms.

Interestingly enough, these later works show two shaping forces at work. First, the framework of movement they describe is essentially that of the *Nāṭyaśāstra*; second, breaking away from the principal interest of that work, they describe regional styles following the *Saṅgītaratnākara.* Recognizing the difference between these types of movements, the later authors term Bharata's tradition as mārga, that is, the way established as of old, and the later tradition as deśī, that is, provincial or regional.

Given that the early as well as the later works on dancing move within the framework of description set up by Bharata, it is essential to examine that framework closely. Yet, given also that by his own admission Bharata does not deal with the many styles peripheral to his central tradition (*NŚ.* 9. 163-64), it is equally essential to examine the later works thoroughly in order to understand the evolution of the dance concepts in India, especially since, as will be argued in this study, it is the later, regional tradition that has directly shaped the styles of dancing we see in contemporary India.

The literature of dancing carries out two main tasks. In the first place, the works identify and describe the body movements required in dancing. Secondly, they also employ, though few discuss with clarity, certain concepts about the nature and categories of dancing. On both levels developments can be seen at various times and I am persuaded by the literature to divide them into three periods. The first period is that which ends with Abhinavagupta in the tenth century of the Christian era. Few works from this period are extant but this scarcity is more than adequately met by the most important of all works in the genre, the *Nāṭyaśāstra,* with which the period began. Appropriately, the end of this period is marked by yet another major contribution to the discussion, Abhinavagupta's commentary on the *Nāṭyaśāstra*. Also, some light on the art is thrown indirectly by references to it in the literatures of alaṁkāra and kāvya, as also in the general prose works of the era. At this time dance was mainly considered to be an auxiliary to drama. The legend of its birth as recorded by Bharata suggests that it existed as an independent art-form.[13] However, while dancing was indeed an independent art-form, it is evident that it was considered chiefly as an art that lent beauty to a dramatic performance.

Although we do not have too many works on dancing from this early period, there is reason to believe that quite a few were actually written. Bharata himself says that the material he does not cover in the *Nāṭyaśāstra* will be dealt with by Kohala in his study :

> शेषमुत्तरतन्त्रेण कोहलस्तु करिष्यति। (*NŚ.* 37. 18.)
> However, Kohala will explain [lit:do] the rest through a supplementary treatise.

This work by Kohala, unfortunately lost, was evidently most authoritative, for virtually every Sanskrit writer on dancing quotes from it or at least refers to it. Also mentioned, though not to the same extent, are treatises by Bhaṭṭatota, Bhaṭṭatanḍu, Śaṅkuka and Lollaṭa, none of which has come down to us. Dattila and Mataṅga are important writers on music who are believed to have written on dancing as well though their works on dance again have not survived.

The second period spans the eleventh to the fifteenth century. It was in this period that most of the extant works on dance and music were written and new trends in dancing recorded. Dance began to be discussed in its

---

13 मयाऽपीदं स्मृतं नृत्तं सन्ध्याकालेषु नृत्यता।
नानाकरणसंयुक्तैरङ्गहारैर्विभूषितम् ॥
पूर्वरङ्गविधावस्मिंस्त्वयासम्यक् प्रयोज्यताम् । *NŚ.* 4. 13-14.
[See p. 109 *infra* for a translation.]

own right rather than as an adjunct to drama, just as music, both vocal and instrumental, was being similarly regarded as an art that had an independent existence outside dramatic performances. These two art-forms comprised a particular discipline that came to be known as saṅgīta, and since they were seen as complementary arts, the manuals on that discipline dealt with both dance and vocal and instrumental music, although the emphasis might vary. Indeed, the *Nṛttaratnāvalī* of Jāya Senāpati is the only work from this period that is wholly devoted to dance alone, and even this is very likely part of a larger project covering music as well, for Jāya himself refers to the companion piece to the work, his *Gītaratnāvalī*.[14]

It was during this second period that a distinction began to be made by writers on dancing between the mārga and deśī styles. The classical style was acknowledged to be the one codified by Bharata in the *Nāṭyaśāstra* and taken to form the core of the entire tradition of the art. But it was also recognized at this time that the many regional and popular styles were equally part of that tradition and therefore needed to be recorded. Another major development recorded in the texts from this period was the appearance of dance dramas. These, discussed in a later chapter, were not simply dramas to which dancing was added as an ornament as in an earlier age but an altogether new genre in which dance permeated the whole form.

In the third period, beginning in the sixteenth century and ending in the nineteenth, the texts record a further development of the tradition, and as we shall see in the course of this study, it is the shape that dance took at this time which we see today. In brief, the texts from this period testify to the growing popularity of the dance, for not only is an increasing variety of regional forms recorded in the manuals but a number of manuals in regional languages begin to appear. In Andhra, in particular, dance flourished throughout this period, as we find from Raghavan's extensive

14 Raghavan, 1965. Introduction, pp. 12,36; text, p. 172.

account of the dance literature in Telugu.[15] Another region from which a number of texts came was Orissa, as noted in a survey by D. N. Patnaik.[16] Dance manuals were produced also in the regional languages of Manipur, Maharashtra and the region now known as Tamil Nadu, and although no systematic account of these texts has been made as yet, their existence attests as much to the codification of the art as to the widespread interest in it. However, while these works in the vernaculars provide a great deal of detailed information about dances of the time, they show no development in the fundamental concepts of dancing. The importance of these regional texts lies in the information they give about regional dance forms, thus providing supplemental information unavailable from Sanskrit sources. However, for the main body of the dance traditions of the time, the extant Sanskrit texts still remain our most comprehensive source. An account of these texts, their particular contributions and their relationship to one another will therefore form the subject of the next chapter.

15 *Ibid.*, Introduction, pp. 18-34.

16 Patnaik, 1971.

Chapter 2

THE LITERATURE OF DANCE

The earliest extant Sanskrit work on music, drama and dance, and also the most influential as a source of both technical description and aesthetic understanding is the *Nāṭyaśāstra,* which is believed to have been written not later than the 2nd century A. D.[1] The work deals with dramaturgy and the arts allied to drama in thirty-seven chapters, of which those of interest to students of dancing are chapters 4, 5, 8-12, 19, 21, 22, 25 and 31. The fourth chapter discusses tāṇḍavavidhi, that is, the rules of tāṇḍava or dancing.[2] In this chapter Bharata mentions five concepts that help to define the art of dancing. These concepts, nṛtta, tāṇḍava, abhinaya, piṇḍībandha and sukumāraprayoga, are discussed in a separate chapter of the present study. Bharata's interest in the fourth chapter is centred on nṛtta, that is, non-representational dancing and valued for the beauty of its form. He describes this dance style in detail, giving the basic units of composite movements known as karaṇas, and the basic choreographic sequences known as aṅgahāras. In addition, he describes group dances and mentions the use of body movements in acting without giving details.[3] Bharata speaks of these movements as necessary parts of the preliminaries of a dramatic presentation.

The fifth chapter of the *Nāṭyaśāstra* continues the discussion of those preliminaries. In the eighth to the twelfth chapter Bharata describes in detail the movements of every part of the body down to the smallest,

---

[1] Kane,1961, p. 47. The date has not been precisely set as yet. See note 10 , chapter 1.

[2] *NŚ*. 4.320.

[3] *NŚ*. 4.279-283.

dividing them into two classes, the aṅgas and the upāṅgas, or major and minor parts of the body. He shows how the different movements are combined into composite movements known as cārīs, maṇḍalas, and sthānas that are in turn combined into karaṇas, which again are put together to create aṅgahāras.

The eighth chapter is devoted to the movements of the head, eyelids, eyebrows, pupils, the nose, cheeks, lips, the chin, the mouth and the neck, while the ninth is given to the movements of the hands, chest, sides, belly, waist, thighs, shanks and the feet. Both chapters describe the use of these movements in conveying meaning, but also included are hand-gestures meant for abstract dancing rather than for acting. The tenth chapter describes cārīs, which are movements using one leg and are used both in dance and drama. Similarly used are sthānas, or postures, which form part of this chapter; examples of these postures occur widely in temple sculpture. Bharata goes on to describe maṇḍalas, which are more complicated movements of the legs involving cārīs. In addition to describing these movements Bharata speaks of the general principles of effective exercise, vyāyāma, as well as aesthetic satisfaction, sauṣṭhava.[4] The eleventh chapter elaborates on maṇḍalas, while the twelfth describes gati, or gaits.

Although Bharata's subject is nṛtta, that is, dancing in its abstract form, in this five chapter long section he explains the meaning attached to individual body movements and thus recognizes by implication the possibility of conveying meaning through dancing.[5] Such uses of body movements for enhancing dramatic expression is termed āṅgikābhinaya by Bharata. That dancing was in fact used for dramatic purposes is evident

[4] *NŚ* . 10. 92-94, 97-103.

[5] *NŚ*.9.219.

from other works on dancing as well as from descriptions of play production.[6]

The nineteenth chapter considers the constituents of lāsya, a dramatic form that is created from delicate body movements and, in Bharata's conception, falls between dance and drama. Chapter twenty-one deals with āhāryābhinaya, that is, the use of costumes, stage properties and other external aids which are essential both to dance and drama. An important concept of presentation discussed in this chapter is the distinction between the lokadharmī and nāṭyadharmī modes of presentation, corresponding to natural and stylized modes.

In chapter twenty-two Bharata takes up the general technique of expression in acting, calling it sāmānyābhinaya, and gives directions for expressing states of mind and responses to sensory experience, such as touching or smelling. These movements are considered to be usually self-explanatory, so that although they are codified into a discipline, they are not seen as stylized, with special, symbolic meanings attached to them. The hand-gestures in this category, for instance, are formed with the purpose of imitating objects. By contrast, chapter twenty-five describes the special mode of citrābhinaya, in which each movement carries a particular meaning specific to it. The thirty-first chapter is partly on tāla, or rhythm, but it also goes back to the subject of lāsya, describing the movements and the music required for each of its several varieties.

As this survey shows, the framework within which Bharata describes dancing is largely that of drama and his interest in discussing even nṛtta appears to lie in examining how it can beautify a dramatic presentation. While the authors who came after him virtually copied his descriptions, they did not continue this approach and in the later works we no longer find dancing treated only as a supplement to drama.

---

[6]See *A.B.* on the *NŚ.* Vol.I. 1956, pp. 181,191.;*DR.* 1.10; *ŚṛP.* vol. II. pp.423-24;*NR.* 1.29;.and Rāghavabhaṭṭa's commentary on *Abhijñānaśakuntalā*,ed. Kale 1902.

The treatise next to the *Nāṭyaśāstra* in time is the *Viṣṇudharmottara Purāṇā.* It has been variously dated but the editor of the text places it between the fifth and the seventh centuries,[7] while Pingree assigns the parts on dancing and painting to the first half of the fifth century; Ludo Rocher has discussed the arguments for the different dates in detail in his volume on the history of Purāṇa literature.[8] Close scrutiny of the text, however, leaves little room for doubt that the *Nāṭyaśāstra* antedates the *Viṣṇudharmottara Purāṇa.* The thirtieth chapter of the *Viṣṇudharmottara Purāṇa* enumerates the rasas as nine; the number given in the *Nāṭyaśāstra* is eight. It is far likelier that Bharata's classification was expanded by the author of the *Viṣṇudharmottara Purāṇa* than that his nine classes were shrunk to eight by Bharata.

The *Viṣṇudharmottara Purāṇa* deals with dancing in its third section, chapters twenty to thirty-four. In chapter twenty the author follows the *Nāṭyaśāstra* in describing the abstract dance form, nṛtta, and in defining its function as one of beautifying a dramatic presentation. But the author differs from Bharata in dividing dance into two categories which he calls nāṭya and lāsya. He thus includes both nāṭya and lāsya in the same genre, that of dance, which is a conceptual departure from Bharata. This chapter also specifies the appropriate places for the performance of each category, discussing aspects of the stage and the presentation of the preliminaries. The discussion includes the characteristics of actors , the four different types of abhinayas, namely, āṅgika, vācika, sāttvika and āhārya, and the names of all the complicated movements necessary for the composition of a dance sequence. In addition, the author briefly touches upon the piṇḍībandhas or group dances mentioned by Bharata and goes on to describe vṛtti, pravṛtti and siddhi, that is style, the means of application and the nature of competence.

---

[7] *VDP,* 1958, G.O.S. ed. P.Shah, vol. I, Introduction, pp.xxvi.

[8] Rocher, 1986, pp. 250-52.

The twenty-first chapter discusses sthānas or postures while lying down, while the twenty-second deals with the sthānas assumed while sitting. The focus of these two chapters seems to be on dramatic presentation. In this the *Viṣṇudharmottara Purāṇa* seems to agree with Bharata in considering the whole subject as part of dramatic presentation. The twenty-third chapter is devoted to postures meant for both men and women. The twenty-fourth chapter lists the movements of the major limbs, the aṅgas, along with the meaning attached to each of them. The major limbs, according to this text, are the head, the neck, the chest, the sides, the waist, the thighs, the shaṅks and the feet. In conclusion, the chapter defines the cārī and the karaṇa, the two vital and complicated movements required in dancing. In the twenty-fifth chapter the movements of the upāṅgas or minor limbs are discussed, including the glances that express rasa and sthāyī and vyabhicāribhāvas, the movements of the pupils, eyebrows, nose, tongue and lips as well as the application of these movements.

The twenty-sixth chapter describes three types of hand-gestures, those made with one hand, those made with both–along with the meanings they can convey–and hand-gestures meant for dancing, which convey no meaning. The twenty-seventh chapter is devoted to the explanation of different kinds of abhinaya and the costumes and decorations necessary for a performance. The next chapter, the twenty-eighth, deals with sāmānyābhinaya, giving general directions for expressing different moods and responses to seeing, touching and smelling objects. Although the author designates this chapter as a discussion of sāmānyābhinaya, he includes citrābhinaya, that is, special presentations. In fact, this chapter is a conflation of the contents of chapters twenty-two and twenty-five of the *Nāṭyaśāstra* and contains extensive quotations from it.[9] The twenty-ninth

---

[9] *NŚ*. 22. 81-5 ; *VDP*. 3. 28. 2-4; *NŚ*. 25. 2-8; *VDP*. 3. 28. 10-15.

chapter describes the gatis, that is, gaits, the thirtieth discusses the nine rasas, and the thirty-first the bhāvas.

A new feature of the treatment of body movements that is added to the discussion of body movements appears in the thirty-second chapter, which deals with what is termed rahasyamudrās, that is, hand-gestures meant for mystical and ritualistic purposes. Continuing the discussion in the thirty-third chapter, the author lists more mudrās, all meant for religious purposes, and calls them mudrāhastas,[10] and associates them with hymns to the gods and goddesses.[11] We must note that the word used in these chapters is not hasta but mudrā, a term connoting religious practices. The use of the term mudrā to denote hand-gestures is found in no other text on dancing. In the medieval period the term mudrā was used in dance literature to mean a pleasing appearance (*NN.* 36a; *SDar.* 7.107). However, in common usage today, all hand-gestures used in dancing are called mudrās and the more accurate term hasta has gone out of use.

The thirty-fourth and final chapter on dancing is devoted to the legend of the origin of dancing. Since the work is devoted to the worship of Viṣṇu, it is not surprising that its author should view Viṣṇu as the propounder of the art of dancing, but in every other text it is Śiva who remains as the god who introduced dancing to mankind.

Our next source of information is a commentary on the *Nāṭyaśāstra* by Abhinavagupta, who lived in Kashmir sometime in the late tenth and early eleventh century A.D.[12] Abhinavagupta's commentary is known as the *Abhinavabhāratī.* It is not known whether the commentary was on the entire *Nāṭyaśāstra;* but what has come down to us follows the *Nāṭyaśāstra* chapter by chapter except for the seventh, the eighth, and the thirty-third to thirty-seventh. It is available now as part of Ramakrishna Kavi's

---

[10] *VDP.* 3. 33. 123.

[11] *Ibid.* 3. 33. 124.

[12] Krishnamachariar, 1974, p. 748.

edition of the *Nāṭyaśāstra* in the Gaekwad Oriental Series. The text is unsatisfactory because of the corrupt state of the mss. from which this edition was prepared.[13] Raghavan has suggested a number of emendations and corrections,[14] which are helpful not only to scholars but to dancers as well, especially in reconstructing the karaṇas of Bharata as explained by Abhinavagupta. For our present purposes the relevant sections are the commentaries on those chapters of the *Nāṭyaśāstra* that deal specifically with dance and dramaturgy.

The importance of Abhinavagupta's work can hardly be overstated. Since a number of works on dancing that are known to have been written after Bharata are now lost, it is difficult to follow the development of the technical discussion of the art of dancing through the early period of its evolution. Abhinavagupta's commentary shows us the changes that took place in the intervening period between his time and Bharata's. In Abhinavagupta's commentary we find more terms representing concepts and categories of dancing than there are in the *Nāṭyaśāstra,* showing that such terms and what they represented had by this time passed into general use, as is also attested by their use in other kinds of literature of the time.[15]

---

[13]Raghavan,1980, p.171.

[14]*Ibid.* pp. 171-92. Raghavan arrived at his emendations of *Abhinavabhāratī* by collating the text of *Abhinavabhāratī* with that of *Nṛttaratnāvalī* in course of preparing his critical edition of the latter text. However, firmer grounds for emendations would be reached if Abhinavagupta's commentary were collated with *Saṅgītaratnākara,* which Raghvan does only in a few instances.

[15]Abhinavagupta quotes Viśākhila on lāsya, *NŚ.* Vol. I. 1956, pp. 197, Kohala on kāvya and past authorities on nṛttakāvya and rāgakāvya, *NŚ.* Vol. I. 1956, pp. 171-84; Daṇḍin in his *Kāvyādarśa* refers to chalika, lāsya and śamyā, *Kāvyādarśa.*, 1. 39; Vararuci, Kālidāsa, Harṣa use lāsya, chalita, śamyā, dvipadī, saṅgītaka etc. in their plays, *Ubhayābhisārikā.*, pp 122-3,134, 141,142 ; *Mālavikāgnimitram.*, Act. I. prose passage following verse 19; *Ratnāvalī.*, Act. I. prose passage following verse 5,12,16; Rājaśekhara in his *Karpūramañjarī* uses carcarī, lāsya and other technical terms related to this art-form, Act. I. 6; III.14, IV. 9,10; Dāmodaragupta in his *Kuṭṭanīmatam* uses

It is evident that by Abhinavagupta's time the dance had proliferated into many more forms than known by Bharata but it is also clear that Abhinavagupta views them as embodiments of the basic concepts stated by Bharata, for he often cites instances of such new categories of dancing to elucidate Bharata's concepts.[16]

For similar elucidations Abhinavagupta also quotes other authorities extensively. Beside Bharata the most important early authority on dancing seems to have been Kohala, whose work, occasionally referred to in the *Nāṭyaśāstra,*[17] is lost. It is through Abhinavagupta's quotations from Kohala that we can reconstruct some of the conceptual developments that were either contemporaneous with Bharata or followed shortly after. Two other authorities quoted by Abhinavagupta, Bhaṭṭatota and Utpaladeva, were teachers to whom he owed his knowledge of dancing. Among other authorities cited are Nandī, Rāhula, Dattila, Nārada, Mataṅga, Viśākhila, Kīrtidhara, Udbhaṭa, Lollaṭa, Śaṅkuka, Bhaṭṭayantra and Rudraṭa, all of whom wrote on music and dance. He uses these authorities critically, drawing upon them for information that helps to elucidate Bharata's sometimes cryptic statements, but often rejecting their views when his own observations provide evidence to the contrary. One of the most illuminating features of Abhinavagupta's work is his practice of citing different views on the same movement. For instance, while explaining the ardhanikuṭṭaka karaṇa which employes añcita of the hands, Śaṅkuka's description, which is different from Bharata's, is included.[18] Abhinavagupta's citation of the two authorities thus shows us that this karaṇa was performed in two different ways.

---

dvipadī 338, 858; carcarī 881; Jayantabhaṭṭa in his *Āgamaḍambaram* describes a dance danced to a carcarī song, Act. II.

[16] *A.B.* on the *NŚ.* Vol.I, 1956, pp.171, 181.

[17] For example, *NŚ.* 1.26; *NŚ.* 37. 18.

[18] *A.B.* on the *NŚ.* Vol.I, 1956, p. 102.

From the range of Abhinavagupta's discussion it is quite apparent that his grasp of the subject was not only extraordinarily thorough but based on direct experience of the art as it was practised in his time. For this reason he explains the *Nāṭyaśāstra* according to the concepts current in his own time. Whether this represents Bharata's thought accurately enough may be debatable, for we have no evidence that the same concepts were prevalent in Bharata's time. In fact, the contrary may be true. For instance, Abhinavagupta speaks of minor categories of drama, for which he uses the terms nṛttakāvya and rāgakāvya,[19] which obviously mean, respectively, plays danced and plays sung. The concept of minor dramas is absent in the *Nāṭyaśāstra,* which makes no mention of nṛttakāvya and rāgakāvya. The reason Abhinavagupta mentions these new developments is to explain the distinction Bharata draws between sukumāraprayoga and tāṇḍava. Again, Abhinavagupta takes lāsya to be a form of dance and not of drama, unlike the *Nāṭyaśāstra,* and his discussion of it shows the evolution of the notion of lāsya after Bharata's time, as noted in the discussion, in a later chapter, on the development of the concept of lāsya through later times. Bharata, as elucidated by Abhinavagupta, is thus not necessarily Bharata himself, for Abhinavagupta not only expands Bharata but interprets him in the light of what he himself knows of dancing. It is, therefore, the evolving reality of the art rather than a description frozen in Bharata's time that is reflected in Abhinavagupta's commentary.

The proliferation of concepts and categories after Bharata's time revealed by Abhinavagupta's commentary is seen particularly clearly in his classification and interpretation of nṛtta, which also throws light upon the development of dance in general. Abhinavagupta classifies nṛtta into the following seven categories: śuddha, that is, pure or abstract dance, gītakādyabhinayonmukha, a dance that expresses the meaning of a song, vādyatālānusārī, a dance that follows instrumental music and rhythm,

[19]*Ibid.* pp.175, 182.

uddhata, a vigorous dance, sukumāra, a delicate dance, masṛṇamiśroddhata, a vigorous dance mixed with delicate movements, and uddhatamiśritamasṛṇanṛtta, a delicate dance mixed with vigorous movements.[20] Since many of these dances were expressive, they required abhinaya or interpretative movements. Such dances, then, fall into the category that later became known as nṛtya.[21] Although Abhinavagupta does not use the term nṛtya, presumably to be consistent with Bharata,[22] who speaks only of nṛtta in the *Nāṭyaśāstra,* Abhinavagupta's descriptions testify to the branching out of the art, as pointed out by K. M. Varma in his detailed discussion of Abhinavagupta's views on abhinaya and nṛtta in detail.[23]

Abhinavagupta provides the details of several dance forms that are mentioned but not described in the *Nāṭyaśāstra.* For instance, he describes bhadrāsana, one of the group dances termed piṇḍībandha by Bharata but not described by him (*NŚ.* 4. 290). Although Abhinavagupta does not use the term bhadrāsana, his description matches that found in a Jainasūtra, the *Rājapraśnīya,* which includes bhadrāsana in its description, in the twenty-third sūtra, of thirty-two varieties of nāṭyavidhis, that is, the features of nāṭya. These thirty-two varieties have been discussed by the editor of the *Saṅgītopaniṣatsāroddhāra* and by V. Rāghavan in his study of the *Śṛṅgāraprakāśa.*[24]

The commentary on the fifth chapter expands Bharata's description of the preliminaries of a dramatic performance and covers such topics as the use of tāla, vocal and instrumental music, and the arousal of the śṛṅgāra

---

20*Ibid.* p.182.

21*DR.* 1.9.

22Varma,1957, p21.

23*Ibid.* pp. 15-22.

24*Sūttāgame,* 1954, pp. 55-6; *Saṅgītopaniṣatsāroddhāra,* 1961, ed. P. Shah, Introduction, pp. xvi.; Raghavan,1963, pp. 572-73.

and raudra rasas in course of depictions of gods and goddesses.[25] The commentaries on the chapters on āṅgikābhinaya, chapters nine to twelve of the *Nāṭyaśāstra* (chapter eight does not have any commentary), do not offer any additional information, although Abhinavagupta's comments help us to visualize the body movements required. By contrast, the commentaries on āhāryābhinaya, sāmānyābhinaya and citrābhinaya (chapters tweny-one, twenty-two and twenty-five) provide details that help us to understand the technicalities of stage presentation. Also treated at some length are Bharata's remarks on lāsya in chapters nineteen and thirty-one; since Abhinavagupta's interpretative approach to lāsya has attracted considerable controversy, it will be considered in the discussion on lāsya later in the present study.

One must remember that like any other commentary Abhinavagupta's commentary is exegetical and absolute reliance on it may mislead attempts to reconstruct the tradition as in Bharata's time. This is particularly necessary to bear in mind because much of the medieval literature of dancing, including the infuential *Saṅgītaratnākara,*is entirely dependent on Abhinavagupta's commentary. As Raghavan says, ". . . the *Saṅgītaratnākara* follows Abhinavagupta so closely that in many places it forms merely a metrical recast of the Abhinavabhāratī."[26] Jāya Senāpati does the same in the discussion of the mārga dance in his *Nṛttaratnāvalī.* So what is often taken today as the influence of the *Nāṭyaśāstra* in these texts is in reality the influence of Abhinavagupta.

Speaking of Abhinavagupta's commentary Raghavan states that "its importance to the student of the history of Nāṭya and Saṅgīta can not be overemphasised." Of particular significance is the fact that Abhinavagupta was from Kashmir, for at that time the study of nāṭya, in Raghavan's words,"had a renaissance in Kashmir in the time of Jayāpīḍa."

---

[25]*A.B.* on the *NŚ.* Vol.I. 1956, pp.207-59.

[26]Raghavan,1980, p.171.

This is borne out by Kalhana, who refers in his *Rājataraṅgiṇī* (iv. 420-84) to a temple presentation of nāṭya by courtesans. Jayāpīḍa, the king of Kashmir, fell in love with one of them, Kamalā, married her, brought her to Kashmir and made her his queen. He was a patron of nāṭya and asked his court-poet Udbhaṭa to write a commentary on the *Nāṭyaśāstra* of Bharata. According to Raghavan, "Udbhaṭa's commentary is the first and it inaugurated an era of vigorous study of the *Nāṭyaśāstra.* This period produced innumerable works and it closed with the time of Abhinavagupta, after which the śāstra began to flourish in Central and South India."[27]

Abhinavagupta, who was a Śaivaite ācārya, turned to dramaturgy and poetics and studied under his first guru Bhaṭṭatota. He extensively quotes from Bhaṭṭatota's work the *Kāvyakautuka,* which is lost, as is the bulk of the literature of this early period that he uses. His work thus brings together the scholarly thought of an entire age and gives us a picture of the evolution of the art of dancing, although the picture is not as clear as we would have liked. Even though his commentary is illuminating in general, there are places where his explanations are not enough to visualize the movements he describes. Since the edited text is often corrupt, the task of understanding is even harder. The movements are sometimes unclear and impossible to reproduce, as in the case of the piṇḍībandhas. However, as the single extant commentary on Bharata's seminal text, Abhinavagupta's work has exerted great influence on subsequent writers on dance and drama. His work came to be accorded the highest authority and to be regarded as the standard work on the subjects, not only in works on music and dancing but on alaṁkāra as well. Hemacandra in his *Kāvyānuśāsana,* Rāmacandra and Guṇacandra in their *Nāṭyadarpaṇa,* and Kallinātha in his commentary on the *Saṅgītaratnākara* continually refer to the views of

[27] *Ibid.* pp. 101-3.

Abhinavagupta.[28] The *Saṅgītaratnākara*'s chapter on dancing is based entirely on it. Śāradātanaya claims that he based his work *Bhāvaprakāśana* on *Abhinavabhāratī*.[29] In fact he did not, but that he should so claim only shows how highly Abhinavagupta was regarded in the medieval period.

Two writers on dancing who are traditionally thought to have preceded Abhinavagupta are Nandikeśvara and Nārada but the chronology is doubtful as are the identities of the authors. The names Nandī and Nārada are part of the legendary history of dancing and it is possible that in some long past period there were indeed sages by these names. Presumably, in an effort to gain acceptance later authors passed off their own works under the names of these legendary sages. Two works on dancing are traditionally attributed to Nandikeśvara, the *Abhinayadarpaṇa* and the *Bharatārṇava.* The *Saṅgītamakaranda,* a work on music and dance, is attributed to "Nārada." Other works have been attributed to "Nārada" but they may be by different authors.[30]

M. Krishnamachariar and V. Raghavan have recorded various works purported to be by "Nandī," [31] but only two of them, the *Abhinayadarpaṇa* and the *Bharatārṇava,* both relevant to our present investigation, are available in edited form. Nandikeśvara has been mentioned by almost every writer on music and dance and Nandī and Bharata have been mentioned side by side in the Kāvyamālā edition of the *Nāṭyaśāstra.* According to Raghavan, "There is a music work called *Nandībharata* noticed by Rice in Mysore and Coorg Catalogue."[32] The Madras Catalogue too mentions one chapter of a work entitled the *Nandībharata*

[28] *KāvyānuśāsanaH,*1938, chapter 8; *Nāṭyadarpaṇa,*1959, p. 25; *Saṅgītaratnākara,* Vol. IV, 1953, 7.880,1062. *Kalānidhi:* Commentary on the *SR.* Vol. IV.1953, pp. 326.

[29] *Bhāvaprakāśana,*1968, pp. 82, 160, 194-5, 313.

[30] Nijenhuis,1977, pp. 19-20.

[31] Krishnamachariar,1974, pp. 825-27; Raghavan,1957, pp. 22-3.

[32] Raghavan,1957, p. 22.

and another work called the *Bharatārthacandrikā* that has a Telugu commentary which takes the form of a conversation between Pārvatī and Nandīkeśvara.[33] His date has not been satisfactorily established so far. In his edition of the *Abhinayadarpaṇa* M. M. Ghosh placed Nandīkeśvara between the fifth and the thirteenth centuries A.D.[34] Nijenhuis has argued for narrowing the date to the twelfth century A.D.[35]

Both the *Abhinayadarpaṇa* and the *Bharatārṇava* are believed to be by Nandīkeśvara,[36] but whether they were written by the same Nandīkeśvara is doubtful because the contents of the two are at odds with each other. Raghavan's view is that the *Abhinayadarpaṇa* is a summary of the *Bharatārṇava,* literally, the ocean of Bharata's art,[37] but this claim is not borne out by comparison of the texts.

If the two works were by the same author, then one would expect them to agree substantially and differ only in the extent of the information given, or in their emphases, for it defies reason to suppose that the same author would give contradictory versions of the same matter in two works without any explanation. Yet the difference between the two works is substantial. While they are on the same subject, they differ significantly in matters of detail. For instance, there are 28 single-hand gestures in the *Abhinayadarpaṇa* but 27 in the *Bharatārṇava;* against the 13 double-hand gestures in the *Abhinayadarpaṇa,* the *Bharatārṇava* describes 16; the nṛttahastas (gestures used in abstract dancing) in the *Abhinayadarpaṇa*

---

[33] *Ibid.* p. 22.

[34] Ghosh, 1957, Introduction, p. 38.

[35] Nijenhuis, 1977, p.11. My own view would put him in twelfth/thirteenth century A.D. See p. 30 *infra*.

[36] Raghavan, 1957, p. 22-3. The edited version of *ADar.* (Ghosh, 1957), however, does not contain any reference either to the name of the text or the author. The text is incomplete and provides no colophon.

[37] Raghavan, 1957, p. 22-3.

are 13 in number while in the *Bharatārṇava* they are 22. Not only are there differences in numbers but also in the names, definitions and applications of the movements. Besides these gestures, the *Abhinayadarpaṇa* describes hastas denoting devas, avatāras, family, different castes and the nine planets. The *Bharatārṇava* omits this entire class of hastas and instead includes an altogether different set of hastas, nānārthdyotakahastas, which convey a medley of meanings as the name indicates. [38] The treatment of the dṛṣṭis is different as well.

In describing the hand gestures meant to denote the planet Śani, one of the navagrahahastas, the *Abhinayadarpaṇa* prescribes the śikhara and triśūla hand-gestures for the two hands while the *Bharatārṇava* prescribes sandaṁśa and alapadma. Budhagraha of the *Abhinayadarpaṇa* requires muṣṭi and patākā while in the *Bharatāṇava* it requires mukula and sandaṁśa. Such discrepancies are common. Nandīkeśvara, the author of the *Abhinayadarpaṇa,* takes eight darśanakarmas from the *Nāṭyaśāstra* and describes them as eight dṛṣṭis, whereas Nandīkeśvara, the author of the *Bharatārṇava,* follows the *Nāṭyaśāstra*'s treatment of the dṛṣṭis and describes thirty-six dṛṣṭis that express rasa and bhāva, aesthetic pleasure and emotions. [39] Gatis or gaits in the *Abhinayadarpaṇa* are compared to animal and human gaits and described in detail following Bharata.[40] By contrast, in its description of the gaits the *Bharatārṇava* focuses on how they are employed in different kinds of tāṇḍavas; the nature of the gaits too are different in this text. [41] The description of tāṇḍava and lāsya, divided into categories, that is given in the *Bharatārṇava* is found in no other text.

---

38 *ADar.* 89-92, 172-75, 248-49; *Bh. Ar.* 1-4, 63-66, 93-96; *ADar.* 204-15, 216-30, 226-31, 231-44, 250-58; *Bh. Ar.* 587-640.

39 *ADar.* 66-67; *Bh.Ar.* 235-40.

40 *ADar.* 309-10.

41 These are described as components of deśī nāṭyas, under deśī tāṇḍavas, which, according to this text, are seven, *Bh.Ar.* 791-868.

The śṛṅganāṭya and aṅgahāra mentioned in this text are two new concepts found nowhere else, as we shall see in a later chapter. The term śṛṅgābhinaya is mentioned in the *Nṛttaratnāvalī* and in the *Nṛtyādhyāya* but none of these authors describe them (*NR.* 2.112; *Nr.Adh.* 141). The cārīs of the *Abhinayadarpaṇa* and the *Bharatārṇava* differ not only in their names but in their definitions as well.[42] The movements of the feet are divided into four types in the *Abhinayadarpaṇa,* namely, maṇḍala, utplavana, sthāna and bhramarī. The *Bharatārṇava* describes twenty-two movements of the feet which are a mixture of Bharata's pāda (feet movements) and cārī, although the *Bharatārṇava* has a separate section on cārī as well.[43] Such discrepancies occur throughout the texts and a comparison even as cursory as this calls into question the assumption of the single authorship of the two works.

Furthermore, we may assign them to different periods. The contents of the *Abhinayadarpaṇa* place it in or close to the medieval period, for we find in it the division of dance into three branches, nāṭya, nṛtta and nṛtya, and this separation did not come about till the early medieval period when the *Daśarpaka* created the distinction, a distinction maintained in the*Saṅgītaratnākara.* Also, the *Abhinayadarpaṇa* views tāṇḍava and lāsya as forms of masculine and feminine dancing, which again was an approach taken not before medieval times. As we shall see later in the detailed discussion of lāsya, it came to be taken as a dance form after Bharata wrote his *Nāṭyaśāstra* and even after the time of the *Viṣṇudharmottarapurāṇa* it continued to be so understood. The use of the term nṛtya to denote a specific art-form came later still. Even Abhinavagupta does not use the term nṛtya, although it is likely that he restricted himself to using only the term nṛtta because in his task of interpreting the *Nāṭyaśāstra* he was bound by Bharata's usage. In the

---

[42]*Bh. Ar.* chapters 8-9, 11-14.

[43]*Ibid.* chapters 4 and 8.

Nāmaliṅgānuśāsana of Amarasiṁha (10th century A.D.)[44] we come across the term nṛtya, but there it is used as a synonym of nāṭya rather than a signifier of an independent art form. Since Amarasiṁha's date has not yet been established beyond question, his use of the term nṛtya does not help us fix a date for the earliest occurrence of the term except that it is likely to have been in use before Abhinavagupta who came after Amarasiṁha.

No text in the first period of the evolution of dancing seems to have dealt with the nature of nṛtya. Dhanañjaya, who was a contemporary of Abhinavagupta, was the first to recognize nṛtya as a distinct category of dance but he said nothing about its nature except that nṛtya belongs to the mārga tradition and is bhāvāśraya, that is, it expresses emotions. The *Abhinayadarpaṇa*'s fuller treatment of nṛtya suggests a later date when the concept had developed beyond Dhanañjaya and Abhinavagupta.

Even more persuasive an argument for placing the *Abhinayadarpaṇa* in the medieval period is that it contains material and expresses views that are characteristic of that period. For example, it talks about the attainment of mokṣa or liberation through the performance of the art. This view is characteristics of musicological works from the medieval period, including the *Saṅgītaratnākara* and the *Abhinayadarpaṇa,* as Katz points out.[45] Since the *Saṅgītaratnākara* has been placed in the thirteenth century it is unlikely that the *Abhinayadarpaṇa* was composed much earlier. Furthermore, the concepts of nāṭya, nṛtta, nṛtya, tāṇḍava and lāsya are introduced in a similar manner and defined in the two works, the *Saṅgītaratnākara* and the *Abhinayadarpaṇa,* and there are verbal parallels as well.[46] M. M. Ghosh believes that the *Saṅgītaratnākara* borrowed

---

[44]Vogel,1974, p.309.

[45]Katz,1987, Vol. II, commentary on verses 18-21.

[46]The editor of the *Saṅgītaratnākara* gives a list of these parallels. See Adyar Library edition, Vol. IV, 1953, pp. 585-87.

from the *Abhinayadarpaṇa* but offers no supporting evidence for his claim and it is impossible to determine which text is the borrower and which the source. The movements of the pratyaṅgas, that is, the minor limbs, are not discussed in the early treatises, the *Nāṭyaśāstra* and the *Viṣṇudharmottara Purāṇa* being silent about them, but are included in medieval works. Both the *Abhinayadarpaṇa* and the *Saṅgītaratnākara* describe pratyaṅgas. They also describe bhramarī as a separate category of movements, which again is a medieval development. This close correspondence between the two texts strongly argues for placing the *Abhinayadarpaṇa* close in time to the *Saṅgītaratnākara* (13th century A.D.), that is, some time in the early medieval period.

We must, however, note that the similarity to the *Saṅgītaratnākara* is not the only distinctive characteristic of the *Abhinayadarpaṇa.* In fact, it occupies an unique position in the literature of classical dancing of India. The author, unlike any other, is concerned exclusively with the performing arts as they apply to dancing, specifically the forms of abhinaya identified by Bharata, with the exception of vācika. While at least twenty-nine texts over a period of eighteen centuries describe the art of dancing, only one text, the *Abhinayadarpaṇa* concentrates entirely on āṅgikābhinaya or the use of body movements in acting and describes how such acting techniques is used in dancing. Judging by the author's concern for performance it seems likely that this text was meant as a textbook for a dancer to learn the technique of mimetic dance. Interestingly enough, that is how it is now used in the training regime of at least one classical style of Indian dancing, Bharatanatyam, although the practitioners claim that they are thereby following Bharata, after whom the style is named. In a number of contemporary Bharatanatyam schools, each student has to learn by rote the entire text of the *Abhinayadarpaṇa* and perform the movements described in it.

The text of the *Abhinayadarpaṇa,* as it is available now, is quite short, with only 324 verses.[47] The text begins with a benediction and short description of the origins of drama, sings its praise, and goes on to describe the different kinds of naṭana (dance), namely, nāṭya, nṛtta, nṛtya. It then speaks of the qualities of the audience, the stage, the performer, the kiṅkiṇīs (ankle-bells), the prayer to be danced. Then the author instructs the performer to begin the performance with various stylized body movements. Next, he establishes the importance of abhinaya and briefly discusses the characteristics of its four kinds. This whole opening section takes up only forty verses and the rest are devoted to describing the movements of the individual parts of the body, which, according to the author, are of vital importance for a performance. That this discussion is meant for dancers and actors is quite apparent for it includes descriptions of the kiṅkiṇīs or ankle bells. Very few texts describe kiṅkiṇīs. Another unique feature of this text is that although in describing the basic hand-gestures and the eyes the author follows the *Nāṭyaśāstra,* his treatment of the movements of the feet comes from a tradition recorded in no other text. He also includes some new gestures found in no other text.[48]

The edition in which the *Bharatārṇava* is at present available has fifteen chapters with 996 verses. To this the editor has added a pariśiṣṭa, an appendix, consisting of 251 verses from a manuscript fragment in the Bhandarkar Oriental Research Institute.[49] The reason for its inclusion is not clear, for while the fragment bears the title *Bharatārṇava,* there is no internal evidence supporting this identification. Against the identification we must note that the material comes from a different school of dancing and does not belong to the school which is represented in the

[47] Ghosh, 1957.

[48] *ADar.* 1957, pp. 204-44. These include devahasta, daśāvatārahasta, jātihasta and bāndhavahasta.

[49] Gairola, 1978.

Abhinayadarpaṇa. To give only one example, the appendix describes a dance sequence which it calls ālāpacārī (*Bh.Ar.* Pariśiṣta 28-37); this sequence is the same as the mukhacāli described in the *Nartananirṇaya* (*NN.* 40a-43a), the 16th century work by Puṇḍarīka Viṭṭhala, and has no parallel in any earlier work.

The beginning of the main text of the *Bharatārṇava* is missing and the text starts from the descriptions of single hand-gestures. The second chapter describes double hand-gestures and the third the hand-gestures used specially in dancing. The fourth chapter gives other varieties of single hand-gestures as taught by Bṛhaspati. It also describes glances and movements of the head and the feet, citing the views of other authorities as well. The fifth chapter describes different postures. The sixth deals with the application of the postures and the applications of combinations of hand gestures. Tāla or rhythm is described in the seventh chapter. The eighth chapter deals with cārī. The ninth describes a new kind of aṅgahāra, of seven types, which is described in no other text. At the end of this chapter the author gives an unusual definition of aṅgahāra as the opinion of the experts: प्रातर्नृत्तप्रकटनैरङ्गहारो विधीयते । (*Bh.Ar.* 9. 584) – aṅgahāra is prescribed as nṛtta performed [lit: displayed] in the morning. The tenth chapter again deals with more hand-gestures that express a variety of meanings. The eleventh and twelfth chapters deal with yet another new form, śṛṅganāṭya, of which nine types are mentioned. This form, again, is described in no other text. The thirteenth chapter describes seven lāsyas and seven tāṇḍavas, this being the only text to describe these divisions. The names of the seven lāsyas given here are found among the deśī dance pieces described in the *Saṅgītaratnākara* and the *Nṛttaratnāvalī.* The description of the deśī dance preraṇi parallels the descriptions found in the *Saṅgītaratnākara* and the *Nṛttaratnāvalī.*[50] The fourteenth chapter describes the use of tāla, gati, karaṇa and cārī in

[50] *SR.* 7. 1303-25; *NR.* 7. 34-58.

delineating śuddha and deśī tāṇḍava, a type of tāṇḍava found only in this text. The treatment of tāla etc. is also entirely new since this text, instead of merely naming the tālas required in dancing as other texts do, prescribes how tālas are to be used in actual dance sequences. The fifteenth chapter is on puṣpāñjali, the right manner of flower offerings, and other such matters relating to presentation. The descriptions of all the movements includes their meaning and application, expect for the nṛttahastas, which are not meant for representational performance.

The appendix seems to be the beginning of a treatise since it opens by prescribing the preliminaries to a performance, including the appropriate arrangements for holding a performance, the manner in which singers should make their entrances and the opening music should be played to tāla, and the kind of competence and training required in the musicians. General instructions concerning movements come next. Instructions follow regarding how the actual performance should begin, with citations from Kohala (*Bh.Ar.* Pariśiṣṭā 37). The rest of this section deals with more hand-gestures, many of them new and found neither in the *Abhinayadarpaṇa* nor in any other text. Two verses in the appendix match verses in the *Abhinayadarpaṇa,*[51] and one of them, on the division of dance into tāṇḍava and lāsya, occurs also in the *Saṅgītaratnākara.*[52]

On the basis of its treatment of several topics,the *Bharatārṇava* seems to be of a later date than the *Abhinayadarpaṇa,* and the appendix later still. Besides the differences between the *Abhinayadarpaṇa* and the *Bharatārṇava* pointed out earlier, we must also note that the *Bharatārṇava* follows the practice of describing dance pieces along with the gaits, rhythm, cārī and karaṇa and tāla recommended for them, which is typical of texts that are later even than the *Saṅgītaratnākara* and the *Nṛttaratnāvalī.* This inclusiveness of the description became common in

---

[51] *Bh.Ar.* Pariśiṣṭa. 1-2; *ADar.*36-7, 247(reiteration of 36)

[52] *Bh.Ar.* Pariśiṣṭa. 38, 39; *SR.* 7. 28, 30.

the literature produced from the sixteenth century onwards. Moreover, some of the technical terms used in the *Bharatārṇava*, as well as in the so-called appendix, such as uḍupa, dhuvāḍa, kuvāḍa and sūlu, are terms that began to appear in the Sanskrit works on dancing around the sixteenth century and not before.

Although the *Abhinayadarpaṇa* and the *Bharatārṇava* seem unquestionably by two different authors and from different periods, the *Bharatārṇava* is as important as the the *Abhinayadarpaṇa* as an instructional manual although it is not so used now, nor do we know if it was ever so used. Nonetheless, its importance as an excellent practical guide can not be denied. If the *Abhinayadarpaṇa* trains a dancer in the basic movements, the *Bharatārṇava* teaches a dancer to compose a dance piece. Both pursue the same purpose of instructing practising artists and not merely of recording the art form of the time. Since its own evidence places the *Bharatārṇava* after the *Abhinayadarpaṇa*, it may be regarded as being complementary to the *Abhinayadarpaṇa*, and this may explain why the unfounded identification of the two as by the same author has persisted for so long.

Another controversial text on music and dance is the *Saṅgītamakaranda* by Nārada. Nārada, as we have noted above, is a mythical name which appears in almost all dance literature in Sanskrit. Nārada appears in the literature of the medieval period as well as in the early period, in the works of Bharata, Dattila, Mataṅga and Abhinavagupta.[53] We have at least two Nāradas, according to Raghavan, one who wrote the *Saṅgītamakaranda* and one who wrote the *Nāradīya Śikṣā*.[54] Raghavan places the Nārada of the *Saṅgītamakaranda* after the seventh century since the text refers to Mātṛgupta, who is believed to have

53Mataṅga, *Bṛhaddeśī*, 2;Lath,1978 p.48, 52, 557; *NŚ*. 5. 32; *A. B.* on the *NŚ*. Vol. I. 1956 p. 221.

54 Raghavan,1957, p. 23.

lived around that time, but it does not specify any date for Mātṛgupta.[55] Nijenhuis suggests that this text was written after the *Saṅgītaratnākara*. She believes that this author is not the same as the one to whom the *Saṅgītaratnākara* refers.[56] Another work by a certain "Nārada," *Catvāriṁśacchatarāganirūpaṇa*, has been placed in the 16th-17th century.[57] Svāmī Prajñānānanda states that there are four works by four different Nāradas: the *Nāradīya Śikṣā* (1st century A.D.), the *Pañcamasārasaṁhitā* (1440 A.D.), the *Saṅgītamakaranda* (14th/15th century A.D) and the *Rāganirūpaṇa* (16th/17th century A.D.)[58] The editor of the *Saṅgītamakaranda*(1920), M. R. Telang, places Nārada, the author of the *Saṅgītamakaranda*, between the 7th and 11th centuries,[59] but this dating remains doubtful. The problem with fixing a date for Nārada is that this is a mythical personage who appears in all the literature of dance and music as an authority and there is more than one Nārada. The whole problem has been compounded by the fact that the edited version is a corrupt text and one that describes a debased style recorded in no other text.

The *Saṅgītamakaranda* has two parts, one on music and the other on dance, each divided into four sections. The whole text is obscure but the dance portion is the most difficult part of this generally difficult work. Many of the difficulties arise from the text as edited. It is hard to get a picture of the tradition but the little we may glimpse shows a decadent style.[60] This seems to be a deśī tradition that was obviously not very highly

---

55 *Ibid.* p.23.

56 Nijenhuis,1977, pp. 13-14.

57 *Ibid.* p.19.

58 *Ibid.* p.20; Prajñānānanda,1963. p. 114.

59 *Saṅgītamakaranda*, 1920, Introduction, p. x.

60 समगैकेति विख्याता हस्तौ वामस्तने धृतौ ।
कैवालं दक्षिणकुचे लग्नौ चुचुकदर्शनम् ॥ *SMak.* 4.4.13.

regarded–possibly because of its vulgar eroticism–since it appears in no other text. The first part of the text is entirely on music. In the first section of the part on dance the author discusses the dance-hall, the audience, the poet, the singer, types of learned spectators, the presiding person, the dance-teacher, the percussionist, the performer, the flower-offering and the origin of the tālas. The second section names the makers of tāla and describes the characteristics of 101 tālas. The third section gives a variety of information on tāla, including the derivation of the word, the essence of tāla, the time, mārga, deśī and other such technicalities of music. The fourth section is devoted to drums but also contains a short final subsection of 33 verses called naṭībhāvanirūpaṇam which is devoted to dance. It describes five double hand-gestures, five single hand-gestures, eight bhramarīs, nine head movements and four feet movements. The text concludes by referring to 33 naṭībhāvas, that is, emotional expressions appropriate for women, but does not elaborate on them. None of the movements described in this text is found in any other text. The technical terms do not match any term found in the existing literature, except for two, cakrabhramarikā and sama (pāda), and even these two are described differently.

As for the date of the *Saṅgītamakaranda,*there are a number of reasons why it must be placed in the medieval period. The text describes dance as nṛtya which is a term found in use not before the time of Dhanañjaya (10th century A.D.),[61] whose *Daśarūpaka* was the first surviving work to define nṛtya. The concept of mokṣa, which we have already noted as a medieval concept, is present in this text.[62] But the strongest reason to place it in the medieval period is that it describes an entire style that falls outside the

[When] the hands hold the left breast it is known as samagaika [and when the hands] touch the right breast to show the nipple it is kaivāla.

[61] Dasgupta, 1962, Vol. I. p. 550.

[62] See p. 29 *supra*; *SMak.* 1.1.24.

tradition described by Bharata and his followers. This new style was part of the deśī tradition and it was only in the medieval period that the deśī type of dancing came to be accepted as one that was worth recording. However, no precise dating of the *Saṅgītamakaranda* has been possible because it contains no material paralleling any other text by means of which terminal dates might be set. However, the type of material it does contain allows the conjecture, supported by at least one musicologist, [63] that it was not written before the *Saṅgītaratnākara.*

The *Daśarūpaka* of Dhanañjaya, a work on dramaturgy, marks the beginning of the second period. Although Abhinavagupta and Dhanañjaya (924-995 A.D)[64] were contemporaries, yet Dhanañjaya must be placed in the second period because in his work we find for the first time how certain concepts had evolved beyond Bharata. The first period is dominated by the concepts enunciated by Bharata, and these form the subject of Abhinavagupta. It is true that Abhinavagupta interprets them in commenting upon the *Nāṭyaśāstra* and thereby develops them, thus indicating that the process of evolution was under way, but the conceptual framework remains entirely that of Bharata. It is in the *Daśarūpaka* that we find the recognition of these new categories and concepts defined for the first time. The most important of these are represented by the terms nṛtya, lāsya, mārga and deśī.

The *Daśarūpaka* has four prakāśas or sections. As the name suggests, the work is on the ten types into which Bharata had divided dramatic literature, and it analyzes their technical features, concentrating on plot construction in particular. A systematic and compact work, it replaced the *Nāṭyaśāstra* for the later authors as a guide to the technicalities of plays. The first chapter, which consists of 68 verses, starts with a benediction and proceeds to offer short definitions of the terms nāṭya, nṛtya, nṛtta,

---

[63]Nijenhuis,1977 , p.14.

[64]Gerow,1977, p. 263.

mārga, tāṇḍava and lāsya. Here Dhanañjaya takes nṛtta and nṛtya as auxiliaries to drama and hence necessary to his study. After defining the terms the author moves on to his main purpose, that of defining and describing nāṭya or drama. According to Dhanañjaya, vastu, netā and rasa, that is, the subject matter, the hero and the aesthetic affect, are the three matters of primary importance and the rest of the first chapter is devoted to the discussion of vastu in detail and of the structural components of a play. The second chapter, in 72 verses, describes the characters in a play, especially the hero, the heroine, their qualities, the method of expressing various emotions etc. Vṛttis or acting styles and the use of language by different characters are also discussed in this chapter. The third chapter, in 70 verses, deals with the varieties of rūpakas or plays and identifies lāsyāṅgas as components of bhāṇa, a major type of play. The fourth chapter, in 87 verses, discusses the nine rasas or aesthetic affects, the eight sthāyībhāvas or mental states, and the thirty-three vyabhicārībhāvas or transitory moods.

The definitions of the terms nṛtta, nṛtya, tāṇḍava and lāsya in Dhanañjaya mark a distinct stage in the evolution of the understanding of dance and drama. Although Dhanañjaya does not elaborate on the concepts he defines, one of his most important contributions is the distinction he draws between nṛtta and nṛtya: . . . .भावाश्रयं नृत्यम् (*DR*. 1. 9.) -- nṛtya is dependant on emotion. He distinguishes nṛtta from nṛtya by saying: नृत्तं ताललयाश्रयम् (*DR*. 1. 9.)-- nṛtta depends on rhythm and tempo. He is thus the first writer known to have used the term nṛtya to denote mimetic dance and also dance-dramas. He further states that nṛtya belongs to the mārga tradition and nṛtta to the deśī.[65] While this is a significant departure from Bharata, Dhanañjaya remains anchored to Bharata's basic view that both nṛtta and nṛtya are auxiliaries to drama. Thus, in principle, Dhanañjaya continues the tradition established by

---

[65] *DR*. 1969 1. 9-10.

Bharata. Dhanañjaya further identifies tāṇḍava and lāsya as subcategories of both nṛtta and nṛtya, tāṇḍava being a vigorous mode of dancing and lāsya a delicate one.[66]

To interpret nṛtta as deśī is a surprising view because nṛtta is accorded the status of mārga in almost all works on dancing on the ground that Bharata describes only nṛtta and distinguishes it from the deśī styles which, he expressly says, do not form his subject.[67] It is not till the thirteenth century that we find another work, the *Saṅgītaratnākara,* calling nṛtya a mārga form of dancing. Still later, in the seventeenth century came the *Saṅgītadarpaṇa,*[68] which was the third and only other text to categorize nṛtta and nṛtya respectively as deśī and mārga, repeating verses from the *Saṅgītaratnākara.* One of the most important pieces of information we get from the *Daśarūpaka* concerns bhāṇa, which is one of the ten major types into which drama is divided by Bharata, who calls it a one-act play. But the *Daśarūpaka* extends our understanding of the type by attributing to it delicate movements and the arousal of śṛṅgārarasa. According to the *Daśarūpaka,* such movements are employed in lāsyāṅgas which thereby generate śṛṅgārarasa. Dhanañjaya further states that lāsyāṅgas are essential parts of bhāṇa.[69] He does not specify the particular aṅgas or features of lāsya, and the ten lāsyāṅgas he names match those found in the *Nāṭyaśāstra,* except one, dvigūḍhaka, which is called dvimūḍhaka in the *Nāṭyaśāstra,* but this may be the result of a scribal error in the *Nāṭyaśāstra.*[70] While Dhanañjaya follows the *Nāṭyaśāstra* in naming the lāsyāṅgas, he ventures in a new direction by

---

66 *DR.* 1.10; 1. 11.

67 अन्ये तु लौकिका ये ते लोकाद् ग्राह्याः सदा बुधैः। *NS.* 25.119.

68 *DR.* 1. 10; *SR.* 7. 27; *SDar.* 7. 94.

69 *DR.* 4. 51-53.

70 *DR.* 4. 52.

relating them to the bhāṇa and thus placing this type of expressive movement in the domain of drama.

The evidence of the *Daśarūpaka* makes it clear that by the tenth century śṛṅgārarasa (aesthetic pleasure of the erotic variety) and kaiśikīvṛtti (graceful style) came to characterize lāsyāṅgas which had become standard parts of bhāṇa. This is confirmed by Abhinavagupta, who cites various authors regarding the development of a certain bhāṇa play.[71] This feature was absent from Bharata's concept of bhāṇa, and he specifically forbids the use of kaiśikīvṛtti.[72] Dhanañjaya is silent on minor dramas, but Dhanika, the commentator on the *Daśarūpaka*, cites seven minor dramas, calling them nṛtyabhedas, without defining them.[73]

Apart from the information mentioned above, this text gives one other that is quite vital to our understanding of the use of gesture language in drama. Gestures obviously formed a very important technique for expressing meaning in the performance of a play. Dhanañjaya mentions tripatākākara, the hands in tripatākā, to indicate janāntika, an aside.[74] That he does not take the trouble to define the term indicates that the use of these gestures was common in his time and therefore required no explanation.

The *Daśarūpaka* reflects considerable changes in the discourse on dancing since Bharata's *Nāṭyaśāstra.* Dhanañjaya's strength lies particularly in the fact that he composed a methodical account of the categories of dance and provided clear, if brief, explanations. Prior to his work, much of the information available, including what we find in

---

[71] *AB.* on the *NŚ,* Vol. I.1956, p. 181. Abhinavagupta's use of both bhāṇa and bhāṇaka for this minor type caused some confusion which continued through the entire literature on dance and drama.

[72] *NŚ.* 18.8-9.

[73] *DR.* 1969, p. 8 (Avaloka of Dhanika).

[74] *DR.* 1.65.

Abhinavagupta, is fragmentary, existing as quotations from lost works or from the general body of literature. Sometimes the information comes in as passing remarks or views not clearly expressed. In Dhanañjaya the concepts and the categories are set down and defined unambiguously enough to suggest that their meanings had come to be generally accepted.

Our next source is the *Śṛṅgāraprakāśa* of Bhoja which is believed to be from the eleventh century.[75] As the name suggests, it is an exposition of śṛṅgārarasa. The term śṛṅgāra here must be understood in the context of Bhoja's "new found theory of the one Rasa of Ahaṁkāra, Abhimāna or Śṛṅgāra as well as the lower śṛṅgāra of Rati."[76] This text is a work in thirty-six chapters and deals with both poetics and dramaturgy. As Raghavan points out, "Bhoja seems to be the first writer, whose work is available to us now, who embraced both branches and wrote in the same work on both."[77] It seems from the treatment of the subject that Bhoja wanted to write a work similar to the *Nāṭyaśāstra.* Like Bharata, Bhoja discusses the characteristics of the Sanskrit language, but does so even more elaborately than Bharata, although–surprisingly–Bhoja omits prosody, which is closely related to poetics.[78] However, he discusses dramaturgy in detail and his analysis of śṛṅgāra is unique, covering as it does the types of śṛṅgāra and its expression.in dramatic presentation. The range and depth of the work has been noted by Raghavan who discusses its contents and compares it with other works on the subject.[79]

The part of the work most relevant to our present study is Bhoja's discussion of the minor types of plays. In the eleventh chapter he describes twenty-four types of drama and their structure which he terms as

---

[75] Raghavan,1956, p. 29.

[76] Raghavan,1978, p. 8.

[77] *Ibid.* 1963, p. 9.

[78] *Ibid.* p.9.

[79] *Ibid.* The comparative study continues through the whole work of Raghavan.

prekṣyaprabandhas, that is, poetical compositions to be seen. These he divides into two subcategories according to the kind of acting necessary, one requiring vākyārthābhinaya and the other padārthābhinaya.[80] Vākyārthābhinaya literally means expressing the meaning of utterances, that is to say, the acting technique required for this type of drama brings out the entire meaning of the play. This is the kind that represents major drama. Padārthābhinaya on the other hand is less demanding and calls for expressing the meaning of the words (in a song) and is employed in minor dramas. Bhoja does not name the class of drama that requires padārthābhinaya, but he does name and describe the twelve varieties within the class. These descriptions show that these varieties are full of delicate and expressive movements. Going back to Dhanañjaya's definition of nṛtya we find that he defines nṛtya as an art requiring padārthābhinaya (*DR*. 1.9). If padārthābhinaya can thus be correlated with nṛtya, which seems plausible, then it is likely that Bhoja viewed as varieties of nṛtya the dramatic types that require padārthābhinaya. Dhanika in his *Avaloka* on the *Daśarūpaka* and Śāradātanaya in his *Bhāvaprakāśana* view these minor dramas as nṛtyabhedas, that is, as various types of nṛtya.[81] Later, Śubhaṅkara refers to these varieties as "nṛtye ratnanakṣatramālā."[82] As these references show, these minor dramatic types were known under many names. Later, however, they were categorized as uparūpakas by Viśvanātha in the *Sāhityadarpaṇa* (fourteenth century A.D.)[83] and we shall examine their relevance to dance in a later chapter. It is in that context that Bhoja's views on the use of padārthābhinaya in prekṣyaprabandhas are of particular significance.

---

80 The text of *Śṛṅgāraprakāśa*, Vol. II.1963, pp.461, 466.

81 *DR. Avaloka*, 1969, p. 8; *Bh.P.* 1968, pp. 255-68.

82 *Saṅgītadāmodara*, 1960, .pp. 79-80.

83 *Sāhityadarpaṇa*, 1923, 6. 4-6.

The *Nāṭyadarpaṇa* of Rāmacandra and Guṇacandra is a treatise on dramaturgy written in the twelfth century.[84] As the name suggests, the text reflects the characteristics of drama. After writing the main text the two authors comment upon their own work to elucidate it. The work is in four chapters and in the third chapter, while discussing āṅgikābhinaya, the authors list by name the movements of the different parts of the body as well as extended sequences and compositions. Their method of listing the terms for movements is to select one or two terms to indicate an entire class and then to state the number of movements in that class, as we find, for instance, in phrases such as: हस्तयोः पताकत्रिपताकादयश्चतुःषष्टिः or स्थिरहस्तपर्यस्तकादयोऽङ्गहारा द्वात्रिंशत् and so on.[85] This list matches the list given in the *Nāṭyaśāstra* and we find that the division of limbs in this work into aṅga and upāṅga is also a continuation of the tradition of the *Nāṭyaśāstra,* although the movements of the limbs are merely named, not described. While it follows the *Nāṭyaśāstra,* in many respects, it also provides additional information. It virtually copies the *Nāṭyaśāstra* in describing āṅgikābhinaya, but names two additional types of major dramas that are not found in the *Nāṭyaśāstra,* raising the number of major dramatic types to twelve. Again, the description of bhāṇa is different from that in the *Nāṭyaśāstra,* and following the tradition that developed after Bharata it includes śṛṅgārarasa and ten lāsyāṅgas as features of bhāṇa. One other major topic that this text introduces is a discussion of the minor types of drama for which it does not have a class name although it describes thirteen varieties of minor drama in detail. [86] The *Nāṭyaśāstra,* as we know, does not describe minor dramas. But that they existed is evidenced by Abhinavagupta's citations in the *Abhinavabhāratī* and in Dhanika's

---

[84] Krishnamachariar, 1974, p. 643.

[85] *Nāṭyadarpaṇa,* 1959, pp.168-69.

[86] *Ibid.* pp. 190-92.

Avaloka on the *Daśarūpaka,*[87] though Dhanika does not describe them. Bhoja was the first to include and describe twelve varieties of minor dramas, giving details, and the *Nāṭyadarpaṇa* was the next work to include them in the category of drama. However, these dramatic types still lacked an accepted class-name. Different names appear in different works, such as nṛtyakāvya and rāgakāvya in the *Abhinavabhāratī,* nṛtyabheda in the *Avaloka* of Dhanika, geyarūpaka in the *Kāvyānuśāsana* of Hemacandra. Rāmacandra and Guṇacandra simply categorize them as anyāni rūpakāṇi, that is, other plays.[88] Even Śāradātanaya, who, writing in the thirteenth century, gives the largest list, consisting of twenty minor dramas, refers to them as nṛtyabhedas.[89] Oddly enough, much later Śubhaṅkara includes both rūpakas and uparūpakas under nṛtya (*SDām.* pp. 79, 80, 99). However, the description in the *Nāṭyadarpaṇa* has lines almost identical with Bhoja's description except that it adds one other minor dramatic type, saṭṭaka.[90] In a later chapter we shall discuss the development of these minor types of plays as well as their nature.

From the inclusion of these minor types in the *Avaloka* of the *Daśarūpaka* and in the *Śṛṅgāraprakāśa,* a practice that is followed by all treatises on music, drama and dance for several centuries, we are justified in surmising that these minor types of dramas were popular and had become well-developed and well established during this second period of our study. This was no doubt the reason why they were recognized by scholars as important enough to be included in works on dramaturgy.

---

[87] Abhinavagupta mentions ten such minor types (*AB.* on the *NŚ.* 1956, pp. 168-84.); Dhanika mentions seven,1969 (*Avaloka* on the *DR.* p. 8).

[88] *AB.* on the *NŚ.*,Vol. I, pp. 171, 175; *Avaloka* on the *DR.* 1969, p. 8; *KAnu.H.* 1938, 8.1; *ND.* 1959, p. 190.

[89] *Bh.P.* 1968, p. 256.

[90] *ND.* 1959, p. 190-92.

However, the precise genre to which they belonged remained a matter of varied opinion.

Another text of great interest from the twelfth century is *Mānasollāsa* by Someśvara, also known as *Abhilaṣitārthacintāmaṇi*.[91] In its one hundred chapters it deals with a variety of subjects that interest the royalty. A guide to royal pastimes, this book has five parts, each containing descriptions of twenty vinodas or pastimes. The fourth part deals with dance and music in chapters sixteen to eighteen. Three others are on vocal and instrumental music and dance and the fifth is on miscellaneous matters. The part called nṛtyavinoda has 457 verses, from 16.4. 949 to 16.4.1406. He introduces us to the subject first by saying when dances should be performed: at every festive occasion, to celebrate conquests, success in competitions and examinations as well as occasions of joy, passion, pleasure and renunciation. Six varieties of dancing are described next and then six types of nartakas. Nartaka here stands for performers in general and includes nartakī (danseuse), naṭa (actor), nartaka (dancer), vaitālika (bard), cāraṇa (wandering performer) and kollāṭika (acrobat). He then describes body movements, dividing them into aṅga, upāṅga and pratyaṅga. The division of the minor limbs into two categories, upāṅga and pratyaṅga, is a new approach. The *Nāṭyaśāstra* divides the body into major and minor limbs and the term Bharata uses for the minor limbs is upāṅga. This division is followed by the *Viṣṇudharmottara Purāṇa.* But Someśvara introduces this further subdivision of pratyaṅgas. This division appears in almost all works on the subject except for the *Nāṭyadarpaṇa* which, as we have noted above, follows the *Nāṭyaśāstra*.[92] The movements of six aṅgas, eight upāṅgas and six pratyaṅgas are discussed in detail, with the meaning and application explained. The one type of movement to which meaning is not

---

91 *Mānasollāsa,* G.O.S. edition, Vol. I. 1958. p. vi.

92 *NŚ.* 8.8; *VDP.* 3.24.65; *ND.* p.168.

attributed is the nṛttahasta, because these movements are meant for adding beauty, not meaning. These are discussed in verses 978-1306. Verses 1307-78 are devoted to describing 21 sthānas and 26 cārīs, of which 16 are described. Verses 1379-99 describe 18 karaṇas of the deśī variety, none of which is found in earlier works. He finishes this section by saying that these should be performed either by a dancer or by the king himself to please his beloved. But performance of the viṣama (acrobatic) and vikaṭa (comic) varieties of dancing should be avoided by the king since they cannot generate śṛṅgārarasa. This suggests that generating śṛṅgārarasa was taken to be a prerequisite for dance. The preferred audience would be connoisseurs of dancing, and dances should be performed inside the palace or a house, or in a pleasant courtyard or a garden. Thus ends the section on dancing.

In the *Mānasollāsa* we find the recognition of four new categories that developed after Bharata, namely, nṛtya, lāsya, mārga and deśī. Nṛtya was first recognized as a distinct category of performance in the *Daśarūpaka*. The *Mānasollāsa* takes the term to represent the whole art of dancing. It is also the first text with a complete and sustained discussion on dancing which treats lāsya as a division of dancing. Someśvara also divides dancing into the mārga and deśī varieties, thus reflecting the growth of the two traditions. The other important contribution of Someśvara is the introduction of the deśī karaṇas, eighteen in number and found in no other text.

However, Someśvara defines neither nṛtya nor nṛtta. The term nṛtta occurs only a few times in the text some of which might have been due to scribal errors since the author does not seem to be concerned with nṛtta except for using the word to form the term nṛttahasta.[93] The term he uses specifically for dancing is nartana, which he divides into six types: nāṭya (mimetic), lāsya (delicate), tāṇḍava (vigorous), viṣama (acrobatic),

[93] *Mānas.* 16.4. 957 ; 1138 ; 1150; 1238; 1262;1269-70; 1277; 1296.

vikaṭa (ludicrous) and laghu (light and graceful). The inclusion of nāṭya as a form of dancing is a continuation from the *Viṣṇudharmottara Purāṇa*'s division of dancing,[94] and the use of the term shows that it obviously had a wider meaning at this time than in later times. We shall reserve its discussion for a later chapter.

A work from this period, but not dated with certainty, which deals with drama is the *Nāṭakalakṣaṇaratnakośa* of Sāgaranandin. From internal evidence Raghavan suggests in his introduction to the translation of the text that Sāgaranandin's date could not have been earlier than that of Abhinavagupta, Dhanañjaya or Bhoja, that is, not earlier than the thirteenth century, nor later than that of Śāradātanaya.[95] The text, as the name suggests, deals with the definition and nature of nāṭaka as well as other varieties of drama in the fullest detail. The author devotes a substantial part of the text to minor dramatic types but does not put them into a separate category. He follows the tradition of the *Nāṭyaśāstra* in his approach to the major dramatic types and also in his discussion of rasa; for example, following Bharata, he does not include śāntarasa, which was a category introduced by Abhinavagupta.

One of the most important contributions of the *Nāṭakalakṣaṇaratnakośa* is that it provides a systematic overview of the literature that preceded it. The same task was undertaken, but not performed methodically, by Śāradātanaya, whom we shall discuss next. The survey in the *Nāṭakalakṣaṇaratnakośa* helps us to understand the views of many earlier writers on many topics of Indian dramaturgy. But Sāgaranandin also has some noteworthy views of his own.[96] We may remember that

---

94 *VDP*. 3. 20. 2.

95 Raghavan's Introduction to the translation of the *Nāṭakalakṣaṇaratnakośa,* Vol. II. 1960, p.7; S. Chattopadhyaya, 1960, puts the lower limit of the date as the eleventh century (Introduction, p.xxxii).

96 *Nāṭakalakṣaṇaratnakośa,* 1960. Vol. II. p.7.

Abhinavagupta did not deal with minor dramas in much detail. Dhanañjaya paid no attention to them. Dhanika simply acknowledged the existence of such types by naming some of them. Bhoja was the first author to discuss the minor varieties of drama and to describe their characteristics, although he did not treat major and minor dramas separately. Sāgaranandin gives us a clear picture of the technical aspects of the plays of his time, noting in particular the technical language of the theatre: "The nāṭakaparibhāṣā or stage jargon, the conventions, the technical terms and the mode of address peculiar to drama, is another subject dealt with in *NLRK* (section 16) for which we are indebted to it; the only other works devoting a separate section to this subject are the *Sāhityasāra* of Sarveśvara and the *Rasārṇavasudhākara* of Singabhūpāla."[97] That his interest lay in technical issues of a practical nature is evident everywhere: "Towards another subject of similar historical nature, the music and dance items of pūrvaraṅga, Sāgaranandin adopts a more practical attitude (1157-1158) which is repeated by Viśvanātha in a more outspoken form in his *Sāhityadarpaṇa*."[98]

The list as well as the descriptions of minor types of drama given in this text, seventeen in all, are similar to what we find in Śāradātanaya's discussion of nṛtyabhedas in his *Bhāvaprakāśana*. In a later chapter of the present study, in which the development of concepts after Bharata is discussed, we shall see how the minor types of plays developed.

The *Nāṭakalakṣaṇaratnakośa* follows the *Nāṭyaśāstra* in all respects but two. In the first place, as we have seen, it discusses minor dramatic types and not only major types as Bharata does. Secondly, the *Nāṭakalakṣaṇaratnakośa* deviates from the *Nāṭyaśāstra* in prescribing lāsyāṅgas for the performance of types of bhāṇa. Bhāṇa, a major dramatic type discussed in the *Nāṭyaśāstra*, has caused a great deal of confusion in

---

97 *Ibid.* p. 8.

98 *Ibid.* p. 8.

the literature, from which the *Nāṭakalakṣaṇaratnakośa* is by no means free. After Bharata, there developed two minor dramatic types, bhāṇaka and bhāṇikā (often referred to as bhāṇa and bhāṇī). These had developed from bhāṇa, as the names indicate, and were similar to it inasmuch as they were one-act plays. What mainly distinguished the two was the application of kaiśikī vṛtti and the arousal of śṛṅgārarasa, both expressly forbidden by Bharata. The *Nāṭakalakṣaṇaratnakośa,* however, reflects the post-Bharata development by including kaiśikī vṛtti and śṛṅgārarasa as features of bhāṇaka and bhāṇikā. Of greater interest to the present work is the fact that the *Nāṭakalakṣaṇaratnakośa* prescribes the use of ten lāsyāṅgas in bhāṇa and bhāṇī. The names and descriptions of the lāsyāṅgas remain virtually unchanged from the *Nāṭyaśāstra,* though the context is entirely different. The *Nāṭakalakṣaṇaratnakośa* thus shows the dramatic use of the lāsya type of dancing that had evidently become part of the tradition.[99]

The *Bhāvaprakāśana* of Śāradātanaya (1175-1250 A.D.)[100] is a compendium of poetics and dramaturgy based on all critical works written before the author's time, that is, the period starting with the *Nāṭyaśāstra.* The author discusses different schools of literary criticism, sometimes accepting other's views and sometimes refuting them or giving his own views. The editor of this text has traced Śāradātanaya's indebtedness to his predecessors in detail in the introduction to the edition.[101] The text contains ten adhikāras or chapters, of which the first three are on bhāva and rasa. The fourth and the fifth are on the characters of the hero and heroine. Of relevance to dancing is a discussion at the end of the fifth chapter on glances that express rasa and bhāva. The sixth chapter discusses the relation between word and meaning. Chapters seven to ten

---

[99] *NLRK.* 2853-98; See also Bose, 1970, p. 15.

[100] Raghavan, 1957, p. 28; *Bh.P.* 1968. G.O.S. ed. Introduction, pp. 72-77.

[101] *Ibid.* pp. 63-71.

all contain material of immediate interest to us. The seventh chapter is on nāṭya which includes dance and music. The eighth chapter discusses major and minor types of dramas, while the ninth chapter discusses in detail the minor types, putting them into a separate category which the author calls nṛtyabhedas. The ninth chapter also includes a discussion on different types of kāvyas or poetic compositions. The tenth and final chapter is of particular interest for it explains the distinction between nṛtta and nṛtya and between mārga and deśī. The information on dance given in the previous chapters is summarized in the tenth, which further describes the characteristics of various kinds of performers and audiences. The chapter also covers a number of topics of general interest, adds a few more words on music, rasa and bhāva, alaṁkāra, and discusses the land known as Bhāratavarṣa, her languages and their use in a dramatic performance.

Although Śāradātanaya is very informative, his treatment of his subjects (particularly, drama and dance) is unsystematic. He often moves abruptly from one topic to another and gives inconsistent information on the same topic at different times, drawing-particularly-upon different sources or theories, which, however, he does not adequately explain. As a result one has to scan the entire text and correlate the scattered discussion to get a cogent overview of his opinions.

An analysis of some topics in the chapters of our interest will clarify my comment on his work. In the seventh chapter he introduces major dramatic forms and puts other forms into a category that he calls nṛtyabheda: नृत्यभेदा भवेयुस्ते डोम्बीश्रीगदितादय: (*Bh.P.* p.181), that is, [spectacles such as] ḍombī, śrīgadita and so on are divisions of nṛtya. He does not comment on their nature in this context since his main interest at this point is the use of rasa and bhāva in these spectacles, in discussing which he follows Bhoja. The plays, called rūpakas, which are dependant on vākyārthābhinaya, literally, expressing the meaning of the sentences, produce rasa and are व्याख्यार्थाभिनयात्मका: that is, they aim at bringing out the total meaning. The पदार्थाभिनयात्मक spectacles, that is, the spectacles expressing the meaning of particular words, are dependant on bhāva. He further says that nṛtya is dependent on emotion: भावाश्रय, a view shared by Dhanañjaya.[102] About nṛtta, however, Śāradātanaya has his own opinions. He believes that nṛtta is dependant on rasa: नृत्तं रसाश्रयम् (*Bh.P.* p. 181.). Not only is this view original to him, it contradicts Bharata's view that, न खल्वर्थकञ्चिन्नृत्तमपेक्षते (*NŚ.* 4.263), that is, nṛtta does not depend on any meaning. Bharata further says that न हि रसादृते कश्चिदर्थः प्रवर्त्तते (*NŚ.* Vol. I, 1956, p.271), that is, no meaning is expressed without [producing] any rasa. Therefore, Śāradātanaya's definition of nṛtta seems to assume that it expresses meaning and does not merely beautify a dramatic presentation. Accordingly, nṛtta can generate rasa.

Śāradātanaya differs not only from Bharata but from all his predecessors and contemporaries. In the *Daśarūpaka* Dhanañjaya views nṛtta as dependant on tāla and laya, rhythm and tempo: नृत्तं ताललयाश्रयम् (*DR.*1. 9) and recognizes only nāṭya as an art-form expressing rasa: नाट्यं रसाश्रयम् (*DR.*1. 9). In the *Saṅgītasamayasāra,* Pārśvadeva, another author who flourished around this time, says that nṛtta depends on tāla, bhāva and laya: तालभावलयायत्तः . . . . (*SSam.* 7.2). That nṛtta is rasāśraya is Śāradātanaya's own interpretation.

After introducing the dramatic forms in the seventh chapter Śāradātanaya elaborates on the preliminaries of dramatic performances which include music and dance. In this part of the discussion he mainly follows Bharata. Śāradātanaya states that the definition of nṛtta and nṛtya are many and given by various authors, which he will discuss later. He views these two art-forms as auxiliary to drama that are used in the preliminaries of a play. In this context he follows the tradition of Bharata.

---

102 *Ibid.* p. 181; *DR.* 1.9.

In the eighth chapter he discusses ten major types of drama that depend on rasa and twenty others that depend on bhāva. He says that all the thirty varieties are often referred to as rūpakas.[103] He discusses all the major types of drama, including bhāṇa, in detail. He states that ten lāsyāṅgas are used in bhāṇa. After describing the ten lāsyāṅgas, following Bharata, he describes four nṛtyabhedas, which he says other authorities discuss. These he includes in the same section on bhāṇa. Not minor types of drama, these nṛtyabhedas are the four piṇḍībandhas or group dances described by Bharata in his fourth chapter and viewed by him as parts of the preliminaries to a play. The descriptions of these four nṛtyabhedas in the *Bhāvaprakāśana,* however, are much more precise and easy to comprehend compared to Bharata's cryptic definition (*NŚ.* 4. 290-91). The discussion ends with instructions for training a dancer in these dances: भद्रासनेन यन्त्रेण तत्तच्छिक्षा विधीयते (*Bh.P.* p. 246) -- the training is prescribed through bhadrāsana and yantra.[104] The actions implied in these terms are hard to visualize through the bare mention of the terms in this text as also in the *Nāṭyaśāstra* and the *Viṣṇudharmotttara Purāṇa* (*VDP.*3.20.55). Abhinavagupta and the *Rājapraśnīya,* one of the Jainasūtras, clarify the terms to some extent, as will be seen in a later chapter of the present study in which the conceptual development of the art of dance will be discussed in detail.

The ninth chapter of the *Bhāvaprakāśana* is devoted to the nṛtyabhedas, that is, the twenty minor varieties of drama mentioned in the seventh chapter. One of these nṛtyabhedas is what he calls bhāṇa, which is different from the bhāṇa that is known as a major dramatic type. The use

---

[103] *Bh.P.* p. 221.

[104] The actions denoted by the terms भद्रासन and यन्त्र are not very clear from the definition of Bharata, and Śāradātanaya has not explained them either. These seem to be formations of figures on the stage by a group of female dancers. Bharata also says that students need proper guidance to be able to perform them (*NŚ.* 4. 290-91). See pp.113-16*infra* for a discussion of the piṇḍībandhas.

of the same term to name both major and minor types, each with a different definition, has caused a great deal of confusion. This chapter gives a detailed description of each kind of these nṛtyabhedas with illustrations from literary works, some of which have survived, like the *Karpūramañjarī* of Rājaśekhara, *Vikramorvaśīyam* of Kālidāsa, *Ratnāvalī* of Harṣa and others.[105] These are major sources for our understanding of the development of dancing.

The last chapter, the tenth, is used to sum up what the author has dealt with so far. He begins by saying: उक्ता नाट्यस्य नृत्तस्य भेदा: सर्वे यथार्थत: (*Bh.P.* p.284)--the varieties of nāṭya and nṛtta have all been explained [by me] in an appropriate manner. In the middle section of the chapter (pp. 295- 302) he summarizes what had been said about dance and drama in the preceding chapters, but adds new interpretations, and these have often confused the issues. However, we shall try to clarify them as far as possible when we examine them more closely in a later chapter.

The *Saṅgītasamayasāra* of Pārśvadeva is the second work devoted to musicology during the second period of our study. This text discusses saṅgīta, that is, gīta (vocal music), vādya (instrumental music) and nṛtta and nṛtya (dance). Besides the *Mānasollāsa,* other works from the second period discussed so far are works on dramaturgy and literary criticism. The *Saṅgītasamayasāra* is the second work of the period to discuss music and dance as separate art-forms and not as art-forms auxiliary to drama.

The date of the author is uncertain. According to Raghavan, Pārśvadeva was a Jaina writer who must have lived between 1165-1330 A. D. because he refers to Bhoja (1010-1050 A.D), Someśvara (about 1131 A.D.), Paramardi (about 1165 A.D.) and Siṁhabhūpāla(about 1330 A.D.)[106] In the introduction to his edition of *Nṛttaratnāvalī,* Raghavan

---

105 *Bh.P,* pp. 238, 244, 269, etc.

106 Raghavan,1956, p, 29.

places Pārśvadeva between Paramardi and Jāya (1253 A.D.)[107] The *Saṅgītasamayasāra* was first edited in 1925 from one manuscript by T. Ganapati Shastri who does not suggest any date for the author. This edition in the Trivandrum Sanskrit Series is often corrupt. A second edition came out in 1977, prepared by Acarya Brihaspati and based on the collation of more manuscripts and of T. Ganapati Shastri's edition. Comparing the text with other relevant works, the editor places Pārśvadeva after Śārṅgadeva and in the later part of the thirteenth century. Pārśvadeva is similarly placed in the thirteenth century by M. Krishnamachariar.[108] From what the *Saṅgītasamayasāra* has to say on the deśī dances it seems likely that Pārśvadeva lived before Jāya in the later part of the twelfth or the earlier part of the thirteenth century.[109]

The two editions of the text differ in the organization of the text, but both versions have essentially the same contents. Nijenhuis has described the content of the work following the 1925 text,[110] one that has too many errors to be reliable. I have followed the later edition in describing the text and its content.

The work is in nine chapters and for the most part it is devoted to vocal and instrumental music. The seventh chapter and the last part of the eighth are of interest to the study of dance. The author quotes frequently from older authorities, such as Kohala (*SSam.* 1.39) and Mataṅga, often without naming the author (*SSam.* 2.1). Among later authorities he refers to Bhoja and Someśvara (*SSam.*1.3).

---

107 Raghavan,1965, *NR.* Introduction, pp. 77-8.

108 Acarya Brihaspati,1977, Introduction, p. 21; Krishnamachariar, 1974, p. 855.

109 Pārśvadeva says that he will discuss all the deśyaṅgas, the features of deśī, which have not been discussed so far by anyone (*SSam.* 7.194). As against the eighteen described by Pārśvadeva, Jāya describes forty-six. (*SSam.* 7. 194-97; *NR.* 6.118-22.)

110 Nijenhuis,1977, p.13.

Beginning with the usual benediction, the first chapter discusses the intricacies of vocal music, such as svara, mūrchanā, jāti, rāga etc. of the mārga or classical tradition. We have already noted in the *Daśarūpaka* that the term mārga is used to refer to the classical tradition. *Saṅgītasamayasāra*'s use of the term in the same sense shows that the term had by this time passed into common usage. The second chapter is devoted to the deśī or regional tradition. In the third chapter the author expands on the theories of various aspects of music, such as svara, ālāpa etc. The fourth chapter deals with rāgas. The fifth discusses the composition of vocal music and the sixth, instrumental music. The seventh chapter is devoted entirely to dancing, which he refers to as nṛtta, its definition and the body movements required, in dealing with all of which it follows the tradition established by Bharata. Like Bharata, Pārśvadeva divides body parts into two:aṅga and upāṅga. He counts all the movements of the different parts of the body and the karaṇas and aṅgahāras following Bharata but while describing them he does not discuss the cārī, sthāna, karaṇa or aṅgahāra from the Bharata tradition but follows the deśī tradition. He seems to take Bharata's tradition as nṛtta and the deśī tradition as nṛtya. He describes the deśīnṛtyas which, according to him, consist of peraṇa, pekkhaṇa, guṇḍalī and daṇḍarāsa.[111] He then discusses the sthānas and cārīs needed for these deśī dances. He uses the term pāla for cārī, a term found in no other text. However, although the discussion starts with the term pāla, it ends with the term cārī.[112] Next, the author describes the utplutikaraṇas, also needed for the deśī dances, other karaṇas with different deśīsthānas, bhramarīs,[113] and moves on to

[111] *SSam.* 7. 130-32.

[112] *SSam.* 7. 157; 7. 180.

[113] *Ibid.* 7. 193-4. While it is mentioned merely as a form of cārī in the *NŚ*. bhramarī became an important movement of dance technique in the medieval period. This is

describing the aṅgas or features of deśī dances, calling them deśyaṅgāni. Jāya, as we shall see later, combines these deśī aṅgas and the aṅgas of lāsya, and putting them into one category calls them deśī lāsyas. After describing the deśī aṅgas, Pārśvadeva describes the aṅgas or parts of peraṇa. Finally, he discusses the instrumental music, drumming in particular, needed for four kinds of deśī dances, namely, peraṇa, pekkhaṇa, guṇḍalī and daṇḍarāsa. The requirements of a good dancer, her physical appearance and the way she should be dressed are also described towards the end of the seventh chapter. The eighth chapter discusses the tāla or rhythm and its varieties, both mārga and deśī. The ninth chapter discusses the sitting arrangements, the qualifications of the audience, the poets, the singers, the dancers, the qualities and faults of a singer, drummers and their qualities and faults and those of the dancers needed for each type of deśī dance. The author warns against making dance and music subjects of gambling matches and ends the text by saying that music brings liberation or mokṣa, a concept characteristic of the medieval period.[114]

One of the most influential works on music and dance from this period is the *Saṅgītaratnākara* of Śārṅgadeva who lived in the thirteenth century under the patronage of the Yādava king Singhana.[115] Followed by most of the writers after Śārṅgadeva's time, it is one of the most important sources or our knowledge of music and dance because there is hardly any other work of the time comparable to the *Saṅgītaratnākara* in its methodical approach. The special strength of the work lies in the author's clear exposition of both music and dance. On music it remains a standard authority. On dancing Śārṅgadeva has less information to offer than his

---

the first text to consider bhramarī as a distinct class of dance movement, with several sub-classes.

114 Katz,1987, commentary on the verses. 18-21.

115 Nijenhuis,1977, p.12; *SR*. Vol. IV, tr. Raja and Burnier, 1976, Preface. p. vii.

contemporary Jāya Senāpati, but what he offers is thoroughly systematic, presenting a clear picture of two traditions, mārga and deśī.

The text is in seven chapters, of which the first six are on vocal and instrumental music. The first chapter deals with nāda (the sound), the second with rāga (musical mode), the third with prakīrṇa (miscellaneous topics relating to music), the fourth with prabandha (composition), the fifth with mārga (classical) and deśī (regional) tāla (rhythm), and the sixth with vādya (musical instruments). The seventh chapter, on dance, is the one that is of interest to us. It has 1678 verses and is an excellent source of our knowledge of both mārga and deśī traditions of dancing in the author's time. In describing the mārga tradition he follows Bharata but he extends our knowledge significantly by giving for the first time a systematic account of the deśī tradition of dancing. Though the *Mānasollāsa* and the *Saṅgītasamayasāra* had previously introduced the deśī style into the traditional account of dancing, it is Śārṅgadeva who systematizes that account. In doing so he combines the material from the *Nāṭyaśāstra* with that from later works and presents a coherent view not found in previous works. Although he follows Bharata in describing the movements of the body, he differs from Bharata in dividing the limbs into three categories, aṅga, upāṅga and pratyaṅga, and not only into aṅga and upāṅga. In this he follows the *Mānasollāsa.* Although the limbs are divided into three categories, no new movements are added to those in the *Nāṭyaśāstra.* He follows Someśvara in using the term nartana for dance, dividing nartana into three categories, nāṭya, nṛtya and nṛtta (*SR.* 7. 3). In narrating the legend about the origin of dance he again follows the *Nāṭyaśāstra,* but differs from it in identifying tāṇḍava as Śiva's dance and lāsya as Pārvatī's. According to Śārṅgadeva, nṛtta and nṛtya can both be of two kinds, tāṇḍava and lāsya (*SR.* 7. 28). Tāṇḍava requires uddhata (forceful) and lāsya requires lalita (delicate) movements (*SR.* 7. 29-30). Nṛtta has three varieties, viṣama, vikaṭa and laghu, identified respectively as rope-dancing, a comic dance, and a dance based on easy karaṇas. Here

Śārṅgadeva is repeating the classification found in the *Mānasollāsa*, except that he uses the term nṛtta, not nartana, as Someśvara does and that he defines them somewhat differently. Śārṅgadeva's description of cārī, sthāna, karaṇa and aṅgahāras of the mārga type are as in the *Nāṭyaśāstra*. But the deśī cārīs, sthānas and utplutikaraṇas are, of course, new, for Bharata does not record the deśī tradition. Some of the thirty-six utplutikaraṇas in the *Saṅgītaratnākara* are the same as those in the *Mānasollāsa* which lists eighteen karaṇas of the deśī variety (*Mānas.* 16. 4. 1384-99). The *Saṅgītasamayasāra* describes eleven deśī karaṇas and mentions five bhramarīs. Bhramarīs are included among utplutikaraṇas by Śārṅgadeva. In the *Nāṭyaśāstra* bhramarī was the name of a cārī, a not particularly complicated revolving movement. Later, more than one bhramarī came into being, all of them being variations of whirling movements. Gradually, these developed into so much more elaborate movements that they came to be recognized as constituting a distinct class, the earliest work to so consider them being *Saṅgītasamayasāra* (7.193); the *Abhinayadarpaṇa* (289-98) too regards them as a distinct group. Their inclusion among the utplutikaraṇas by Śārṅgadeva shows that by his time bhramarīs were so developed and important that they had come to be regarded as a form of karaṇas.

After the description of the sthānas which include sitting and lying postures that are appropriate to drama, the author discusses vṛttis or styles of presentation and conventions. This is followed by a description of maṇḍala (combination of cārīs) and then of ten lāsyāṅgas of the deśī variety. Jāya, who was a contemporary of Śārṅgadeva, gives us a list of forty-six lāsyāṅgas, and Pārśvadeva, who preceded both, gives us twenty deśī aṅgas requiring similar movements,[116] but it is Śārṅgadeva's list of ten lāsyāṅgas that continued to be reproduced by a number of later authors.

[116] *NR.* 6. 117-73; *SSam.* 7. 194-216.

After describing the lāsyāṅgas Śārṅgadeva explains the importance of aesthetic beauty, lays down the rules of exercise, and describes the qualities and faults of a performer (including a description of her make-up and costume), and those of the teacher and the group of supporting performers. Then he describes the sequential process of a performance, including the musical accompaniment, in the pure mode or śuddhapaddhati(*SR.* 7. 1260-73).

Next described are gauṇḍalī and peraṇi. These two dances seem to be the commonest pieces of dancing in the deśī tradition, for they are found in almost all the works from the *Saṅgitasamayasāra* in the twelfth/thirteenth century down to the *Śivatattvaratnākara* in the early eighteenth century. Peraṇi in particular has had a long life, for literature from the Andhra Province records it till the end of the nineteenth century and a number of present day dancers have attempted to revive it.[117] Its popularity in that region is also suggested by the widespread use of one of the fast movements essential to it, gharghara, which requires special movements of ankle bells. In the sixteenth century work, the *Nartananirṇaya*, Puṇḍarīka Viṭṭhala remarks that gharghara was a distinctive feature of the deśī dances of the Drāviḍa region (*NN.* 50a-b). The same movement is an essential feature of today's Kathak dancing[118] in which it is known as tatkār. Gauṇḍalī dance certainly survived till the eighteenth century[119] but no current practice of it is known.

After describing these two dance pieces, Śārṅgadeva deals with the qualifications of the ācārya (the teacher), the naṭa (the actor), the nartaka (the dancer), the vaitālika (a general entertainer), the cāraṇa (an expert in understanding gharghara) and the kohlāṭika (a performer who specializes in bhramarī, rope-walking and dancing with a dagger). Next, he describes

---

117 *NR.*,1965, Introduction, p.137-41.

118 *Classical and Folk Dances of India*,1953, Part III, pp. 25-27.

119 *ŚTR.* 6.3. 15-16.

the audience and the sitting arrangements. Finally, he discusses rasas (nine in number), sthāyībhāvas (thirty-three in number) and the definition of sattva (the essence) and sāttvikabhāvas (eight in number). The chapter concludes with final prayers.

The *Saṅgītaratnākara* has a highly important supplement in the form of a commentary on it called *Kalānidhi* and written in the fourteenth century by Kallinātha. The commentator quotes from Kohala to expand Śārṅgadeva's description of arm movements and adds an entire section on vartanā, of which thirty-one (*SR.* pp.105-10) are given, and another section on cālaka, which are fifty in number (*SR.* pp.111-24). Kallinātha quotes Kohala again with respect to cārī, adding a new cārī called madhupacārī, of which twenty-five are described (*SR.* pp.313-17). Except for the *Kalānidhi,* the only texts that include these cārīs are the *Nṛtyādhyāya* of Aśokamalla and the *Nṛtyaratnakośa* of Mahārāṇā Kumbhā, which, however, use the term muḍupacārī for the same movements.[120]

Close in time to the *Saṅgītaratnākara* was the *Nṛttaratnāvalī* of Jāya Senāpati which was written in the thirteenth century A.D.[121] The authors were contemporaries and as Raghavan points out, Jāya must have known of Śārṅgadeva's work. But Jāya makes no mention of Śārṅgadeva's work,[122] very likely because of the rivalry between the two neighbouring states where they lived. Whereas the *Saṅgītaratnākara* is a text that deals with saṅgīta, that is, all three musical arts, namely, vocal and instrumental music, and dance, the *Nṛttaratnāvalī* concentrates on dancing. The

---

[120] *Nr.Adh.* 1080-1115, *NRK.* 2. 3. 1-37. *NRK.* quotes Kohala after Kalānidhi, acknowledging the source at the beginning of the chapter. The lines match those in the edition of the *SR.* 1953, pp. 313-317; *NRK*. calls them muḍupa.

[121] *NR.* 1965, Introduction, pp. 8-12; Krishnamachariar, 1974, p. 855.

[122] *NR.* 1965, Introduction, pp. 73-4. Śārṅgadeva's patron was the Yādava king while Jāya's patron was the Kākatīya king; these were the rulers of two neighbouring states in South India.

Saṅgītaratnākara's single chapter on dancing is a comprehensive study of dance but a concise one. By contrast, the *Nṛttaratnāvalī* devotes all eight chapters to dance and discusses vocal or instrumental music only in the context of dance.

The *Nṛttaratnāvalī* has eight chapters devoted entirely to dancing and covers two traditions. The first four chapters of the text discuss the mārga tradition following the *Nāṭyaśāstra* and the other four discuss the deśī. The tradition of Bharata is regarded as mārga while the tradition comprising regional and popular styles is called deśī, the latter being a subject on which Jāya is particularly informative. This is the only work that deals exclusively with dance in such detail. The text has been critically edited by V. Raghavan who gives a great deal of related information on the subject in his introduction. Of particular help is Raghavan's comparison of Jāya's work with the work of some of his contemporaries in the field.

The first chapter begins with the customary benediction, praising dance as an art-form and defining nāṭya. The four modes of abhinaya, i.e., āṅgika, vācika, āhārya and sāttvika, the six forms of dancing–nṛtta, nṛtya, mārga, deśī, tāṇḍava and lāsya–are then discussed in detail. Chapter two deals with abhinaya. Since āṅgika abhinaya or body movements are the most relevant to dance, Jāya describes in detail the movements of the major and minor limbs, six aṅgas, six pratyaṅgas and six upāṅgas. He also describes the hand-gestures in this chapter, in course of which he quotes other authors, such as Abhinavagupta, Kīrtidhara and others.[123] The third chapter is on cārīs (movements of one leg), sthānas (postures), nyāya (rules of performance), vyāyāma (exercise), sauṣṭhava (grace), more sthānas and maṇḍalas (combinations of cārīs). The fourth chapter describes karaṇas (dance-units) and aṅgahāras (sequences of dance-units) and ends with recakas (extending movements of the neck, the hands, the

[123] *NR*. 2. 182; 2. 183; 2. 214; 2. 265; 2. 275. Jāya refers frequently to a " muni," which seems to indicate Bharata, *NR*. 2. 4, 202, 213, 215, 273.

waist and the feet) mainly in the lines of the *Nāṭyaśāstra.* In general, Jāya's treatment of the mārga tradition is faithful to Bharata and is precise and systematic.

The second half of the text is devoted to the deśī tradition, in dealing with which the author is just as organized and informative as he is with mārga. The fifth chapter, which is the first on the deśī tradition, starts by defining the term deśī. Deśī sthānas, utplutikaraṇas (deśī karaṇas) and bhramarīs (pirouettes) are described. We have already noted how bhramarīs became popular and came to be regarded as a separate category comprising several varieties. We may note that one such variety, cakrabhramarī, a fast pirouette, has survived as a distinctive feature of the Kathak style. A variations of the movement appears also in the Maṇipurī style which employs slow revolving movements, but bhramarīs are no longer important in other classical styles of dancing in India today.[124] In this chapter, the fifth, the author refers to his other work, the *Gītaratnāvalī,* which has not come down to us.

The sixth chapter deals with movements of the feet. These deśīpādas, as they are called in this work, are often described as deśī cārīs in the later texts. Cārīs are the movements of one leg which necessarily include foot movements as well but cārīs and pādas are always treated as separate movements in the Bharata tradition. Jāya has a separate section on deśī cārīs, describing cārīs not found in works preceding his. His descriptions of deśī pāṭamaṇis (foot movements) are his own as well.[125] From the descriptions of the deśīpādas, pāṭamaṇis and cārīs one can say that pādas involve simple floor contacts of the feet; pāṭamaṇis involve striking the ground with the feet and cārīs involve movements of one leg extended. He then describes forty-six varieties of deśī lāsyāṅgas which include the deśī

---

[124] The movement in Kathak comparable to the cakrabhramarī is called cakkar. See p. 213.

[125] Raghavan,1965, p.174. fn.

lāsyāṅgas described in the *Saṅgītaratnākara* and the deśī aṅgas found in the *Saṅgītasamayasāra.* Gatis or gaits are described next.

The seventh chapter discusses auspicious dates for beginning dance lessons (the term he uses here is nṛtya), the characteristics of the stage and some general discussion on presentation, the time and location of dance performances, the worship of Gaṇeśa, methods of practice, the qualifications desirable in a dancer, dance costume, hand-gestures for practice and the accompanying vocal and instrumental music. The chapter then concentrates on describing individual dance pieces, calling them deśīnṛtta. These include peraṇi, pekkhaṇa, sūḍa, rāsaka, carcarī, nāṭyarāsaka, śivapriya, ciṇṭu, kanduka, bhāṇḍikā, ghaṭisani, cāraṇa, bahurūpa, kollāṭa and gauṇḍalī. We come across only a few of these in the *Saṅgītaratnākara* and the *Saṅgītasamayasāra.* Most of them occur later in the *Nṛttaratnakośa.*[126] The chapter concludes with the description of the stage, its types and shapes, the audience and the presiding dignitary. The eighth and final chapter provides more information regarding presentation in general, the recital, the appropriate time for its presentation, the arrival of the chief guest and the welcome accorded the king, other members of the audience, the qualities required in a dancer, her costume, the orchestra, the sitting arrangements, the entrance of a dancer, the use of three curtains on the stage and their removal.[127] The chapter ends with advice on honouring the dancer, the musicians and the poet.

Although it may seem that the author has not made any significant contribution while dealing with the mārga tradition since he follows Bharata, this is not true. The description of each karaṇa of the mārga

---

126 See p.81 *infra.*

127 This feature of using and removing the curtains held by performers other than the dancer is still very much in use in various dance styles of South India. Kathakali, the classical dance style of Kerala, is the commonest example.

tradition is unique. This happens to be the first of the very few texts which describe karaṇas along with cārīs, hand-gestures and foot movements in such a way that by following the directions a karaṇa can be reproduced. Not only does Jāya elaborate on the actual performance of the karaṇas, he quotes the views of earlier writers, which is helpful in tracing the evolution of dance. In a later chapter we shall discuss his treatment of the karaṇas and deśī dances, in which context his contribution is particularly important.

The *Sāhityadarpaṇa* of Viśvanātha, written in the fourteenth century, is the last treatise from the second period, one principally on poetics, to be considered here. A work that deals also with dramaturgy,[128] the *Sāhityadarpaṇa* is one of the most illuminating works on poetics. According to Gerow, "With Viśvanātha, the period of poetics beginning with Mammaṭa, marked by a concern to regularize and codify alaṁkāravidyā as a śāstra, may be said to have reached its conclusion." Gerow views this text as the "second best known Indian poetic text."[129] As the name suggests, the work is meant to be a mirror of literature, that is, a work on literary theory. The text is divided into ten chapters: i. the nature of kāvya (a poetic composition), ii. vākya (a sentence), iii. rasa and bhāva (aesthetic affect and emotional expression), iv. dhvani (sound), v. vyañjanā (rhetorical expression), vi. dṛśyakāvya (a poetic composition to be seen), vii. doṣa (the defects of a kāvya), viii. guṇa (the qualities of a kāvya), ix. rīti (style) and x. alaṁkāra (poetics). Of these ten, the sixth chapter, which is concerned with dṛśyakāvya, is of interest to us. Viśvanātha divides kāvya into two groups, dṛśya and śravya, that is, poetic compositions to be seen and poetic compositions to be heard. The dṛśyakāvyas are divided into two categories again, rūpaka and uparūpaka. Rūpakas are said to be of ten types, which is a division inherited from

---

128 Dasgupta, 1947, Vol. I, p. 566.

129 Gerow, 1977, pp. 281, 283.

Bharata. However, Viśvanātha considers lāsyāṅgas as parts of bhāṇa like other writers who associate lāsyāṅgas with bhāṇa.

The major contribution of Viśvanātha is that he gives a class name to minor types of rūpakas, which he calls uparūpakas, a term that became standard in the works of the authors after him and continues to be used by Sanskrit scholars. These uparūpakas are eighteen in number, they employ dancing, and they are described in detail.[130] Since they comprise a major genre relevant to the study of dancing, we shall reserve them for detailed study in a later chapter.

The *Saṅgītopaniṣatsāroddhāra* is a treatise on music and dance written in the fourteenth century (1350 A.D.) by the Jaina writer Sudhākalaśa. The writer says that it is an abridged version of his previous and larger work, *Saṅgītopaniṣat,* written in 1324 A.D.[131] No copy of it is known to exist. The abridged version does not record anything new, or anything that had not already been said by Śārṅgadeva or Jāya who preceded Sudhākalaśa by about a hundred years. Nor does the author give any information on the development of the art that must have taken place during these hundred years. The *Saṅgītopaniṣatsāroddhāra* is not concerned with two traditions, mārga and deśī. Surprisingly, the author does not even seem to recognize the development of the separate traditions of mārga and deśī dance. He mostly repeats the information gathered till his time by his predecessors, with a few minor variations. Nevertheless, the text is useful as an organized and succinct report.

The work is in six chapters, the first four of which are on gīta or vocal music and its technicalities, on tāla or rhythm, and on the origin of vādya or musical instruments. The fifth and the sixth are devoted to dancing and these are the two chapters which are of interest to us. In the fifth chapter, which contains 141 verses, the author begins with the praise of Jinapati.

---

130 *SD.* 6.3-312.

131 *Saṅgītopaniṣatsāroddhāra,* 1961, Introduction, p. v; see also the text, *SUS.* 6. 152.

The term he uses for dance is nṛtya (*SUS.* 5. 2). After a few verses, giving the legend of the origin of dance, the author defines three varieties of an art-form consisting of nṛtta, nṛtya and nāṭya. The author derives the term nṛtya from the root nṛt and defines the art as gātrasya vikṣepaḥ, i.e., movements of the body.[132] According to him, nṛtta is danced by men, nṛtya by women, while nāṭya is nāṭaka, performed by both men and women. He considers both lāsya and tāṇḍava to be forms of nṛtya and says that lāsya originated from Gaurī (=Pārvatī) and tāṇḍava from Rudra (=Śiva). Lāsya is sukumāra or delicate while tāṇḍava, he says, has the qualities of viṣama.[133] Evidently, viṣama had a different connotation for Sudhākalaśa, for he views viṣama as "difficult or vigorous" movements as opposed to Śārṅgadeva's view of viṣama as an "acrobatic" style that included such performances as rope-walking. Jāya, however, connects viṣama with tāṇḍava while referring to viṣamatāṇḍava as a feature of a deśī dance called peraṇi, although he does not explain its nature.[134]

The rest of the fifth chapter is devoted to describing the movements of the limbs, which are divided into aṅga, upāṅga and pratyaṅga, as is customary in the texts of the medieval period. Sudhākalaśa does not say anything about their application and ends the chapter with a description of six sthānas. However, his treatment of two classes of movements, movements of the feet and the postures, differs from that of other texts. Pādas, or the positions of the feet, and pādakarmas, or the actions of the feet, are described separately in this text in contrast both with the *Nāṭyaśāstra* and the *Saṅgītaratnākara,* which describe positions as well as movements of the feet under one category called pāda.[135] Further, Sudhākalaśa treats sthānas and sthānakas as separate categories of

[132] *SUS.* 5. 6.

[133] *SUS.* 5.10.

[134] *SR.* 7. 31; *NR.* 7. 63.

[135] *SUS.* 5.126-34.

postures which no other writer does. According to him, sthānas are postures meant for women while sthānakas are postures meant for men. He adds no new postures, although his descriptions of the movements vary in details from other accounts.[136]

The sixth chapter mainly defines karaṇas and aṅgahāras. Karaṇas, according to Sudhākalaśa, are components of lāsyāṅgas and nṛtya. He lists one hundred and eight karaṇas but actually describes one hundred and five. In some details the karaṇas occasionally differ from those found in the *Nāṭyaśāstra* and the works that followed it, including the *Saṅgītaratnākara*. Some have different names and movements.[137] The number of the aṅgahāras is the same as in the *Nāṭyaśāstra* but some names are different,[138] although what these new aṅgahāras were cannot be ascertained, for they are described neither in this work nor in any other. That Sudhākalaśa was recording contemporary traditions is apparent from his treatment of the bhramarīs, which he puts in a group of six. Most of them have the same names as in the *Saṅgītaratnākara*, with a few variations.[139] We have already noticed in the earlier treatises that bhramarī had developed from a simple cārī movement to a separate category which included a variety of whirling movements. The *Saṅgītasamayasāra* was the first text to collect them into one group. It places them between the descriptions of the utplutikaraṇas (karaṇas involving leaps and recognized as deśīkaraṇas) and the deśī aṅgas

---

[136] *SUS.* 5.135-40.

[137] *SUS.* 6. 2; 6. 6-111; Karaṇas such as ardhasūci and alāta, for instance, use different cārīs in the tradition described in the *Nāṭyaśāstra* and the *Saṅgītaratnākara*. See Bose, 1970, pp. 108-35; karaṇas such as uruślista and kaṭirecita etc. are new. These may have come from a different tradition.

[138] *SUS.* 6.115-19. Haripriya, ālipallava, bhujaṅgatrasta, jayadarpa, vilasanmada and mahodvṛtta are new names but since they are not described we do not know what they were like. They are described in no other text.

[139] *SUS.* 6.120-22.

(features of deśī).[140] The *Saṅgītaratnākara* describes seven bharamarīs which it places with the utplutikaraṇas, while the *Nṛttaratnāvalī* treats them separately as a group of thirteen variations.[141] The *Saṅgītopaniṣatsāroddhāra* also treats them separately from the utpluti or deśīkaraṇas. After the bhramarīs cārīs are named but not described.

Concluding the descriptions of the dance movements and their sequences at this point, the author makes an interesting remark. He states that theory and practice are as important to a dancer as they are to a theorist. He then passes on to nartakabhāṣā and nṛtyabhāvas, that is, special languages and expressions, and provides examples from the western part of India where he lived.[142] The paddhati or presentation technique is described next. At the end, the text follows the contemporary practice of other works by providing the usual description of the presiding dignitary, the audience, the vāggeyakāra[143] (a musician who also composes music) and the gandharvarañjaka (knowledgeable in a variety of music and thus an entertaining performer). The text comes to an end with a final prayer and the verse stating that it is an abridged version of the author's larger work, the *Saṅgītopaniṣat.*

The *Saṅgītacandra* is a work containing 2168 verses by Śuklapaṇḍita, also known as Vipradāsa. He has been placed in the fourteenth century by the editor of the currently available edition who follows Ramakrishna Kavi. Kavi believes that Kumbhakarṇa based his work on the

140 There are five such bhramarīs. *SSam.* 7. 193.

141 *SR.* 7. 755; 7. 775-82; *NR.* 5. 83-105.

142 *SUS.* 6. 129-32. See Bose, 1970, p. 4.

143 *SUS.* 6. 143. The editor has chosen vāṅmayakāraka to refer to a composer musician. The word for this type of musician found in other texts is vāggeyakāraka. (*SR.* 7. 347; *NR.*8. 29). One of the MSS. of the *SUS.* reads gāggeyakāraka, very likely a scribal error.

Saṅgītacandra.[144] But it is hard to say for certain who quoted from whom since the traditions recorded by the two authors seem to have come more or less from the same period. No evidence, internal or external, is available regarding the author's date or land of origin. The single manuscript in which the text exists does name the author but not at the beginning or the end, which are the sections where the author's particulars usually appear. The lack of such information may be due to the evidently unsatisfactory state of the manuscript which seems to have a number of scribal errors unemended in the current edition.[145]

The text begins with a benediction and recounts the origin of the nāṭyaveda. It then lists the proposed subjects of discussion, and gives the rules for building the dance-hall, performing the pūjā, and describes the qualifications of the presiding person and the audience. The author then explains the conduct of the pūrvaraṅga or the preliminaries following the *Nāṭyaśāstra* and mentions the four abhinayas and the four vṛttis. This introductory section ends at verse 388. From the next verse, verse 389, the author begins to describe nṛtya which he takes to represent the entire art of dance. He first divides nṛtya into two, mārganṛtya which expresses rasa, and nāṭyanṛtya, which expresses bhāva (389-94). He next describes natural and stylized movements and then adds a third variety of nṛtya, calling it deśīya nṛtya. All three varieties of nṛtya can again be divided into tāṇḍava and lāsya (395-410). Viṣama, vikaṭa and laghu are then referred to as varieties of nṛtta, a term not used so far (411-13). The author then moves on to describe movements of the major and minor limbs, which cover verses 414-1046. In describing the movements of the body he follows the *Nāṭyaśāstra,* but in his list of hand-gestures he adds a few new gestures that fall outside the *Nāṭyaśāstra.* These he takes from other sources, which he does not, however, consider reliable. He recommends

144 *Saṅgītacandra,* Introduction, p. viii.

145 For instance, kolkāṭika is not emended to the correct form, *SC.* 2. 107.

the appropriate dress and make-up for the dancer but gives no details (853-4). To this list of body movements he adds a new one, a movement of the soles of the feet (1024-25).

After describing the movements of the limbs, he describes the sthānas or postures(1047-1149), which he calls essential to dance since a dance begins with a posture and proceeds to a cārī. The sthānas include postures meant for men and women, postures for lying and sitting, all of which may be of both mārga and deśī varieties. Cārīs of the mārga and deśī varieties are described next in verses 1150-1272. Karaṇas of the mārga and deśī varieties are described in verses 1273-1517, followed by maṇḍalas in verses 1518-80. Movements in the mārga tradition are described after Bharata.

Four types of nyāya or rules for depicting battle-scenes are discussed next in 1581- 98, a topic that seems to be the author's own contribution. Aṅgahāra comes next (1596-1709), followed by descriptions of the four recakas (1710-16). Then the author discusses how the performer may represent the nine rasas (1717-1936) and the forty-one bhāvas (1937-2027). The description of the dance teacher and the preceptor comes next (2028-32), followed by the rules of practice(2033-40). In verses 2041-57 the author identifies the qualities required in a performer as well as her possible strengths and shortcomings. This is followed by a description of the dancer's ornaments (2058-69).

In the next section the author discusses the deśī forms, beginning with ten lāsyāṅgas (2070-96). While he mainly follows the *Saṅgītaratnākara* here, he adds three new types of rekhā (2097-99). This is followed by a description of the peraṇi dance (2100-2102), after which the author again discusses (2103-2114) the characteristics of various performers as well as others connected with performances, such as, a naṭa (actor), a nartaka (dancer), a vaitālika (critic and entertainer), a cāraṇa (musician), a kolkāṭika (correctly, a kohlāṭika, an acrobatic dancer) and the troupe. He then discusses the techniques, respectively, of a śuddha or pure performance (2116-2128), and the peraṇī and gauṇḍalī, which are dances in the deśī style (2129-2165). The text ends by saying in verse 2166 that dance is an erotic art, an observation made by no other writer.

The work differs from its contemporaries in regarding dance merely as an art auxiliary to drama and in ignoring music. This is surprising because by the time this work was written, dance had already developed into a separate art form that made use of vocal and instrumental music and was no longer merely one of the components of a dramatic performance. Vipradāsa's treatment of dance as a part of the pūrvaraṅga of a drama is closer to the position taken in the *Nāṭyaśāstra.* However, the division of the limbs into three categories and the description of deśī dancing are signs of the medieval approach to dancing in which Vipradāsa is a follower of Śārṅgadeva.

A major work of the medieval period, which originated in eastern India and influenced a number of works in that region, is the *Saṅgītadāmodara* by Śubhaṅkara. The editors of the text believe that the author lived sometime in the fifteenth century in Bengal. Nijenhuis suggests that the author may have lived sometime in the early part of the sixteenth century.[146] That he influenced an extensive body of musical literature through several centuries, particularly in Bengal and Orissa, has been established.[147] He was quoted by Bhavānanda Thākur, author of *Sadarpakandarpa,* by Ghanaśyāmadāsa, author of *Bhaktiratnākara,* by Rāmgopāl Dās, author of *Rasakalpavallī* and by Puruṣottamamiśra, author of *Saṅgītanārāyaṇa,* all from the eastern region.[148] Such was its popularity that not only was it studied by these Vaiṣṇava authors from Bengal but, as Nijenhuis tells us, it was even translated into Persian. She also points out the importance of the anthropomorphic images of the rāgas

---

[146] *Saṅgītadāmodara,* 1960, Introduction, p. 15; Nijenhuis, 1977, p.18.

[147] Nijenhuis, 1977, p.19.

[148] *SDām.*1960, Introduction, p. 15. Katz, 1987, Introduction, p. i.

that appear in the dhyānaślokas on rāgas in this text. It is on these images that the rāgamālā miniature paintings are based.[149]

Although the *Saṅgītadāmodara* is principally a work on music and dance, it includes substantial discussions on drama as well. It has five chapters, the first of which is on bhāva or emotional expression. The second describes the nāyaka or the hero, the nāyikā or the heroine, the sakhi or the friend of the heroine, and then explains the meaning of nāda or sound and gīta or vocal music. The third chapter is an exposition of the intricacies of the grammar of vocal music, which includes svara, rāga, and tāla among other subjects. The fourth chapter describes vādya, nṛtya and nāṭya. The fifth chapter is devoted partly to more technicalities of music and partly to rasa or aesthetic affect.

For our purpose the fourth chapter is the important one, where the author describes dancing under two headings, aṅgahāra and nṛtya. Aṅgahāra, in this context, is defined as aṅgavikṣepa, movements of the body. Under this heading the author includes āṅgikābhinaya because it means acting by using the movements of the limbs. The limbs are divided into major and minor limbs, aṅga, upāṅga and pratyaṅga. The author then names the sthānas or postures, the cārīs or movements executed with one leg, the karaṇas or the coordinated movements of the hands and the feet (dance units), maṇḍalas or the combination of cārīs, and aṅgahāras or sequences of dance units. These are described after Bharata[150] but Śubhaṅkara adds one more class of movements to his list. This category, viṣama alaga, consists of difficult movements and does not belong to the styles described by Bharata and his followers. Śubhaṅkara mentions thirteen such movements.[151] He states that nṛtya is deśī or regional and it has two subdivisions called tāṇḍava and lāsya. Tāṇḍava is puṁnṛtya, that

---

149 Nijenhuis, 1977, p. 19.

150 *SDām.* p. 61-68; cf. *NŚ.* chapters 8-12.

151 *SDām.* p. 69-70.

is, danced by men, and lāsya is strīnṛtya, that is, danced by women. Following the usual practice of most medieval texts, the *Saṅgītadāmodara* subdivides tāṇḍava into peraṇi and bahurūpa and describes them briefly. But the corresponding subdivision of lāsya into churita and yauvata, again discussed briefly, is a new feature introduced by the *Saṅgītadāmodara.*[152]

The author then moves on to describe nāṭya, which includes the major and minor types of drama. While describing the preliminary parts of nāṭya, the author again speaks of nṛtya as it is performed for the ritual of flower offerings, specifying for it the performance of māṇḍalī, which involves lāsyāṅgas as well.[153] The term māṇḍalī is very likely a scribal error for guṇḍalī or gauṇḍalī, for the particular dance described in the *Saṅgītadāmodara* as māṇḍalī is similar to the guṇḍalī or gauṇḍalī described in most medieval works on dancing.[154] The author mentions twenty-seven rūpakas and uparūpakas, major and minor types of dramas. He classifies them under the heading nṛtye nakṣatramālā, the gemlike starry garland of nṛtya, and describes them in detail. The lāsyāṅgas are described in detail, as is bhāṇa, one of the major types of drama. Śubhaṅkara's treatment of bhāṇa agrees with that of the authors who came after Bharata rather than with that of Bharata himself and includes lāsyāṅgas as one of the features of bhāṇa.[155] However, in describing the ten rūpakas he follows Bharata. Seven of the seventeen minor types of dramas, that is, uparūpakas, described in this text employ dancing. All seventeen are described in detail. The concluding verse of the fourth

---

[152] *Ibid.* p. 69.

[153] *Ibid.* p. 73.

[154] See Bose, 1970, p. 185, fn. 57. The dancer was called a guṇḍalī and her dance was gauṇḍalī, but often the dance is also called guṇḍalī.

[155] *SDām.* pp. 79; 85-7.

chapter before the closing prayer again refers to all these dramatic types as nṛtye ratnanakṣatramālā.[156]

Besides *Saṅgītadāmodara* Śubhaṅkara wrote two other treatises, the *Saṁgānasāra,* an unedited manuscript mentioned in the catalogue of the Asiatic Society of Bengal and the *Hastamuktāvalī,* [157] which adds to the discussion in the *Saṅgītadāmodara.* In the section of the *Saṅgītadāmodara* in which the author lists hand-gestures he directs the reader to the *Hastamuktāvalī* for a fuller discussion (*SDām.* p.63).

As its title indicates, the *Hastamuktāvalī* deals only with hand-gestures. Nijenhuis is not altogether accurate in thinking that this text contains dancing,[158] for it describes hand-gestures that are applicable both to dance and drama. Beginning with a few verses of benediction the author states the subject of his discussion, which is hasta, that is, gestures of the hands. The number and the names of the gestures mentioned in his *Saṅgītadāmodara* match the material here, while the actual descriptions and the application of the gestures in general match the discussion in the *Nāṭyaśāstra.* According to the author, there are thirty single and fourteen double hand gestures that signify words as well as emotions. The author then describes twenty-seven nṛttahastas, hand gestures meant for dancing, which express no meaning. This text was obviously quite popular since a certain Rāghava Rāya acknowledges that his *Hastaratnāvalī* is based on the *Hastamuktāvalī.* The Bodleian Library has a copy of the *Hastaratnāvalī* which seems to be a virtual copy of the *Hastamuktāvalī* insofar as the portions on the single and double hand gestures are concerned.[159] However, Rāghava Rāya's contribution, as Maheśvar

---

156 *SDām.* pp. 79, 91-6, 99.

157 Neog, 1952-59.

158 Nijenhuis, 1977, p. 19.

159 See Bose, 1964, pp. 57-87 for the discussion of *Hastaratnāvalī,* 1970, p. 6.; 47-67.

Neog notes, lies in his explanation of the applications of the gestures.[160] The applications of the hand-gestures described in the *Hastamuktāvalī* are very elaborate, which shows that the hand-gestures had become so important that it was necessary to write a separate work on these alone.

Another important work from this period is what is known as the *Nṛtyādhyāya* of Aśokamalla, which is part of a larger work. The edition currently available was prepared from a single manuscript which lacks the beginning and the colophon of the text.[161] Because of the missing colophon the actual title of the work is not known, and the title by which it is known, *Nṛtyādhyāya,* was given by the editor. Fortunately, the author's name is known from his own references to himself in the text.[162] The editor has placed the author in the fourteenth century A.D.[163] and comparisons with other works, known to be from the fourteenth/fifteenth centuries supports this view. For instance, most of the deśī lāsyāṅgas, thirty-seven in all, described in the *Nṛtyādhyāya* are also found in the section on deśī aṅgas in the *Saṅgītasamayasāra,* and among the deśīlāsyas of the *Nṛttaratnāvalī.* The *Saṅgītaratnākara* describes fewer lāsyāṅgas but they too are found in the list of deśī lāsyāṅgas in the *Nṛtyādhyāya.* Furthermore, a number of lines in the *Nṛtyādhyāya.* closely match lines in the *Saṅgītaratnākara.*[164] The *Nṛtyādhyāya* has a reference to the commentary of Siṁhabhūpāla on the *Saṅgītaratnākara* (*Nr.Adh.* verse 695) which, as the editor points out, places the author after Siṁhabhūpāla, who is believed to have lived in the fourteenth century. The *Nṛtyaratnakośa* and the *Nṛtyādhyāya* both quote the same prākṛt verse

---

[160] Neog, 1952-59.

[161] *Nṛtyādhyāya,* 1963, Introduction, pp. 9-10.

[162] *Ibid.* verses 695, 707, 1272.

[163] *Nṛ.Adh.*, 1963, Introduction, p. 10.

[164] *Ibid.* verses1513-65; *SSam.* 7. 194-216; *SR.* 7. 1206-15; *NR.* 6. 117-73; *Nr. Adh.* verse 1301; *SR.* 7. 745.

while describing the mārga lāsyāṅgas, although neither author mentions the other. They may both have quoted from the same source. We cannot determine whether Maharāṇā Kumbhā, who wrote the *Nṛtyaratnakośa* and lived in the fifteenth century, was before or after Aśokamalla. However, the internal evidence strongly suggests that Aśokamalla came after Pārśvadeva, Śārṅgadeva, Jāya and Siṁhabhūpāla.

The *Nṛtyādhyāya* consists of 1611 verses, with the beginning and the end of the text missing. Although the beginning is missing, the contents reflect the deśī tradition of dance recorded in the *Saṅgītaratnākara* and the *Nṛttaratnāvalī*. The text starts with the hand gestures followed by the movements of the major and minor limbs, that is, aṅga, upāṅga and pratyaṅga. These take up 614 verses and resemble the descriptions in the *Saṅgītaratnākara* and the *Nṛttaratnāvalī*. Verses 615 to 707 describe vicitrābhinaya (various ways of acting), dividing the contents into bhāvābhinaya (emotional expression) and indriyābhinaya (expressing through the sense organs). These seem to be summarized versions of the chapters in the *Nāṭyaśāstra* (*NŚ.* chs. 22 and 25) on sāmānyābhinaya and citrābhinaya. Verses 708 to 753 describe thirty-six vartanās or arm movements, of which twenty-five are claimed to be derived from Hanuman and the other eleven from other authors. The first twenty-five are similar to the arm movements described in Kallinātha's commentary on the *Saṅgītaratnākara* (*SR.* Vol. IV pp. 105-10) where Kallinātha cites Kohala as his source. These are also found in the *Nṛtyaratnakośa*. Cālanas or cālakas, another type of arm movement, are fifty-five in number and described from verses 754 to 862. The first fifty are similar to what we find in Kallinātha (*SR.*Vol. IV. pp. 111-23). Sthānas or postures are described next, from verses 863 to 948, which include postures meant for men (six) and women (eight), reclining postures (six) and deśī sthānas (twentythree). The deśī and mārga varieties of cārīs, one hundred and eleven in all, including twenty-five muḍupacārīs, are described in verses 949 to 1115. The same descriptions of the muḍupacārīs are found in

Kallinātha's commentary on the *Saṅgītaratnākara* where the term given is madhupacārī (*SR*.Vol. IV, pp. 313-17). In verses 1116 to 1305 the author describes one hundred and eight karaṇas after Bharata. Verses 1306 to 1342 describe twenty-seven deśī karaṇas. The text has a lacuna at this point but the editor has supplied us with descriptions of the other eleven deśī karaṇas (*Nr. Adh.* pp. 138-39), taking them from the *Bharatakośa.* The descriptions of the first few aṅgahāras are also missing, which the editor has supplied from the *Saṅgītaratnākara* (*SR.* 7. 789-808; *Nr. Adh.* pp. 140-41.). Verses 1343 to 1415 describe the rest of the aṅgahāras, thirty-two in all. In the next five verses, 1416-1420, the author talks about the musical accompaniment for the aṅgahāras. Four recakas are described next in verses 1421 to 1426. Twenty maṇḍalas are described next in 1427 to 1486. Verses 1487 to 1512 describe mārga lāsyāṅgas while verses 1513 to 1565 describe 37 deśīlāsyāṅgas. The text ends with descriptions of the closing movements known as kalāsas which are covered in verses 1566 to 1611. The last variety of kalāsa is missing from the text but the editor has supplied the missing part the description of the last variety of kalāsa from the *Nṛtyaratnakośa* (*Nr. Adh.* pp. 172-73; *NRK.* 4.1.83-5).[165]

This is one of the few texts to refer to śṛṅgābhinaya (*Nr.Adh.* verse. 141). The *Bhartārṇava* has one whole chapter on śṛṅgābhinaya (chapter 12). The *Nṛttaratnāvalī* also refers to śṛṅga in passing while describing the application of the kartarīmukha hand (*NR.* 2.112) but offers no detail. Kalāsa is another movement which is described in the *Nṛtyādhyāya* in detail, the only other text that describes them in similar detail being the *Nṛtyaratnakośa.* Kalāsas are not defined but this term is in use today in Kathākali as a concluding part; the same function is indicated by Kallinātha's explanation of the term.[166]

---

[165] An exhaustive discussion of the last three movements have already been noted by the present writer. See Bose, 1970, pp. 167-83.

[166] *SR.* Vol. IV, p. 381, commentary on verse 1292: कलासयेत् नर्तनं समापयेदित्यर्थः ।

The *Nṛtyaratnakośa* of Mahārāṇā Kumbhā can be taken as the last work of the second period. It is part of a larger work, the *Saṅgītarāja*, which closely follows the *Saṅgītaratnākara*. According to Nijenhuis, who gives an account of the work in her monograph, "This large work comprising 16,000 verses is divided into five chapters on: 1. pāṭhya (recitation), 2. gīta (vocal music), 3. vādya, 4. nṛtya and 5. rasa."[167] Mahārāṇā Kumbhā, who was a scholar king of the fifteenth century, is generally acknowledged as the author and the case for this attribution has been made at length by the editor of the text.[168] The same attribution appear in both Raghavan and Nijenhuis but Kunhan Raja believes the author to be Kālasena.[169]

The fourth chapter, which is on nṛtya, is divided into four ullāsas or parts, each consisting of four parīkṣaṇas or sections. Each section starts with a benedictory verse. The first section of the first part, in 811 verses, discusses a variety of subjects and concludes with a description of the movements of aṅgas or major limbs. Beginning with the benediction, the first 123 verses describe the origin of the śāstra of nāṭya, the rules of building the performance-hall, the qualifications of the person presiding and the audience. Also discussed are the preliminaries to the performance, which are described in detail following the *Nāṭyaśāstra*. The author then defines nāṭya, nṛtya and nṛtta (verses 124-170). Nāṭya, according to him, is to be understood as abhinaya, नाट्येनाभिनयम् (*NRK*.1.1.128), nṛtya as rasa, नृत्यशब्देन च रसं पुन: (*NRK*.1.1.128) and nṛtta consists of the combination of karaṇas and aṅgahāras, करणाङ्गहारनिचयैर्नृत्तम् (*NRK*.1.1.129). Verses 171 to 212 describe piṇḍībandhas or group dances, which are performed by sixteen female

---

167 Nijenhuis, 1977, p.16-18.

168 *Nṛtyaratnakośa*, Vol. II, 1968, pp. 2-5.

169 Raghavan, 1960, pp. 11-12; Nijenhuis, 1977, p. 16; *NRK*. Vol. II, 1968, Introduction, pp. 2-5.

dancers as part of the preliminaries. More details about the preliminaries are given in verses 213 to 276. The terms nṛtya, and nṛtta are explained in verses 277 to 286, nṛtya being identified as the mārga style and nṛtta as deśī. In so classifying them the author follows the *Daśarūpaka* and the *Saṅgītaratnākara*.[170] Lāsya and tāṇḍava, and viṣama, vikaṭa and laghu as varieties of tāṇḍava, are described in verses 287 to 296. Sāmānyābhinaya or the general style of acting comes next (verses 297-315), followed by citrābhinaya which means a special acting style (verses 316-18), āhāryābhinaya or the use of costume, make-up and stage-properties (verses 319-25), vṛttis or styles (326-31) and sāttvikabhāva or the representation of emotions(verses 332-433). The rest of the verses are devoted to āṅgikābhinaya or the movements of the body (434-811). The author repeats the same verses in many places in the same chapter (285-86 repeated in 448, 287-92 repeated in 459-64). Although the author has followed the *Saṅgītaratnākara* in listing the aṇgas or the major limbs, he adds a new one, which is dhammilla or braid (502-4). The dramatic applications of the movements of the aṅgas or major limbs are also described. Some additional hand-gestures are also described, the source of most of which is identified as the *Bṛhaddeśī*. They are also found in the *Saṅgītaratnākara,* which, however, acknowledges them as borrowed from an unidentified source(*SR*.7.284-5; *NRK*.1.1.513-15; 755). The *Nṛtyaratnakośa* uses the term nṛtyahasta and not nṛttahasta for hand-gestures employed in dancing, which include three new hand-gestures, añjana, jayanta and candraka (*NRK*. 1.1.774-8), found in no other text.

The second section of the first part discusses in 89 verses nine pratyaṅgas or minor limbs. It includes vartanās or the movements of arms, which the author acknowledges as taken from the *Kalānidhi,* Kallinātha's commentary on the *Saṅgītaratnākara* (*NRK*. 1.2.27.). The third section of the first part, consisting of 159 verses, is on upāṅgas, another division of

---

[170] *DR*. 1.9; *SR*. 7.26-28.

minor limbs, which are said to be twelve. The fourth and final section of the first part, consisting of 43 verses, is on āhāryābhinaya or costume, make-up and stage properties. The first twenty eight verses discuss āhāryābhinaya but the rest deal with various actions and positions of the hands, namely, pracāra, karaṇa, karma, kṣetra (*NRK.* 1.4. 29-42).

The second part begins its first section, of 92 verses, with a benediction, which is followed by a description of the sthānakas or postures, which include mārga and deśī types of postures meant for men and women, for sitting and reclining. The second section of the second part, in 63 verses, is on mārga cārī. The third section of this part, in 61 verses, is on deśī. An appendix of 37 verses to this section, which, according to the author, quotes from the *Kalānidhi,* gives descriptions of the movements of recakas, that is, oscillating movements, and the muḍupa or deśī cārīs.[171] The fourth section, consisting of 62 verses, is on maṇḍala or the combination of cārīs. All of these descriptions so far, follow the *Saṅgītaratnākara* in the main.

The third part begins its first section, which consists of 188 verses, with a set of three benedictory verses, after which karaṇas or dance-units are described, according to the author, after Bharata (*NRK.*3.1.2). The author refers to this set of karaṇas as śuddha (literally, pure) karaṇas, by which he means the mārga variety. The second section of the third part describes the deśī variety of karaṇas in 51 verses that include descriptions of nine bhramarīs. This section has an appendix of 23 verses attached to it, describing thirteen more bhramarīs which the author says he has taken from *Ānandasañjīvana* (*NRK.* Vol. II, p. 169-72). The third section of the third part discusses aṅgahāras in 106 verses and at the end of the section the author states that the aṅgahāras are meant specifically for the preliminaries to a play (*NRK.* 3.3. 103-5). In the last verse of this section

---

171 Muḍupacārī is the same as madhupacārī. *NRK.* pp. 134-38; *SR.* pp. 313-17; *Nṛ. Adh.* pp.108-12.

(*NRK.* 3.3. 106) Kumbhā gives directions for the application of four aṅgahāras, directions that had never appeared before in any previous work. The fourth section of this part describes in 8 verses the recakas or oscillating movements.

The fourth part starts its first section, of 85 verses, with a long benediction, which is followed by detailed discussions of four vṛttis or styles and six kalāsas (dance movements with which a performance concludes) with twenty-two sub-varieties. There are 7 more verses appended to this section giving the definitions of an upādhyāya (instructor), an ācārya (preceptor), a naṭa (actor), a nartaka (dancer) and a vaitālika (a critic who is knowledgeable in music and can amuse the audience). The second section is in 52 verses. In this the author discusses different presentation techniques and rules, then describes a dance called peraṇī, and ends with the definition of a kohlāṭika, that is, a performer who is able to perform acrobatic movements. The third section of this part has 193 verses, the first 85 of which describe the lāsyāṅgas, of the mārga variety (twelve in number) as well as the deśī (thirty-six in number). In verses 86-105 the author discusses different gatis or gaits, in describing which he says he is following Bharata. This is followed by a description of the deśī nṛtyabhedas in verses 106-123. The term nṛtyabheda is used by Dhanika and Śāradātanaya to denote minor dramas that require dancing.[172] But Kumbhā uses it to mean dancing. Of the six nṛtyabhedas described in this text, śivapriya comes from the *Nṛttaratnāvalī,* which describes it as a deśī dance. It occurs in no other text. Dohaka is also a new name which is not mentioned in any other text. The rest are described in all other texts that discuss minor dramas.[173] Verses 124-128 discuss the technical language used by the dancers. Four features of deśīnṛtyas are

---

[172] See pp. 167-9 *infra.*

[173] The nṛtyabhedas are śivapriya, rāsaka, nāṭyarāsaka, daṇḍarāsaka, carcarī and dohaka; *NRK.*106-123.

described next, followed by deśīgītanṛtyavidhi which describes six varieties of regional dances following specific tālas and the music appropriate to them, along with general directions for such presentations in verses 129-144.

From the above discussion it seems that this author divides the minor dramas that employed dance and expressive dance of the deśī variety into two different categories, respectively, deśī nṛtyabheda and deśīnṛtya, the latter being a category used by what he calls "other" authorities. The rest of the verses are on the nine rasas and their expression through body movements. The fourth and the final section of the fourth and last part of the treatise has 88 verses. In this section the author attempts to define the ideal performer, explains the aesthetic concept known as rekhā or the lines of body movements that enhance beauty, enumerates the qualities and faults of a performer, discusses make-up, different schools of performing artists, their qualities and faults, the śuddhapaddhati or the pure way of presentation, the gauṇḍalīvidhi or the regional variation called gauṇḍalī, explains how instructions are given to performers and ends with a final prayer.

The beginning of the third period in the evolution of the concept of dance is marked by the *Nartananirṇaya* of Puṇḍarīka Viṭṭhala who lived in the late sixteenth to the early seventeenth century.[174] Till Mahārāṇā Kumbha's *Nṛtyaratnakośa* the major divisions of the art as conceived by

---

[174]Krishnamachariar, 1974, p. 865. This text remained unedited and unpublished until recently. Dr. S. Satyanārāyaṇa brought out an edition in early 1987 in Kannada script prepared from one full and four fragmentary MSS.. A detailed account of the fourth chapter of the text appears in the present writer's dissertation (Oxford, 1964) and in her book on classical Indian dancing (1970). A critical edition based upon 15 MSS. is under preparation by the present writer. References to the 4th chapter of the text in the present study are to the India Office Library, London manuscript (MS. 5197). References to other chapters are to the Asiatic Society, Calcutta MS.(MS. III. D.5) and to the Jaipur Khasmahal Library MS.(MS. 6885).

scholars were mārga and deśī, that is, the canonical style and the regional or popular styles. The *Nartananirṇaya* marks a major conceptual departure by dividing dance primarily by structural principle into two divisions, namely, bandha, or styles that rigidly adhered to set rules of composition, and anibandha, styles that did not do so and allowed innovations by the dancer. Many of the works on dancing written after the *Nartananirṇaya* still followed the approach of the *Nāṭyaśāstra* as found in the *Saṅgītaratnākara* but the *Nartananirṇaya*'s approach to categories of dancing became part of their conceptual framework.

Puṇḍarīka Viṭṭhala is believed to have come from southern India and later he became a court poet in the courts of Man Singh of Jaipur and his brother Madho Singh. He wrote several texts on music under the patronage of these rulers but still later moved on to Akbar's court. His three works on music, the *Sadrāgacandrodaya,* the *Rāgamālā* and the *Rāgamañjarī* are well-known. He is believed to have written two more texts on music, the *Rāganārāyaṇa* and the *Saṅgītavṛttaratnākara.* He also wrote a lexicon titled the *Śīghrabodhinīnāmamālā* and a treatise called the *Dūtīkarmaprakāśa* on the characters of the heroine and the hero.[175]

The *Nartananirṇaya* was written in the sixteenth century to please the emperor Akbar, according to Puṇḍrīka's statement at the end of the text.[176] Like most works before it, the *Nartananirṇaya* discusses the various types of acting, namely, āhāryābhinaya, sāttvikābhinaya and āṅgikābhinaya, and in doing so it follows the *Nāṭyaśāstra* as interpreted in the *Saṅgītaratnākara.* However, instead of following the usual practice of reproducing the *Nāṭyaśāstra*'s (and in the case of later texts, the *Saṅgītaratnākara*'s rendering of the *Nāṭyaśāstra*'s material) descriptions of the 108 karaṇas and the 32 aṅgahāras created by combining them, the

---

175 Krishnamachariar, 1974, p. 865; Raghavan, 1960., pp. 15-16.

176 अकबरनृपरुच्यर्थं भूलोके सरलसंगीतम् ।
कृतमिदं बहुतरभेदं सुहृदां हृदये सुखं भूयात् ॥ (*Nartananirṇaya.* 53b).

Nartananirṇaya selects only 16 of the karaṇas as those needed in bandhanṛtya, of which it describes several varieties. The text then proceeds to describe the distinctive features of the various kinds of anibandhanṛtya. From these descriptions of dance compositions there emerge striking similarities with the classical dance styles of the present time, as demonstrated in a later chapter of the present study. This text thus provides the link so far missing between the older and the present day traditions of classical Indian dancing.

At the beginning of the first chapter, the author declares his plan to write on five topics, namely, tāla or rhythm, vādya or instrumental music, gīta or vocal music, nartana or dance and nāṭya or drama.[177] However, he never wrote the fifth chapter, that on nāṭya, nor gave any reason for the omission, leaving the treatise with four chapters, the last of which is the one on dance.[178] The text begins with a set of 34 verses, written in a variety of metres, in praise of Akbar and his ancestors.[179] The first chapter, consisting of 259 verses, is on rhythm, the second, in 116 verses, is on drums and the third, in 579 verses, is on vocal music. The fourth chapter, the largest one, has 916 verses that deal with dancing. This chapter starts by defining nartana, a term used by the author to mean dance. Nartana is divided into nāṭya, nṛtya and nṛtta, of which the last is again divided into three, viṣama, vikaṭa and laghu. All the types are defined and the author reproduces in the first ten verses the *Saṅgītaratnākara*'s view that nṛtya and nṛtta may both have varieties of tāṇḍava and lāsya. In verses 11 to 206 abhinaya is discussed, with the sāttvika, āhārya and āṅgika types of abhinaya described in detail but not vācika as it is not employed in nartana. Citrābhinaya is then described in

---

[177] *Nartananirṇaya*. 1a (Calcutta.MS.).

[178] *Nartananirṇaya*. 53b (London.MS.).

179 This part is contained in the Jaipur.MS. but not in the Kannada edition, which is based on only one full and four fragmentary manuscripts.

verses 207 to 238. The author does not divide the movements of the limbs into the movements of aṅga, upāṅga or pratyaṅga but in verses 239 to 244, where he lists his topics of discussion, he mentions the movements of the parts of the body which, in his view, are of importance. These include the movements of the head, the eyes, the eyebrows, the arms, the hand-gestures and other actions of the hands, the waist and the feet. It also discusses the function of the colour of the face. The list further includes more complicated movements generated from the combination of the movements of the parts of the body, such as the sthānas or postures, cārīs or the movements of one leg, karaṇas or dance-units and recakas or oscillating movements. Also in the list are the dance-hall, the characteristics of a good dancer, rekhā or the lines created by the movements of the body, the lāsyāṅgas or features of lāsya, sauṣṭhava or standing without any movement, citrakalāsa or concluding movement, mudrā or natural grace, pramāṇa or harmony, the audience, the person presiding, sitting arrangements, the troupe of musicians, the flute, the entrance of a dancer and various dance-sequences. The actual discussions of these topics is in verses 245 to 656. Most of the material comes either from the *Nāṭyaśāstra* or the *Saṅgītaratnākara.* The original matter that the author contributes to our knowledge comes after this when he begins to describe the opening dance item, the dancer's entrance into the stage. This is where he divides nṛtta into two categories, bandha and anibandha. Under bandhanṛtta he puts mukhacāli, urupa, dhuvāḍa, viḍulāgava, śabdacāli (later discussed as śabdanṛtta), śabdaprabandha, svaramaṇṭha, gītaprabandha, cindu, dharu and dhruvapada. Their descriptions in verses 668 to 874 show them to be highly structured dance pieces.[180] A group of five bhramarīs is also discussed (794 to 98) between the discussions on viḍulāgava and śabdanṛtta.

---

[180]See Bose, 1970, pp. 149-161 for details.

Next, anibandha dance is discussed in verses 875 to 898 with its forms given, namely, nāmāvalī, yati, different neris, kaivartana, murū, tālarūpaka, guṇḍāla, kamala, natajānuka, maṇḍī, muḍupa, muraṇḍarī, kuḍupa, tiryakaraṇa, lāvaṇī and baṭu. These have fewer details compared to the discussion of the bandhanṛttas. At the end of these descriptions the author refers to these sequences as anibandha urūpas, evidently using the term urūpa to denote a broad category of dance. Urūpa is described only in two works, in this text and in a later work, the *Saṅgītamakaranda* of Vedasūri.[181] Finally, Puṇḍarīka Viṭṭhala ends the work with two more dance sequences, jakkaḍī and rāsa,which he includes under anibandha dance (875 to 912). Throughout these descriptions the terms nṛtta and nṛtya are used interchangeably. The last four verses of the text are in praise of the patron and contain a final prayer.

The *Rasakaumudī* of Śrīkaṇṭha is another text from the third period. The author was a contemporary and student of Puṇḍarīka [182]and was a court poet of Śatruśalya (Jam Sattarsal of Navanagar near Dvārakā) who lived in the late sixteenth and the early seventeenth centuries.[183] He refers to Puṇḍarīka as his teacher whom he follows in defining music.[184] The editor of the text thinks that Śrīkaṇṭha, like his teacher, was originally from the South and moved to western India.[185]

The *Rasakaumudī* is a work in ten chapters divided into two parts, pūrva and uttarakhaṇḍa, each consisting of five chapters. The first part deals with vocal and instrumental music and dance. The second part deals

---

181 In some of the copies of the manuscripts of this text the term urūpa is spelt as urupa or uḍupa.

182 श्रीमद् विट्ठलदेवस्य प्रसादाच्च गुरोर्मया।
श्रीकण्ठेनोच्यते कामं तालकादिनिर्णयः ॥ *RK*. 4.96.

183 *Rasakaumudī*, 1963, G.O.S. ed. 143. Introduction, pp. 8-9.

184 *Ibid*. p. 8. *RK*. 4.80.

185 *RK*. Introduction, p. 8.

with drama, rasa, the seasons and the proper conduct of a king. The first chapter, in 91 verses, deals with general matters pertaining to music. The second, in 219 verses, explains the nature of rāga and the technicalities of making and playing the vīṇā. The third chapter consists of 150 verses discussing further intricacies of vocal music. The fourth chapter, in 190 verses, discusses vādya or musical instruments, with details borrowed extensively from the *Nartananirṇaya.*

Chapter five is the part that holds our interest most since it deals with dancing. Consisting of 356 verses, this is the longest chapter. Beginning with verses in praise of Kṛṣṇa, the author relates the origin of nāṭya following the *Saṅgītaratnākara.* This is followed by a description of the stage, and of the initial presentation by the principal dancer and others. The author recommends the ārabhaṭī style of presentation for the initial part of the performance. Dancers from different regions are described next, followed by āṅgikābhinaya or the use of body movements in acting, which include the movements of the head, the hands and the feet. The author lists the number of movements prescribed for the minor limbs without giving any details. He mentions ten divisions of nāṭya but calls only the first variety nāṭya. The ten divisions of nāṭya that he mentions are nāṭya, nṛtya, nṛtta, tāṇḍava, lāsya, viṣama, vikaṭa, laghu, peraṇi and gauṇḍalī. He describes four kinds of abhinayas and then reproduces verbatim verses from the *Nartananirṇaya* that give general instructions on acting, for which Puṇḍarīka had drawn upon the discussion on sāmānyābhinaya in the *Nāṭyaśāstra* (chapter 22).[186] Before describing any dance-sequence, Śrīkaṇṭha describes the essence or prāṇa of a nṛtya (nṛtya here stands for the art of dance). Next, puṣpāñjali or the flower-offering on the stage, the rules of exercise, make-up, and presentation techniques are described, followed by the definitions of 108 karaṇas. The author then presents a list of cārīs, maṇḍalas and sthānas, adding that there

[186] *RK.* 5. 145-161; *NN.* 3b-12a.

can be many more varieties of karaṇas, aṅgahāra, cārī and maṇḍala. Then he proceeds to describe utplutikaraṇas, aṅgahāras, cārīs, recakas, sthānas, maṇḍalas and lāsyāṅgas. In describing lāsyāṅgas he follows the *Nartananirṇaya.* He divides gatis or gaits into three different types, uttama, madhyama and adhama and refers to the use of three tempos. Thus ends the chapter on dancing and the first part of the text, in which he keeps referring to Bharata as the authority followed.

The sixth chapter is very short, consisting of 5 verses and, as the editor of the text points out, it serves as a connecting link between the first and the second parts of the text with a benedictory verse and an introduction to the subject of the next chapter, which is rasa. The seventh chapter, in 26 verses, is devoted to the discussion of the nine rasas. The author discusses Śṛṅgārarasa, giving its varieties in detail and pays less attention to the other rasas. The eighth chapter, in 31 verses, begins with a discussion of how to enhance the beauty of a woman in sixteen different ways. This he refers to as Śṛṅgāravarṇana. It includes taking a bath, putting on make-up, wearing jewellery, dressing and giving the finishing touch by chewing on a betel leaf (in order to redden the lips). The author adds shrewdness to the list of qualities necessary in a good performer and instructs the performer to use appropriate emotional expressions. The ninth chapter describes the six seasons in 59 verses after justifying the inclusion of this subject. According to the author, the seasons should be enjoyed and the joy of the seasons can be expressed through different costumes worn to represent different seasons. The tenth and last chapter has 48 verses and deals with royal conduct and the daily programme of a king. The reason given for including this subject is that a king should know and enjoy the art of dancing. The chapter and the text end with a final prayer.

The contribution of Śrīkaṇṭha to dance scholarship is not substantial in terms of the definitions and categories of dance that he presents, nor of the descriptions of body movements. His chief contribution lies in his discussion of the concept of prāṇa, or the essence of a performance, which sums up what a dancer should aim at while performing. The ten prāṇas are listed in the following couplet:

> रेखा च स्थिरता वेगो भ्रमरी दृष्टि+रस्मय:+।
> प्रीतिर्मेधा वचो गीतं नृत्ये प्राणा दशोदिता: ॥
>
> (*RK.* 5. 162)
>
> The line, the steadiness, the swiftness, the pirouettes, the glances, the desirous [smile], the pleasing [appearance], the intellect, the speech and the song constitute the ten vital spirits of a nṛtya.

It is interesting to note that the fourth essential prāṇa is bhramarī, which by this time must have become a movement of such vital importance in dance that it was exalted to the status of a prāṇa. It is unfortunate that Śrīkaṇṭha leaves it undiscussed, especially as he is the first author to speak of prāṇa.

Śrīkaṇṭha's other contribution is his detailed instructions for make-up and stage presentation, his approach to both subjects being original. Regarding the second, for instance, he says:

> माल्यकारो यथा माल्यं वध्नाति कुसुमोत्करै: ।
> सुधी कुर्यात् तथा नाटचमङ्गोपाङ्गै रसादिभि: ॥
>
> (*RK.* 5. 183)
>
> Just as [the way] a garland maker makes a garland with the help of flowers a performer [literally, the skilled one] should act in the same way with [the movements of] the major and minor limbs and [expressions of] rasa etc.

The work also has the virtue of being a systematic and organized approach to the subject. However, as we have noted in summarizing the work, it is a derivative piece of writing, the author relying heavily on Puṇḍarīka for the most part.

The *Saṅgītadarpaṇa* of Dāmodara is a work on music and dance. He is believed to have been a descendant of Kallinātha, the commentator on the *Saṅgītaratnākara*. Dāmodara was a poet at Jahangir 's court, which places him in the seventeenth century.[187] A complete manuscript is known to exist in the Bibliotheque Nationale of Paris; a fragment containing three chapters on instrumental music, rhythm and dancing is in the Bodleian Library at Oxford.[188] The readings of the two manuscripts are virtually the same. One edition of the full text, an unsatisfactory one, as Rāghavan points out, was brought out in 1952 by the Saraswati Mahal Library of Tanjore. Nijenhuis ascribes the work to Haribhaṭṭa, who was indeed, as reported by Raghavan, the author of a work called the *Saṅgītadarpaṇa*.[189] The two works are almost identical, which permits the conjecture that either Harībhaṭṭa and Dāmodara were one and the same person, or Haribhaṭṭa "made his own version of Dāmodara's work."[190] According to Raghavan, the Tanjore edition is from the manuscript that bears the name of Haribhaṭṭa. Generally speaking, the *Saṅgītadarpaṇa* is ascribed to Dāmodara by most scholars, including Raghavan. Comparison between the chapter on dancing of the edited version with that of the Bodleian MS. shows that the two are identical.

The Paris manuscript has seven chapters while the manuscript examined by Raghavan is said to have six. The edited text of the

---

[187] Krishnamachariar, 1974,.p.866.

[188] See Bose, 1964, pp.16-18; 1970, p. 5. *Saṅgtadarpaṇa* of Dāmodara, Bibliotheque Nationale, Paris, MS.No. 771; Bodleian Library , Oxford, MS. No. Mill. 47.d.

[189] Raghavan, 1960, pp. 20-21.; Nijenhuis, 1977, p. 27.

[190] Raghavan, 1960, p. 21.

Saṅgītadarpaṇa has seven chapters,[191] the first on svara or the science and philosophy of sound, the second on rāga or musical modes, the third on prakīrṇa or miscellaneous technicalities of music, the fourth on prabandha or composition, the fifth on vādya or instrumental music, the sixth on tāla or rhythm and the seventh on nṛtya or dancing. The first chapter has 150 verses and starts with a benediction and proceeds to define the term saṅgīta to explain its division into mārga and deśī. The origins of rāga or musical mode, nāda or sound and other technical intricacies of vocal music are discussed, and the chapter ends with a verse that lists seven birds and animals that represent the seven musical notes. The same verse is also found in the *Nartananirṇaya*.[192] The second chapter (verses 151-289) begins with a verse defining rāga, which is found in the *Saṅgītaratnākara* and the *Nartananirṇaya*. This chapter describes the anthropomorphic images of the rāgas and rāgiṇīs as well as their structures. Kriṣṇamāchariar and Rāghavan state that Dāmodara borrowed his anthropomorphic description of musical modes from Somanātha's *Rāgavibodha*.[193] Chapter three (verses 290-352) discusses a variety of subjects, including ālāpa, the use of the voice, the qualities of a singer and the characteristics of a musical composition. The fourth chapter (verses 353-531) discusses the details of musical composition. The fifth chapter (verses 532-615) is on vādya or instrumental music and describes the vīṇā and other stringed instruments, different kinds of flutes, their characteristic sounds, the compositions appropriate to them, drums and so on. Here the author again quotes extensively from the *Nartananirṇaya*, though he does not name it as his source. The sixth chapter is on tāla. In

---

191 Raghavan reports that six chapters and the chapter on tāla is missing from his list, 1960, p 21. The Paris MS. has seven chapters.

192 *SDar.*1. 150; cf. *NN.* 20a. There are a number of verses which seem to be quoted from the *Nartananirṇaya*.

193 Raghavan, 1960, p. 21; Krishnamachariar, 1974, p.866.

verses 616-798 it defines the term tāla, explains its derivation, and describes ten prāṇas, mārga tālas and, finally, deśī tālas. At the end of this section appears a description of 120 tālas, of which the source is the *Saṅgītaratnākara*. This is followed by another set of 103 tālas described according to other authorities (pp. 149-70). In the section that follows, other technicalities of tālas are described.

The final and seventh chapter, in 282 verses, is the one on dancing. The chapter begins with a benediction followed by a detailed description of the opening dance called mukhacāli which is very similar to the mukhacāli described in *Nartananirṇaya* in greater detail. That the descriptions in the two works come from the same tradition is shown by the fact that the song to be illustrated by hand-gestures is the same in both the texts. Next, verse 53 lists ten types of dancing but does so confusingly. The verse identifies nāṭya, nṛtya, tāṇḍava, nṛtta and lāsya as types of nartana. It then divides nṛtya into five types, namely, viṣama, vikaṭa, laghu, peraṇi and goṇḍalī (a variant form of the word gauṇḍalī), which are deśī forms. This division might thus seem to indicate that nartana is the general class name and that nṛtya is a subdivision. But the verse concludes by stating that all ten types mentioned are types of nṛtya. Evidently, then, the text is using the terms nartana and nṛtya interchangeably in this verse.

Verses 54-93 describe bhāva, rasa, mukharāga, the four types of abhinaya, and explains the meaning of lokadharmī or natural and nāṭyadharmī or stylized presentations. Verses 94-96 define nṛtya and nṛtta. Here, nṛtya is considered to be a mārga style which portrays emotions through body movements. Nṛtta, on the other hand, is based on tāla and laya and expresses no meaning. Verses 97-103 list the movements of aṅga, upāṅga and pratyaṅga, followed in verses 104-11 by definitions of rekhā (the imaginary lines described by the body in motion), pramāṇa (harmony), and the ten prāṇas (the vitalizing power of a performance) to be instilled into a dance by the dancer. Prāṇa is discussed, as we have seen, also in the *Rasakaumudī*. Gatis are described from verses 112-23 in the manner of the *Nartananirṇaya.* Tāṇḍava and lāsya are defined with quotations from the *Saṅgītaratnākara* in verses 124-25. The author views them as dances for men and women, respectively. In verses 126-30 mukharāgas or the colour of the face, nāndī or the opening verse and the characteristics of an actor are described. The rest of verses 131-282 describe dance pieces. Most of these descriptions are taken from the *Nartananirṇaya.* The author then describes yatinṛtya, śabdacāli, uḍupas, dhruvāḍas, śabdanṛtya, camatkāranṛtta, śabdanṛtta, gītanṛtya, svarābhinaya, svaramaṇṭhanṛtya, sūḍanṛtya, dhruvagītanṛtya, one after the other, classifying them under the śuddha or pure dance style (verses 131-240). Deśīnṛtyas are described next, which include cindu, kaṭṭarī (dharu is a variety of this type) and vaipota (verses 241-61). Finally, bandhanṛtya, kalpanṛtya, jakkarī, peraṇī and goṇḍalī are described (verses 261-82).

While it is evident that there is no original material on dancing in the *Saṅgītadarpaṇa,* either in terms of information or interpretation, the work is valuable as an illustration of an approach to dancing that began with the *Nartananirṇaya.* As shown above, the author follows the *Nartananirṇaya* as well as the *Rasakaumudī,* which itself borrowed the views of the *Nartananirṇaya,* in showing a growing interest in such aesthetic elements as rekhā, pramāṇa and prāṇa. Generally speaking, then, we find from the *Nartananirṇaya* onwards a great stress laid on the responsibility of the dancer for creating the artistic effect.

Saṅgītanārāyaṇa is a seventeenth century text by Purṣottama Miśra, a poet at the court of Gajapati Nārāyaṇadeva of Orissa.[194] The work is in four chapters and deals with music and dance. Chapter one (546 verses), called gītanirṇaya, is devoted to the technicalities of vocal music, such as nāda, śruti, svara, grāma, rāga, gīta and tāla. The second chapter, vādyanirṇaya (131 verses), discusses vādya or instrumental music. The

[194] Katz, 1987, Introduction, p. iii -vi.

third chapter, nāṭyanirṇaya, in 828 verses, deals with nāṭya or mimetic art, which includes dancing. The fourth chapter (verses unnumbered, pp.176-200), śuddhaprabandhodāharaṇa, is on prabandha or composition. The first edition of the text was brought out by the Saṅgīt Nāṭak Academy of Orissa in 1966. A scholarly edition of only the musicological parts of the text has been recently prepared by Jonathan Katz but not yet published. There is no satisfactory edition of the part on dancing. However, the edition prepared in Orissa gives us a fair idea of the contents of that part.

The third chapter, on dance and mimetic art, begins by relating the origin of the nāṭyaveda. Similar verses are also found in the *Abhinayadarpaṇa* (*SN*.3.2,3; *ADar*.2, 3). Next, the author divides nartana into nāṭya, nṛtya and nṛtta and defines them, citing various authorities. He then defines mārga and deśī along the lines of the *Saṅgītaratnākara* and also refers to the views of Kohala (3.3-11). As examples the author names twenty mārga-nāṭyas, which include ten rūpakas and ten other varieties of dramatic presentation, for which no class-name is given.[195] Sixteen varieties of deśīnāṭyas are given as those identified by Dattila.[196] Twelve names of deśīnṛttas are given next, some of which are the same as types of mārganāṭya and deśīnāṭya.[197] The names of ten mārganāṭyas (excluding rūpakas), sixteen deśīnāṭyas and twelve deśīnṛttas are cited as found in various texts as examples of minor dramas (3.12-20). The names of the deśīnṛttas are those of the nṛtyabhedas in the *Avaloka* of Dhanika, in

[195] Ten varieties of mārganāṭyas, not included in the rūpakas, are Nāṭikā, Prakaraṇikā, Bhāṇikā, Hāsikā, Viyoginī, Ḍimikā, Utsāhavatī, Citrā, Jugupsitā and Vicitrā. *SN*. 3. 14-15.

[196] The sixteen varieties of deśīnāṭyas are: Saṭṭaka, Troṭaka, Goṣṭhī, Vṛndaka, Śilpaka, Prekṣaṇa, Saṁlāpaka (sallāpaka?), Hallīśa, Rāsaka, Ullāpyaka, Śrīgadita, Nāṭyarāsaka, Durmallī, Prasthāna, Kāvya and Lāsika. *SN*.3. 15-18.

[197] Ḍomikā, Bhāṇikā, Prasthānaka, Bhāṇaka, Lāsikā, Rāsikā, Durmallikā, Vidagdhā, Śilpinī, Hasti(Daṇḍi)nī, Ulmukī (Bhillukī), Tumbikā are cited as the twelve deśīnṛttas. *SN*.3. 18-20.

the *Bhāvaprakāśa* and in the *Saṅgītadāmodara*.[198] The use of the term nṛtta in this context in the *Saṅgītanārāyaṇa* seems to be a scribal error. Not only do the varieties mentioned above appear in the category of nṛtya in other texts, but the *Saṅgītanārāyaṇa* itself recognizes nṛtta as a different branch, as we see only a few verses later where the types of nṛtta are discussed along the lines of the *Saṅgītaratnākara*. Although Puruṣottama borrows frequently from others, the classification of the dramatic arts into three categories is entirely his own, as is his mention of so many dramatic types, which we find in no other work.

Tāṇḍava and lāsya are next defined and described as two types of nṛtta. Two kinds of tāṇḍava, preraṇī and bahurūpa, and two kinds of lāsya, sphurita and yauvata, are discussed in detail (3. 21-28). Nṛtta is then described, with its three varieties, viṣama, vikaṭa and laghu (3.29-30). Tāṇḍava and lāsya are designated as dances for men and women following the *Saṅgītadāmodara* (3.31; *SDām.* p.69). A new set of nāṭyas, known as prakāranāṭyas are mentioned next and their names are given as kāṣṭhā, jākaḍī (same as the jakkaḍī mentioned in the *Nartanirṇaya*), śāvara, kurañjī and mattāvalī. These are in fact dance pieces, of which only jākaḍī was recorded by earlier authors. After describing these dances the author refers to them as deśīnṛtya (3. 31-36), of which a definition is then given (3.37). We may note that this author records two kinds of deśī dances, namely, deśīnṛtta and deśīnṛtya.

The author then describes the nāṭyaśālā or the dance-hall and the sitting arrangements for the audience (3. 38-52). The qualifications desirable in spectators are enumerated (3. 53-61). The author then describes the talents and defects of performers, particularly the principal dancers, reviewing dancers from different regions. Then he describes how the training of a dancer begins(3. 62-83). He speaks of the work of the teacher and mentions the use of the curtain (3. 84-90). Four types of

---

[198] *DR.* 1969, p.8; *Bh.P.* 1968. pp. 255-69 ; *SDām.* 1960, pp. 91-96.

abhinayas are also mentioned. The type of abhinaya known as āhārya or the use of costume, make-up and stage accessories is described at great length (3. 90-175). The languages used for different characters in a play and the forms of addressing one another are then described (3.176-201). The author also suggests names for characters which will express their distinctive traits (3. 202-13). Vṛttis or styles of presentation come next (3. 214-19). The author says that since sandhi, bindu, patākā etc. (terms that mark the structural divisions of a play) and the pūrvaraṅga (the preliminaries to a play) are not relevant to nartana or dancing, he will not even mention them (3. 220). This suggests that the use of nartana or dance in the pūrvaraṅga of a play was no longer of vital importance when this text was written. Instead, the art of dance must have been very much a part of the total presentation of saṅgīta, that is, a comprehensive recital of vocal and instrumental music and dance. The interdependence of dance and music can be seen from the early medieval period and as we analyse the texts it becomes much more apparent that in the later medieval period there was no need for any author to describe saṅgīta primarily as a part of a dramatic presentation.

The author proceeds with the characteristics of the best, mediocre and worst performers. The method for entering the stage follows, which this text borrows line for line from the *Saṅgītaratnākara* and the *Nartananirṇaya.*[199] The actions that are to be avoided on stage are specified next. The ideal time for the presentation of a nāṭya is then mentioned.[200] The author adds that the spectator has to remember to encourage the dancer by showing his appreciation; otherwise many misfortunes may befall him (3. 221-255). Āṅgikābhinaya is then described in detail (3. 255-728) with the divisions of limbs into aṅga, upāṅga and

---

[199] *SN.* 3. 235-8; *SR.* 7. 1260-63; *NN.* 40a.

[200] Nāṭya in this context refers to dance, a common practice of the writers on dancing through its history, which is followed in naming the present-day style Bharatnatyam.

pratyaṅga. Next, the author identifies five features of nṛtya, namely, sthānaka, cārī, karaṇa, maṇḍala and aṅgahāra, and he does so, as he himself says, by following the path shown by Bharata. Sthāna is then defined and its different types are described with the names of 52 mārga and deśī sthānas given but no details (3. 731-43). Cāri is then defined and two lines are quoted from the *Saṅgītadāmodara* and the *Saṅgītaratnākara*.[201] The names of 32 mārga and 54 deśī cārīs are given without any description (3. 744-64) but with a passing reference to Bharata. Karaṇas are explained next, Śārṅgadeva being cited as the source and the names of 108 karaṇas are given (3. 765-82). The author prescribes the talapuṣpapuṭa karaṇa for the worship at the beginning of the performance and the gaṅgāvataraṇa karaṇa as part of the benediction with which a performance should conclude (3. 784-5). The names of thirty-six utpluti or deśī karaṇas are given next (3. 786- 92). Seven bhramarīs are included in the list of utplutikaraṇas as in the *Saṅgītaratnākara*.[202] Next, in verses 793-96, thirty-two kalāsakaraṇas are mentioned. Kalāsas occur in other works but are never thought of as karaṇas, which is a very different way of looking at these movements and unique to this text.[203] The author then defines maṇḍala and lists twenty varieties, quoting lines from the *Saṅgītadāmodara* (3. 797-801; *SDām*.p. 67). The author describes aṅgahāras next (3. 802-17), quoting lines from Śārṅgadeva and Śubhaṅkara.[204] Recakas are then described in detail. The chapter ends with verses, again from Dāmodara, prescribing methods of practice, eating light food etc.[205] The author finally talks about nyāya or the use of

---

201 *SN*. 3. 745; *SDām*. p. 64; *SN*. 3. 783-4; *SR*. 7. 748-9.

202 *SN*. 3. 791-2; *SR*. 7. 755.

203 Kalāsas are described in detail in the *Nṛtyādhyāya* and in the *Nṛtyaratnakośa*. *Nr.Adh*. 1570-1613; *NRK*. 4. 1. 37-85.

204 *SN*. 3. 797-8; *SDām*. p. 67; *SN*. 3. 804; *SR*.7. 791; *SN*. 3. 808; *SDām*. p. 68.

205 *SN*. 3. 823; *SDām*. p. 66.

appropriate movements and ends his discussion out of concern for the length of the text.

The new information given by this author relates to the different varieties of mārga and deśīnāṭya, deśīnṛtta (3.12-20), five varieties of prakāranāṭya, also known as deśīnṛtya (3.31-36), and kalāsakaraṇa (3. 793-96). Although he devotes a large number of verses to descriptions, the information does not add much to the knowledge we have already gathered from other texts insofar as the movements of the limbs are concerned.

The next work on our list is the *Saṅgītamakaranda* of Vedasūri which was written in the early seventeenth century. From Raghavan's account, written in 1932-33 (repr. 1956,1957, 1960, 1961), it appears that the only extant part is the chapter on dancing, which has several prakaraṇas or sections. Raghavan reports that on examining the manuscripts he found that the chapter on dance discussed rasadṛṣṭis, gatis, cārīs, hastas, various dances and lastly rasas. He also mentions that Śāhajī, father of the Maratha leader Śivājī, was Vedasūri's patron.[206] Krishnamachariar repeats this information but adds that Vedasūri was the son of Ananta and a grandson of Dāmodara, author of the *Saṅgītadarpaṇa.*[207] The text was edited by K.V. Vasudeva Shastri and published in several parts in the *Journal of the Saraswati Mahal Library,* Tanjore in volumes VI.3; X. 1; X.2 and X.3 and XII from 1955 to 1957.

Of these, only some parts have been available to me. The first section available (X.2) starts from verse 65 and describes the sixth gati, mṛgī. This description is different from any discussion of gati that we have come across so far. The author treats each gati like a dance sequence and describes the gati with all its components of movements. For instance, while describing the mṛgī gati the author gives all the movements necessary for its presentation, such as the appropriate karaṇa, sthāna,

---

206 Raghavan, 1961, pp. 21-23.

207 Krishnamachariar, 1974, p.867.

cārī, the hand-gestures, the head movements and glances. The rest of the gatis are described in the same way. In all he describes the eleven gatis that, he says, are recognized by schools of dancing. This is followed by a description of two cālakas of the arms, laharīcakra and nīrājitapadma (the names are new) that are necessary for maṇḍalasthānaka. At the end of this section the author describes the abhinaya or miming of a verse in the same way that Puṇḍarīka Viṭṭhala in *Nartananirṇaya* has described the abhinaya of a śloka,[208] each word of which is to be expressed by an appropriate hand-gesture. This first prakaraṇa or section ends with a description of the mukhacāli or the opening dance-sequence. The first description of mukhacāli in dance literature occurs in the *Nartananirṇaya*. The second prakaraṇa of the *Saṅgītamakaranda* describes the aṅgahāras which are to be performed in the preliminaries of a play. According to the author, this dance requires twelve karaṇas, which are described in detail.[209] The rest of this section is devoted to the description of the aṅgahāras.

In the next prakaraṇa the author says that after performing the aṅgahāranartana, uḍupa in lakṣmītāla is to be performed and describes in detail the dance along with the required tāla. Next to be described is the dance called nāmāvalī which, according to the author, is taken from Kohala's description. A closer source, however, is Puṇḍarīka's *Nartananirṇaya*. Nāmāvalī can be performed in four, five or six khaṇḍas or units of tālas, each of which is described in the *Saṅgītamakaranda* with its appropriate rhythmic syllables, for which the *Saṅgītadarpaṇa* is cited

---

[208] See *Nartananirṇaya*. 42b.

[209] The twelve karaṇas are vaiśākharecita, vṛścika, vṛścikakuṭṭita, ākṣiptaka, cakramaṇḍala, uromaṇḍala, āvarta, kuñcita, dolāpāda, vivṛta, vinivṛtta and kaṭicchinna. Interestingly, although these karaṇas are from the list found in the Bharata tradition, they are different from the group of sixteen described in the *Nartananirṇaya*. Obviously, the style that is described in the *Saṅgītamakaranda* is different from the style described in the *Nartananirṇaya*. *NN*. 32b-33b.

as the source. Next comes śabdacāli nṛtta, followed by the dances termed neris. A new dance sequence called hastaneri, not found in any other text, is described. This dance requires twenty-four kinds of hand-gestures, ten varieties of sthānas, six types of cārīs, various movements of the different parts of the body and different gatis done in a slow tempo and to āditāla. The author begins to describe the twenty-four hand gestures required for this dance. Unfortunately, the edited text to which I had access breaks off after the description of the seventh hand-gesture.

Although the whole text has not been available to me, the portions examined here are sufficient to show that the author's approach to his subject was unusually full in the detailed instructions he gives for the actual performance of dance movements. He seems to have been interested mainly in the structure of dance compositions as combinations of smaller movements. He describes these movements step by step, and includes with each movement the appropriate rhythm and tempo.

Yet another seventeenth century work that deals with, among other subjects, music and dance is the *Śivatattvaratnākara.* The author was Bāsavarāja, a king who reigned between 1684-1710 A.D. The text has been edited by Narayanaswamy Sastry in three volumes and in the introduction to the first volume H. Deverappa tells us that Bāsavarāja's kingdom was known as Keladi which stretched across "the whole coast of Kanara from Goa in the North to Cannanore in the South as also parts of the Shimoga district of Mysore.[210]

The text consists of nine kallolas or sections with several taraṅgas or subsections each. Altogether a hundred and one such subsections cover a variety of subjects. Dance is described in the sixth chapter in several taraṅgas or subsections numbering 3-6 while music is described in 7-9. The third taraṅga of the sixth chapter has 56 verses, the fourth has 114, the

---

210 *Śivatattvaratnākara*, 1964, Vol. I, Introduction, p. ii.

fifth has 101 and the 6th and final taraṅga, the one that is most relevant to our study, has 100 verses.

The third taraṅga of the sixth chapter begins with a definition of dance for which the author uses the term naṭana (6.3.1) and which he equates with both nṛtta and nāṭya (6.3.5; 6.3.7). Here he explains the nature of dance, writes in praise of the art, relates its origin and discusses verbal acting. Nāṭya and nṛtta are continually used interchangeably (6.3.5-9). Next, mārganṛtta is described, divided into tāṇḍava and lāsya, followed by a description of deśīnṛtta. Then the author describes the seating arrangements for the king, the queen, and the rājavilāsinīs or women of the royal court. Next he provides a traditional description of the characteristics of the nartaka and nartakī or the male and female dancers (6.3. 9-33), but adds a personal note to it by stating that the nartakīs who come from Lāṭa, Gūrjara, Saurāṣṭra and Mahārāṣṭra are the best (uttama), presumably in terms of competence, while the dancers from the central and northern regions are mediocre (madhyama). The worst (adhama) dancers, according to him, come from Karṇāṭa, Drāviḍa and Andhra (6.3. 33).[211] The author then discusses at length the appearance and the qualities of a nartakī (6.3. 34-39). Next he describes how to begin a performance by bowing to Śiva (6.3. 40-45), and gives the number of the drummers needed, naming the different drums as huḍukkā, kāhala, karaḍā, cañcu (6.3.45-48). For initiating the performance the author recommends a set of six rāgas, beginning with śrī or dhruvā and following up with śrī, madhyama, nāṭa, karṇāṭagolaka and chāyānāṭa (6.3.48-50). In the same subsection the terms for the movements of aṅga, upāṅga and pratyaṅga are mentioned, as are the sthānas, cārīs, maṇḍalas, pādas,

---

211 This seems surprising in view of the widespread cultivation of the art, which can be inferred from the fact that at least from the medieval period a number of manuals were produced from the south and were still being produced when this text was written. Further, we find references to highly developed dance styles from those regions. See Raghavan, 1965, Introduction, pp. 18-34.

aṅgahāras and recakas. Departing from the usual practice of dance manuals, the author also includes in this section a brief discussion of the method of teaching dancing. All of these the author promises to discuss in the following sections (6.3.50-56).

The fourth taraṅga deals with the movements of the head and its parts in 114 verses. The fifth taraṅga describes, in 101 verses, hand-gestures and the movements of the arms and prescribes their applications. Unlike other works, the *Śivatattvaratnākara* first describes the nṛttahastas or the hand-gestures specially meant for dancing, and then describes the others, that is, the single and double hand-gestures. The sixth taraṅga discusses the rest of the major and minor limbs (6.6.1-43), finishing with the movements of the feet and moves on to describing sthānas (6.6.43-85). In discussing the movements of the limbs the author mostly follows the *Nāṭyaśāstra* and *Saṅgītaratnākara.* The author mentions deśī sthānas as they appear in the *Saṅgītaratnākara* but does not describe them. Cārīs and maṇḍalas are discussed next but no deśī varieties (6.6.86-99) are given. The author at this point expresses concern about the length of his work and says that there are 108 karaṇas but does not name them. However, he states that 16 of these karaṇas are better known than the others; we may recall that in the *Nartananirṇaya,* Puṇḍarīka describes a set of 16 karaṇas that constitute bandhanṛtta (6.6.100; *NN.* 32b). Whether the 16 karaṇas considered by Bāsavarāja as the most prominent were the same as the karaṇas required for bandhanṛtta cannot be known but the coincidence is worth noting. As we shall see in a later chapter, the bandhanṛtta described in the *Nartananirṇaya* is very likely closely related to the style now known as Odissi. If indeed the 16 karaṇas selected by Bāsavarāja were elements of bandhanṛtta, then there is reason to believe that this style was practiced in Western as well as Eastern India at the time this author wrote.

The *Saṅgītasārasaṅgraha* is a late work by a "Bengali Vaiṣṇava lyric poet and composer Narahari Cakravartī, alias Ghanaśyāmadāsa" who lived in the early nineteenth century.[212] It is in six chapters which deal mostly with music, and as Nijenhuis points out, it is a compilation of materials drawn from older works on music from the eastern part of India, mainly from Orissa and Bengal. The text offers very little to add to our knowledge of the concept or descriptions of movements or sequences. But it does show that informed interest in certain dance styles continued from the medieval times till the early nineteenth century in Eastern India.

The chapters deal with the following subjects: vocal music, instrumental music, dance and drama, body movements, language and metre. Of these, chapters 3 and 4 are of interest to us. The third chapter (pp. 63-69) starts with a benediction, relates the origin of nāṭyaveda, which the author refers to as the fifth veda, and mentions the division of nartana (dance) into nāṭya, nṛtya and nṛtta. These terms as well as mārga and deśī are explained with quotations from Kohala. Ten mārganāṭyas, sixteen deśīnāṭyas and twelve nṛtyas are mentioned, the information being taken from the *Saṅgītanārāyaṇa*[213] Nṛtta is divided into the usual three categories, namely, viṣama, vikaṭa and laghu. Tāṇḍava and lāsya, which the author says can be both nṛtta and nṛtya, are discussed in detail along with their varieties. Tāṇḍava and lāsya are referred to as dances for men and women respectively. Tāṇḍava has two varieties, preraṇi and bahurūpa, and lāsya has sphurita [214] and yauvata; these are taken from the *Saṅgītadāmodara.* The author quotes from the *Saṅgītadāmodara, Saṅgītakaumudī* and the *Saṅgītasāra* to describe these dances. He gives a list of dance pieces from the late medieval period, which includes kāṣṭhā, jākaḍī, śabda, karañjī and mattāvalīnṛtya. These again are from the *Saṅgītanārāyaṇa.*[215] Jākaḍī and śabdanṛtya are found in other texts as

---

212 Nijenhuis, 1977, p. 35; Katz, 1987, Introduction, pp. xxii-xiii.

213 *SN.* 3. 12-20; *SSār.Sam.* pp.63-69.

214 *SDām.* has churita, p. 69.

215 *SN.* 3. 31-36; *SSārSam.* pp.63-69.

well.[216] In describing dance movements the author mainly follows the *Saṅgītadāmodara* and the *Saṅgītaratnākara.* He quotes from *Kaumudī* (i.e., *Saṅgītakaumudī*) to say that different regions have different varieties of nṛtya according to the taste of the particular region.[217]

The fourth chapter (pp. 70-90) discusses aṅgahāra, by which the author means aṅgas, upāṅgas and pratyaṅgas, or the major and minor limbs. In this he follows the *Saṅgītadāmodara.*[218] The applications of some of these movements are also described. The author finishes the chapter by mentioning the five components of a dance which are sthānaka, cārī, karaṇa, maṇḍala and aṅgahāra; the term aṅgahāra, in this context, stands for the basic dance sequence. He does not discuss them in detail since he is concerned about the length of the work.

No survey of Sanskrit treatises on dancing can hope to be entirely comprehensive since many of the earliest works are lost. As the present survey has indicated, the lost work by Kohala was clearly a source of abiding authority on which contemporaries as well as later writers continued to draw. The medieval period has fared better, for most of the treatises written in that period are extant and most are available in modern editions. In the later period a number of manuals were produced, some in Sanskrit and some in the vernacular languages, many of which are still unedited and available only as manuscripts scattered through libraries all over India and a few in libraries outside India. Raghavan has described some of these manuals on dancing in his survey of saṅgīta literature in Sanskrit, and some vernacular works in the introduction to his edition of the *Nṛttaratnāvalī.*[219]

---

216 *NN.* 47b-48a (śabdanṛtta), 53a (Jakkaḍī); *SDar.*7. 268-71 (Jakkaḍī); *SMakV.* ch.2.

217 *SN.*3.37.

218 *SSārSam.* .pp.70-90.; *SDām.* .pp. 61-9.

219 Raghavan, 1956-61; *NR.*1965, Introduction, pp. 18-34.

The present survey covers the majority of Sanskrit works that directly deal with dancing, leaving out only those from the late period (16th -17th century) that fail to provide new information or to show any originality of approach. Also omitted, for fear of needless duplication, are certain eighteenth century texts that have been exhaustively described by Kapila Vatsyayan. Her survey, as earlier mentioned, may be used to great advantage to complement the present survey.[220] The present survey has also left out works in regional languages since they do not form part of the Sanskrit tradition that is the subject of this study. But the considerable number of these vernacular dance manuals produced in the late medieval times and through the nineteenth century in Andhra, Tamilnadu, Kerala, Orissa, Bengal and Manipur attest to the importance and popularity of the art.[221]

The relevance of dance treatises is not limited to dance historians and critics but extends to the actual dancers. At the present time, practitioners of each of the modern styles claim to have their own manuals which they follow, some written in Sanskrit some in the languages of the regions where they originated. The Bharatanatyam dancers follow the text of the *Abhinayadarpaṇa* of Nandīkeśvara for learning the movements of the body, Odissi dancers seem to follow the *Abhinayacandrikā* of Maheśvara

220 Vatsyayan, 1968, pp.32-37, has used the *Nāṭyaśāstra* of Bharata, the *Abhinayadarpaṇa* of Nandīkeśvara, the *Saṅgītaratnākara* of Śārṅgadeva, the *Saṅgītamakaranda* of Vedasūri, the *Nāṭyaśāstrasaṁgraha* of Govindācārya, the *Hastalakṣaṇadīpikā* (followed by the Kathākali dancers), the *Hastamuktāvalī* of Śubhaṅkara(followed by the Manipurī dancers) and the *Balarāmabharata* of Balarāma Varmā (followed by the Mohiniāṭṭam dancers) to compare the theories offered. The present researcher has given an account of the *Nāṭyaśāstrasaṁgraha* in her earlier studies (1964, 1970). This text is left out f rom the present study. The *Hastalakṣaṇadīpikā* and the *Balarāmabharata* are left out since Vatsāyayan's book provides the details of their content.

221 Patnaik, 1971; *Classical and Folk Dances of India*, 1963, part i, 'Bharatanatyam,' p. 29; part ii, 'Kathakali,' p. 10; part iv, 'Odissi,' p.20; part v, 'Manipuri,' p.39.

Mahāpātra, Kathak dancers refer to *Nartanasarvasva* as their guidebook (though no copy of it has been found so far), and Kathakali and Mohinīattam dancers follow – among other manuals – the *Hastalakṣaṇadīpikā* and *Balarāmabharatam* as their guidebook.[222] This reliance of dancers on the śāstra of dancing is a product of the tradition of discourse established in the Sanskrit treatises, which has resulted in simultaneously providing theoretical exposition and practical guidance.

The literature of dancing surveyed here is important as the major repository of information but more important still as the only record and the only measure of the changes through which dancing has evolved in India. In terms both of techniques and concepts we see the phenomenon of steady change in the art and it is only by studying the treatises in their chronological sequence that we may trace the details of that evolution. The present survey thus forms the necessary background to the study undertaken here of the particular features and underlying principles of classical Indian dancing. To understand these features and principles, this study will closely examine the terms, relating to both concepts and techniques, found in the texts of the subject, which are charted below.

---

[222]The sources for the various styles are as follows. Kathak: 'Kathak,' Vatsyayan, 1956, pp. 74-88, and 'Bhārater Śāstrīya Nṛtyakalā,' Kothari, 1987, p. 60; Mohinīattam: 'Mohiniaattam,' Rele, 1981, pp. 69-70; Kathakali: 'The Tradition: ABrief Historical Survey,' Khokar, 1963, pt. II, p. 10; Odissi: 'A Glimpse Into Odissi Dance,' Miśra, 1981, p. .90; Bharatanātyam: 'Śāstra and Prayoga: The Use of Abhinayadarpaṇa,' Bose, 1988.

Work	Date(approximate)	Author
Nāṭyaśāstra	2nd/ 3rd c. A. D.	Bharata
Viṣṇudharmottara Purāṇa	5th c. A. D.(section on dance)	
Abhinavabharatī	10th-11th c. A.D.	Abhinavagupta
Daśarūpaka	10th c. A.D.	Dhanañjaya
Śṛṅgāraprakāśa	11th c. A.D.	Bhoja
Nāṭyadarpaṇa	12th c. A.D.	Rāmacandra and Guṇacandra
Mānasollāsa	12th c. A.D.	Someśvara
Nāṭakalakṣaṇaratnakośa	12th/13th c. A.D.	Sāgaranandin
Bhāvaprakāśana	around13th c. A.D.	Śāradātanaya
Saṅgītasamayasāra	12th-13th c. A.D.	Pārśvadeva
Saṅgītaratnākara	13th c. A.D	Śārṅgadeva
Nṛttaratnāvalī	13th c. A.D	Jāya Senāpati
Abhinayadarpaṇa	around13th c. A.D.	Nandīkeśvara
Saṅgītamakaranda	13th/14th c. A.D.	Nārada
Sāhityadarpaṇa	14th c. A.D.	Viśvanātha Kavirāja
Saṅgītopaniṣatsāroddhāra	14th c. A.D.	Sudhākalaśa
Saṅgītacandra	14/15th c. A.D.	Vipradāsa
Saṅgītadāmodara	15th c. A.D.	Śubhaṅkara
Hastamuktāvalī	15th c. A.D.	Śubhaṅkara
Nṛtyādhyāya	14th/15th c. A.D.	Aśokamalla
Nṛtyaratnakośa	15th c. A.D.	Mahārāṇā Kumbhā
Bharatārṇava	16th c. A.D.	Nandīkeśvara
Nartananirṇaya	16th-17th c. A.D.	Puṇḍarīka Viṭṭhala
Rasakaumudī	16th-17th c. A.D.	Śrīkaṇṭha
Saṅgītadarpaṇa	17th c. A.D.	Dāmodara
Saṅgītanārāyaṇa	17th c. A.D.	Puruṣottama Miśra
Saṅgītamakaranda	17th c. A.D.	Vedasūri
Śivatattvaratnākara	17th/18th c. A.D.	Bāsavarāja
Saṅgītasārasaṁgraha	19th c. A.D.	Ghanaśyāmadāsa

Chapter 3

THE *NĀṬYAŚĀSTRA* AND THE CONCEPT OF DANCE

The *Nāṭyaśāstra* of Bharata is not only the earliest but also the most extensive work on all aspects of drama, dance and music. Its influence has been so great on all subsequent works on the performing arts that not one of the many treatises on dancing has attempted to describe dancing without adhering to the framework of discussion laid down by Bharata and often borrowing substantially from his work. That the impact of the *Nāṭyaśāstra* is so deep and permanent is due to the fact that it combines theory and practice, formulating concepts of dance as it describes its technique. These concepts must be closely examined since they have remained central to all discussions on dancing.

These concepts may be set in the context of Bharata's comprehensive view of drama, dance and music by noting the place that Bharata accords these arts in the social structure. According to him, the drama is the fifth Veda, which was created by Brahmā for those castes that did not have access to the Vedas proper:

> न वेदव्यवहारोऽयं संश्राव्यः शूद्रजातिषु ।
> तस्मात् सृजापरं वेदं पञ्चमं सार्ववर्णिकम् ॥
> एवमस्त्विति . . . . .
>
> (*NŚ.* 1. 12-13)
>
> The Vedas [lit: the use of this Veda] are not to be heard by [lit:in] the śūdra castes. Therefore [please] create another Veda, the fifth, meant for all the varṇas. "Let it be thus," [said]. . . . .

Bharata calls this fifth Veda the nāṭyaveda: nāṭyākhyam pañcamam vedam . . (*NŚ*. 1. 15).

Dance is seen by Bharata as an introduction to dramatic performance. It was Śiva, he says, who prescribed the addition of dance to the preliminaries of a dramatic performance in order to add beauty to it.

> मयाऽपीदं स्मृतं नृत्तं[1] सन्ध्याकालेषु नृत्यता ।
> नानाकरणसंयुक्तैरङ्गहारैर्विभूषितम् ॥
> पूर्वरङ्गविधावस्मिंस्त्वया सम्यक् प्रयोज्यताम् ।
>
> (*NŚ*. 4.13 -14)
>
> And I have also propagated this [art of] dancing embellished with aṅgahāras consisting of a number of karaṇas while performing dances in the evening. Apply this art (i.e., dance) in an appropritate manner in the rites of these preliminaries of [a drama].

Although references to dancers and dance are scattered through early literature,[2] it was Bharata who first treated dance systematically, defining it as an art-form which consisted of beautiful movements of the body performed to rhythm and to vocal or instrumental music or to both, and which may be mimetic or purely decorative. This definition rests upon five major terms: nṛtta, tāṇḍava, piṇḍībandha, abhinaya and sukumāraprayoga. Although most of these are familiar terms, the concepts behind them have been obscured by time and often by confusing

---

[1] Nṛtta is the term, not nṛtya, that Bharata uses consistently throughout his work to denote dancing. The term nṛtya appears only twice in the G. O. S. edition of the *NŚ* (4.13, and 30), and seems to have been a scribal error. See Bose, 1970, p.8; Varma, 1957, p.21. The Kāśī edition has nṛtta, which supports this view. Nṛtta and nṛtya are different concepts and the latter did not become current till the tenth century A.D.

[2] See Bose, 1970, pp. 1-4.

commentary. To understand the tradition of art described by Bharata, one must clarify the concepts.

Bharata's most significant statements on dance occur in the fourth chapter of the *Nāṭyaśāstra,* which is devoted entirely to this subject. Dance, we are told, was created for beauty's sake: शोभां प्रजनयेदिति नृत्तं प्रवर्त्तितम् ।[3] The terms he uses for this dance are two–nṛtta and tāṇḍava:

रेचका अङ्गहाराश्च पिण्डीबन्धास्तथैव च ॥
सृष्ट्वा भगवता दत्तास्तण्डवे मुनये तदा ।
तेनापि हि ततः सम्यग् गानभाण्डसमन्वितः ॥
नृत्तप्रयोगः सृष्टो यः स ताण्डव इति स्मृतः ।

(*NŚ.* 4. 259-61)

Recakas, aṅgahāras and the piṇḍībandhas were created by god [Śiva] and then given to the sage Taṇḍu. That method of dancing which was then created by him [=Taṇḍu] accompanied by appropriate songs and drums, is known as Tāṇḍava.

Taken as a karmadhāraya samāsa, the compound nṛttaprayoga in the last line of this passage equates tāṇḍava with nṛtta.[4] Nṛtta is described as an art-form which is beautified with aṅgahāras made of various karaṇas. He then describes these karaṇas and aṅgahāras in detail: हस्तपादसमायोगो नृत्तस्य करणं भवेत् । – the coordinated movement of the hands and feet makes the karaṇa of a dance.[5] A karaṇa is the basic unit of dancing and the movements that constitute karaṇas are clearly prescribed. A combination of karaṇas, numbering six to nine, makes an aṅgahāra, which

---

[3] *NŚ.* 4.264.

[4] ताण्डवमिति सर्वं नृत्तमुच्यते । (*AB.* on the *NŚ.* G. O. S ed., 1956, Vol. I, p. 180).

[5] *NŚ.* 4.30

can be described as a basic dance-sequence.[6] Bharata states that such sequences beautify a dramatic performance when they are included in the pūrvaraṅga or preliminaries, which can be presented with or without dance. When there is no dance but songs are sung, a pūrvaraṅga is known as śuddha or pure. The kind that has dancing in it is called citra or mixed.[7] In this fourth chapter Bharata deals with the citra type of pūrvaraṅga. In the same chapter Bharata says that sthānas, cārīs and nṛttahastas prescribed in the discussion of vyāyāma or exercise (in the chapters on āṅgikābhinaya, chapters eight to twelve) should be applied to a karaṇa.[8] Sthānas are the basic postures or stances in a dance.[9] Cārīs are executed with one leg: एकपादप्रचारो यः सा चारीत्यभिसंज्ञिता[10] The different gestures of hands meant solely for the use in nṛtta are known as nṛttahastas: करणे तु प्रयोक्तव्या नृत्तहस्ता विशेषतः। -- in a karaṇa nṛttahastas are to be applied in particular.[11] Bharata describes these karaṇas and aṅgahāras in detail and then describes another movement called recaka. Recakas, defined as the basic movements of the feet, hips, hands and neck, seem to be quite fundamental to dancing, for Bharata has included them in his chapter on dance.[12] He states his view clearly about the nature of nṛtta by saying that aṅgahāras, recakas and piṇḍībandhas done together in an appropriate manner form nṛtta (*NŚ*. 4. 259-61).

After listing and discussing the constituent movements of dancing, Bharata returns to the structure of the pūrvaraṅga as a whole. Here he

---

[6] *NŚ*. 4.33.

[7] *NŚ*. 4.15-16.

[8] *NŚ*. 4.169-71.

[9] *NŚ* does not define sthāna as such but from the descriptions of the sthānas in chapter ten of the *NŚ* the movement can be understood (*NŚ*. 10. 50-71).

[10] *NŚ*. 10.3.

[11] *NŚ*..9.210.

[12] *NŚ*. 4.248-49.

introduces another term, piṇḍībandha. Piṇḍībandhas are group dances that constitute a distinct phase of the preliminaries following the introductory dancing and they are of four types: piṇḍī, latā, śṛṅkhalā, and bhedyaka (*NŚ.* 4. 287-89). The purpose of these dances is to invoke the blessings of the gods. Bharata relates how, after disrupting Dakṣas's sacrifice ceremony, Maheśvara danced in the evening with aṅgahāras set to rhythm and tempo. Evidently, Bharata is taking it for granted that Śiva was accompanied in his dancing by his followers, and that this performance created a number of group dances or piṇḍībandhas, for Bharata goes on to say that Śiva's gaṇas or disciples, such as Nandī and Bhadramukha, saw the piṇḍībandhas and named the variations of one type of piṇḍībandha known as piṇḍī, that is, a cluster. They named each variation of the cluster after a god or a goddess. These piṇḍīs, named in this way by Śiva's disciples, are then listed by Bharata who adds that other piṇḍīs should be similarly named after other gods or goddesses. Emphasizing the mythological status of Taṇḍu as the archetypal dancer among mortals, Bharata tells us that recaka, aṅgahāra and piṇḍībandhas were created and given to Taṇḍu and it was thus that with songs and drums the art of dance was created. While describing the performance of tāṇḍava he again elaborates on piṇḍīs.[13]

The presentation of the preliminaries seems to be an elaborate performance which calls for, beside the singers and drummers, one principal female dancer and a group of other female dancers. The group of dancers is required to enter and dance in a variety of formations which are known as piṇḍībandhas. Such formation dancing is prescribed only for female dancers and considered appropriate only for this particular part of the entire stage presentation. Piṇḍībandhas are dedicated to different gods who are denoted by their emblems, which are represented by the formations created by the dancers. In addition, the dancers form into

---

[13] *NŚ.* 4. 279-91.

ritualistic diagrams. Bharata states that in order to be able to create such formations in an appropriate manner, these dancers require careful and thorough training.[14] Piṇḍībandhas thus have a auspicious purpose in the main, to invoke the blessings of the gods, and that Bharata should include them as necessary parts of the stage-presentation adds to our understanding of the function of dancing as an art in Bharata's time.

Elaborating on the piṇḍībandhas, Bharata says that different yonis, bhadrāsana and yantra are to be applied in composing piṅḍībandhas. The use of the first two refers to the formation of auspicious diagrams. Yantra is a term for mystical diagrams in tāntric and Buddhist usage. If we take the word in that sense then it fits in with yoni and bhadrāsana as the name of a figure formed by a group of dancers. Raghavan, however, takes yantra to mean mechanical aids in his discussion of the uparūpakas of the Jaina tradition. The editor of the *Saṅgītopaniṣatsāroddhāra* gives a list of thirty-two varieties of dance dramas which includes bhadrāsana. These are from the Jainasūtra named *Rājapraśnīya*, as noted also by Raghavan. Following this text, Raghavan has described this bhadrāsana as the "execution of rows or garland-like formations made up of groups resembling moon, sun, swans, stars, pearls, gems and so on."[15] In Abhinavagupta's commentary we find references to a formation like a stick grasped in the beak of a swan.[16]

Bharata divides piṇḍībandha into four classes:

पिण्डीनां विधयश्चैव चत्वारः सम्प्रकीर्त्तिताः ॥
पिण्डी शृङ्खलिका चैव लताबन्धोऽथ भेद्यकः ।
पिण्डीबन्धस्तु पिण्डत्वाद् गुल्मः शृङ्खलिका भवेत् ॥
जालोपनद्धा च लता सनृत्तो भेद्यकः स्मृतः। (*NŚ.* 4. 287-89)

---

[14] *NŚ.* 4. 252- 59; 4. 287- 91.

[15] Raghavan 1963, pp. 572- 74. See also *SUS.*,1961, Introduction, xvi-xvii.

[16] *AB.* on *NŚ.* 1956, Vol. I., p. 191.

> The practice of piṇḍīs can be of four types: piṇḍī, śṛṅkhalikā, latābandha and bhedyaka. Piṇḍībandha is [lit.: from] a roundish mass, śṛṅkhalikā is [like a] cluster, latā is entwined [lit.: bound] in a net and bhedyaka is known to be [performed with] nṛtta.

The precise nature of the formations is not easy to understand from this passage. Abhinavagupta has a fairly long commentary on it which is not much clearer.[17] Attempting a better explanation, V. Rāghavan in his introduction to *Nṛttaratnāvalī* has suggested an improved reading of the edited version of the commentary on piṇḍībandhas as given in Ramakrishna Kavi's edition of the *Nāṭyaśāstra*. The passage in Kavi's edition is:

> नर्तकीयोज्यः परस्परसम्वन्धः एव पिण्डीबन्धद्वयप्रकारः
> सजातीयो वा एकता(ना)लावबद्धकमलयुगलवत् विजातीयो वा
> हंसवदनपरिगृहीतनालनलिनवत् गुल्मः शृङ्खलिकाशब्दवाच्यः ।
> नर्तकीत्रयप्रयोज्यस्तु ततोऽपि
> वैचित्र्यसहिष्णुत्वाज्जालवद्विचित्रतां
> गच्छत्पूर्ववत्सजातीयविजातीयात्मा लताबन्धः
> चतुष्टयप्रयोज्यस्तु . . .

Raghavan emends it thus:

> नर्तकीयोज्यः परस्परसम्वन्ध एव पिण्डीबन्धः, सजातीयो वा
> एकनालाबद्धकमलयुगलवत्, विजातीयो वा
> हंसवदनपरिगृहीतनालनलिनवत् । गुल्मः
> शृङ्खलिकाशब्दवाच्यः नर्तकीत्रयप्रयोज्यस्तु। ततोऽपि

---

17 *Ibid.* 191.

> वैचित्र्यसहिष्णुत्वात् विचित्रतां गच्छत्
> सजातीयविजातीयात्मा लताबन्धश्चतुष्टयप्रयोज्यस्तु . . .[18]
> The employment of female dancers joining with one another [in a dance figure] is Piṇḍībandha, the symmetrical [form of the figure] like a pair of lotuses joined in one stalk, the asymmertric like a lotus stalk held in the beak of a swan. Gulma is expressed by the word chain to be performed by three female dancers. Through its capacity for diversity, latābandha of symmetrical and asymmetrical nature, [and] demonstrated by four [female dancers] becomes more entertaining . . . . .

In his study of *Śṛṅgāraprakāśa,* Raghavan further attempts to explain the characteristics of piṇḍībandhas by citing Bhoja. Bhoja, he says, defines the piṇḍībandhas as group dances used in presenting the rāsaka, nāṭyarāsaka and lāsya types of minor drama (that is, padārthābhinayātmaka prekṣyaprabandha).[19] We may recall that in Bharata's account piṇḍībandhas are parts of the preliminaries to a dramatic performance (as is all dancing), not of the presentation of the dramas themselves. Neither Bhoja's mention of piṇḍībandhas nor Raghavan's commentary throws any more light on the nature of piṇḍībandhas and all we know to any degree of certainty is that these were group dances that were used in Bharata's time in the citra type of pūrvaraṅga but had come to be part of the technique of minor dramas by Bhoja's time. As we shall find later in the course of discussing the minor types of drama such as rāgakāvyas, nṛttakāvyas, nṛtyabhedas and uparūpakas, these group dances formed a major part of dramatic

---

[18] *Ibid.* 191; *NR.*1965, Introduction, pp.143.

[19] *Śṛ.P.* 1963, pp. 563; 588-89.

presentation for centuries. Even today some of them survive, as for instance in the rāsa dance of Gujrat, Rajasthan, Vrindavan and Mathura and in Kathak and Manipuri.

In describing nṛtta, tāṇḍava and piṇḍībandha Bharata is concerned with the process of dancing as described in terms of the physical structure of movements. Our understanding of the process is augmented by two other concepts that deal with the affective quality of the art, namely, sukumāraprayoga and abhinaya.

The concept of sukumāraprayoga is invoked in the context of Śiva's dance. According to the legend cited by Bharata, Śiva's dance, which comprises aṅgahāras and recakas, inspires Pārvatī who demonstrates a different way of dancing by employing graceful and delicate movements:

> रेचकैरङ्गहारैश्च नृत्यन्तं वीक्ष्य शङ्करम् ॥
> सुकुमारप्रयोगेण नृत्यन्तीं चैव पार्वतीम् ।
>
> (*NŚ*. 4. 249-50)
>
> On seeing Śaṅkara dancing with recakas and aṅgahāras and on seeing Pārvatī dancing with delicacy . . .

Beyond the use of the adjective sukumāra Bharata does not provide any clue to the nature of Pārvatī's dance and goes on to describe the whole sequence of the dance that is included in the pūrvaraṅga along with drumming, singing etc. Abhinavagupta is not much help either. All he says is that since Śaṅkara's dance lacked grace, Pārvatī demonstrated that quality by giving a performance that was characterized by delicate movements.[20] This implies that Pārvatī's dance falls into a separate category. However, Pārvatī's dance is different not because she uses movements different from those of Śiva, but because she uses the same

[20] *AB*. on *NŚ*. 1956, Vol. I., p. 164.

movements more delicately. The difference is thus stylistic not substantive.

The significance of sukumāraprayoga is not entirely clear in this passage. Later on in his discourse Bharata does offer some explanation of sukumāra when he says:

> स्त्रीपुंसयोस्तु संलापो यस्तु कामसमुद्भवः ।
> तज्ज्ञेयं सुकुमारं हि शृङ्गाररससम्भवम् ॥
>
> (*NŚ*. 4. 303)
>
> The conversation, which is generated from the passion between a man and a woman is known as sukumāra that arises from the erotic sentiment.

Such a sentiment, he says, can be represented in a performance by applying the aṅgahāras shown by Pārvatī: देवीकृतैरङ्गहारैर्ललितैस्तत् प्रयोजयेत् । -- which is to be applied with delicate aṅgahāras created by the goddess (=Pārvatī).[21] The emphasis here is on the affective function of sukumāra. Necessarily, then, by relating sukumāra to dancing Bharata is shifting conceptual areas, from the structure to the function–at least one function–of dancing. By itself Bharata's statement does not clarify the nature of the application. Abhinavagupta tries to clarify the nature of sukumāra by giving some examples from the rāgakāvyas which later, in the medieval period, came to be known as uparūpakas or minor types of drama. From the examples of the rāgakāvyas given by Abhinavagupta one may say that these required graceful and delicate movements. He further cites some aṅgahāras which employ less vigorous movements as examples of delicate aṅgahāras[22] but no other detail can be found. If one tries out these so called aṅgahāras, the delicate nature of the movements can be

---

[21] *NŚ*. 4. 312.

[22] *AB*. on *NŚ*. 1956, Vol. I. p. 201.

perceived, although it is difficult to fully understand through verbal description an art-form which relies entirely on visual experience for its effect. That is why sukumāraprayoga and its nature gave rise to a great deal of confusion in the later texts concerning what constituted the delicacy of movements. In the next chapter of the present study this confusion has been discussed in detail.

The other concept that relates to the quality rather than the structure of dance is the vital one of abhinaya. The term abhinaya denotes the method of expressing ideas through gestures and is explained in the *Nāṭyaśāstra* as:

> ...प्राप्त्यर्थमर्थानां तज्ज्ञैरभिनयः कृतः ।
>
> (*NŚ.* 4. 261.)
>
> ... abhinaya is created by the experts to understand the meaning [lit:when the meaning is aimed at] [of the kāvya].

Bharata attempts to address questions asked by the sages who seem puzzled when they find that nṛtta has no connection either with the total meaning of the accompanying songs, nor even with the meaning of individual words or sentences. They ask again, why then was nṛtta created?

> न गीतकार्थसम्बन्धं न चाप्यर्थस्य भावकम् ॥
> कस्मात् नृत्तं कृतं. . .
>
> (*NŚ.* 4. 262-63)
>
> [Nṛtta] does not have any connection with the meaning of the song nor does it express the meaning of the [words]. Why is nṛtta created?

To this Bharata's answer is:

> . . . . . न खल्वर्थं कंचिन्नृत्तमपेक्षते ॥

> किं तु शोभां प्रजनयेदिति नृत्तं प्रवर्त्तितम् ।
>
> (*NŚ.* 4. 262-63).
>
> . . . . . nṛtta requires no meaning at all but [it was] to produce beauty [that] nṛtta was created.

Abhinaya is explained by Bharata not only as a particular mode of performance but also as a distinct phase of stage-presentation. We have seen how in the preliminaries the aṅgahāras are performed at first and then the piṇḍībandhas. To perform the aṅgahāras the main nartakī enters and dances with pure karaṇas. She then performs abhinaya to a song without the accompaniment of drums:

> यत्राभिनेयं गीतं स्यात् तत्र वाद्यं न योजयेत् ।
>
> (*NŚ.* 4. 276)
>
> Where a song is to be acted drumming should not be applied.

She first performs nṛtta and then abhinaya, after which she makes an exit. Then female dancers enter and make different group formations. Bharata says that until the piṇḍīs are formed, paryastaka (i.e., body movements that do not express ideas) is performed by these dancers.[23] Bharata describes in the fullest detail the entire sequence of this performance of the preliminaries with songs, instrumental music, tāla etc. He then clarifies his concept of nṛtta, tāṇḍava and abhinaya.

Bharata's statement that nṛtta has no connection either with the total meaning of the accompanying songs, nor even with the meaning of individual words or sentences leaves unanswered the question whether nṛtta has any function of communication. Here we are confronting a basic problem of art, that of its semantic purpose. David Smith has tried to give

---

[23] *Ibid.* p.188: अभिनयशून्यमा(आ)ङ्गिकविधिः पर्यस्तकः ।

an answer to this question posed by the sages while discussing tāṇḍava in his study of *Haravijayam.* He views nṛtta as a superior art-form that does not look for any purpose: "The dance does not imitate anything in real life, but is a self-subsistent creation free from any practical aim. It is the natural expression, through the movements of the limbs, of a given state of mind. . . . Even if Śiva dances abhinaya, mimetic dance, there are still no grounds for enquiry into the meaning of this dance, since dancing Śiva is all there really is."[24] In support of this point of view Smith quotes the following verse:

करणाङ्गहारविधिभिः सविस्तरैः
सकलासु शङ्कर ! निशासु नृत्यता ।
क्रियते त्वयानुकृतिरात्मनो विभो !
सचराचरं जगदवाप्य तस्थुषः ॥

(*Haravijayam,* 6. 180)

O beneficent Śiva !
every night you dance
with the whole range of karaṇas and aṅgahāras,
yet, O Lord!
there is nothing for you to imitate
but yourself
for you pervade, you are, the entire universe.[25]

Given the self-subsistent nature of Śiva that Smith points out, the question of meaning (or the lack of it) seems beside the point. However, the question of purpose still remains. In fact, Bharata attributes purpose to nṛtta. This is clear in the distinction he draws between the dance as demonstrated, respectively, by Śiva and Pārvatī. The dance taught by Śiva

---

24 Smith, 1985, p. 250.

25 *Ibid.* p. 251.

to Taṇḍu, that is, tāṇḍava, aims at devastuti, that is, praise-offerings to the gods. It does so because dancing of this type creates beauty of form and is like any other beautiful object, such as flowers, that are offered to the gods. Thus, tāṇḍava has purpose but no meaning because it is not conceived by Bharata as a vehicle of feelings or emotions.

Emotional signification seems to be the business of the dance demonstrated by Pārvatī. The respective functions of the two styles are quite explicitly stated :

> देवस्तुत्याश्रयकृतं यदङ्गं तु भवेदथ ।
> माहेश्वरैरङ्गहारैरुद्धतैस्तत् प्रयोजयेत् ।
> यत्तु शृङ्गारसम्बन्धं गानं स्त्रीपुरुषाश्रयम् ।
> देवीकृतैरङ्गहारैर्ललितैस्तत् प्रयोजयेत् ॥
>
> (*NŚ*. 4.312)
>
> Whatever part [of a play; here, the pūrvaraṅga] is for praising gods, that [one] should perform with the vigorous aṅgahāras created by Maheśvara, while a song related to erotic sentiment involving [lit.: depending on] man and woman should be performed with the aṅgahāras created by Devī.

While tāṇḍava is exclusively intended for worship as an offering valued for the beauty of its form, Pārvatī's dance is used for human communication and is valued for its ability to express emotions. As we go from Śiva's dance to Pārvatī's, we find the emphasis shifting from the metaphysical to the material, from form to content. Bharata 's concept of sukumāraprayoga sets Pārvatī's kind of dancing in a context of human relations where सुकुमारप्रयोगश्च शृङ्गाररससम्भवः-- the application of delicate (movements) generates the erotic sentiment (*NŚ*. 4.269). This does open up the possibility of the expressive use of nṛtta which is seen in the references to the application of delicate movements in the dramatic literature of all periods. The dramatic potentiality of sukumāraprayoga brings dance movements within the orbit of acting or abhinaya.

In speaking of dancing while discussing pūrvarāṅga in the fourth chapter, Bharata prescribes two styles of presentation: uddhata and lalita. Uddhata aṅgahāras are used for devastuti in a pūrvaraṅga. In a pūrvaraṅga, lalita or delicate movements are employed to depict the feelings between a man and woman. This distinction between the styles that are appropriate, respectively, to the portrayal of gods and the depiction of human beings in love is drawn again in the discussion of the pūrvaraṅga in the fifth chapter. There Bharata says:

> शृङ्गारस्य प्रचारणाच्चारी सम्परिकीर्त्तिता ।
> रौद्रप्रचारणाच्चापि महाचारीति कीर्तिता ॥
>
> (*NŚ*. 5.27)
>
> Cārī is known to manifest śṛṅgāra [rasa] and mahācārī
> is known to manifest raudra [rasa] as well.

It is important to bear in mind that Bharata places the entire discussion on vigorous dancing in the context of the pūrvaraṅga, not in that of drama proper. As the following discussion shows, the nature of abhinaya pertaining to the dance in the pūrvaraṅga may seem confusing if the.uddhata and lalita styles are extended to drama proper. As Abhinavagupta explains,uddhata, which is the style of Śiva, obviously indicates vigorous dancing with forceful aṅgahāras while lalita is the style of Pārvatī and is characterized by delicate aṅgahāras.[26] Uddhata is used in devastuti and lalita is used in presenting love scenes.

The classification of dance into uddhata and lalita also suggests a distinction between masculine and feminine modes of expression, first because of their physical characteristics and second, because of their

---

[26] *AB*. on *NŚ*. 1956,Vol.I.p.201.

creation, respectively, by a male and a female deity. Though Bharata does not explicitly correlate uddhata with manly actions or lalita with feminine moods, the correlation seems implied in the use of the terms themselves and has been recognized by later authors, following the lead of Abhinavagupta. As an example of tāṇḍava Abhinavagupta cites a minor dramatic form in which the action is performed by a masculine figure, whereas for the lalita style he cites a dramatic form in which the corresponding figure is feminine. The association of uddhata and lalita with, respectively, masculine and feminine qualities is evident, though it is stated somewhat obliquely, specially in the case of the uddhata style. Explaining that tāṇḍava is usually directed at devastuti and expressed through uddhata aṅgahāras, Abhinavagupta refers to their use in bhāṇakas (or bhāṇas, as he later calls them), which, according to him, are rāgakāvyas. In support of his view he cites the cirantanas, that is, traditional authorities, according to whom avatāras such as Nṛsiṁha (the man-lion incarnation of Viṣṇu) and the Boar are signified by uddhata aṅgahāras. To illustrate sukumāra Abhinavagupta refers to ḍombikā, a minor dramatic form which shows how a woman performs the actions of flattering a king.[27]

Bhāṇaka and ḍombikā later came to be known as types of nṛtyabhedas or uparūpakas, minor dramatic types[28] in which the emphasis is on body movements. Whether Bharata himself had actual dramas such as these in mind is doubtful. In the first place, he is speaking of dancing as part not of the drama proper but of the citra type of pūrvaraṇga. In the second place, it is not known whether there were any such types as bhāṇaka or ḍombikā in Bharata's time, for in his discussion of dramatic types he does not include them, nor indeed the class of uparūpakas to which they belonged.

---

[27] *Ibid.* pp. 180-81.

[28] *DR.* 1969, p. 8; *BhP.* 1930, p. 255.

The genre that Bharata discusses is rūpaka, that is, major dramatic types. One such type is bhāṇa. Because of the similarity of the terms bhāṇa and bhāṇaka, one might be led, as Abhinavagupta was, to assume the use of uddhata aṅgahāras in bhāṇa. But this seems highly unlikely. Bhāṇa is a play acted by a single character. The actor can either present his own feelings or those of others by conversing with imaginary persons with suitable movements. The character considered by Bharata as appropriate for this kind of play is that of a viṭa, a knave, or a dhūrta, a rogue.[29] It is hard to believe that Bharata is thinking of bhāṇa as the proper place for the use of uddhata aṅgahāras, which he considers suitable for devastuti. If bhāṇakas employed the uddhata style as mentioned by Abhinavagupta, such a use was evidently a later development for which the *Nāṭyaśāstra* provides no basis. Ḍombikā is nowhere mentioned in the *Nāṭyaśāstra.* It would seem that by Abhinavagupta's time the uddhata and lalita styles referred to genres not included in Bharata's own framework of discussion. However, because of a confusing statement in a later chapter of the *Nāṭyaśāstra,* it is possible to assume mistakenly that Bharata authorizes the use of uddhata and lalita in bhāṇa.[30] In that chapter Bharata describes the types of lāsya which involve delicate and expressive movements and quite often use nṛtta as well. Here Bharata compares lāsya with bhāṇa. The similarity lies in the fact that both forms use one character. But the types of lāsya as described by Bharata are not such as to accommodate a character like the viṭa,[31] and there is no justification for equating lāsya with bhāṇa or for attributing to bhāṇa the same qualities of abhinaya. A fuller discussion of the term lāsya is reserved for a later chapter but at this point we may note that this mainly involved female performers who often expressed their feelings with delicate and

---

29 *NŚ.* 18. 108-10.

30 *NŚ.* 19. 117-18.

31 *NŚ.* 19. 121-35.

meaningful body movements and sometimes performed pure nṛtta as well. What is important here is that lāsya possessed qualities of both dance and drama. Abhinaya was, therefore, specially appropriate to it.

What, then, was abhinaya thought to be? The use of the term abhinaya is of vital importance in the *Nāṭyaśāstra*, which covers more than one idea under the term. Bharata discusses abhinaya first in the fourth chapter and then in chapters eight to thirteen. In the fourth chapter he uses the term [32] to denote expressive movements of the body in the preliminaries of a play. Abhinaya is performed to a song where drumming is specifically prohibited. Tāṇḍava, that is, nṛtta is performed to the beat of drums while abhinaya is done to express the meaning of the songs. Both are used in the preliminaries.[33] Beyond this Bharata does not deal with the nature of abhinaya in the fourth chapter.

After the discussion of nṛtta Bharata discusses the performance of pūrvaraṅga in full detail in the rest of the fourth and in the fifth chapter. In the sixth and the seventh chapters the subject is rasa and bhāva–aesthetic affect and emotion. The next five chapters are devoted to abhinaya. In his eighth chapter he defines abhinaya and describes its nature. Abhinaya, he says, can be of four kinds:

> आङ्गिको वाचिकश्चैव ह्याहार्यः सात्त्विकस्तथा ।
> ज्ञेयस्त्वभिनयो विप्राश्चतुर्धा परिकीर्त्तितः ॥
>
> (*NŚ*. 8. 10)
>
> O brahmins! Āṅgika, vācika, āhārya and sāttvika– these are known to be the four abhinayas.

---

[32] *NŚ*. 4. 261; 276; 283; 294; 297; 300; 316.

[33] *NŚ*. 4. 276-77; 300.

Reminding the reader that sāttvika has already been discussed in the chapter on bhāva, here he takes up āṅgika.[34] He devotes five chapters to the body movements (āṅgikābhinaya). Every movement of each part of the body that can be moved to beautify or express or do both is codified here. These show the emphasis given to the body movements at the time when this text was written.

From Bharata's arrangement of the topics it appears that he considers the creation of beauty in a stage-presentation as of primary importance. That is why he discusses nṛtta first because it creates śobhā or beauty and thus captures the mind of the audience. The next important issue in his mind is the arousal of feelings, emotions, aesthetic pleasure and affect. Accordingly, rasa and bhāva are the subjects of the succeeding chapters. How are emotions and aesthetic pleasure recreated and communicated ? Bharata answers, through the movements of the body, through glances, hand-gestures etc. He describes in minute detail the movements of the smallest parts of the body, such as the upper lip, lower lip, eyelid, etc., all of which can express feelings. It is hard to believe that these movements can express any feelings by themselves but once they are put together they may indeed form a harmonious whole to enhance communication. However, the most expressive of all are the movements of the hands and the glances, according to Bharata, and he devotes most of his discussion of āṅgika to them.[35] The entire literature of dance has followed Bharata in this. Although most of these movements are used to express meaning he does not forget about nṛtta here. He devotes a section of hand-gestures reserved specially for abstract nṛtta. He describes sthānas and cārīs which are components of the karaṇas and therefore of the aṅgahāras as well.

---

[34] *NŚ*. 8. 11.

[35] *NŚ*. chapters 8 & 9.

Āṇgikābhinaya, according to Bharata, can be of three kinds: śānra, mukhaja and ceṣṭākṛta–that is, by means of the limbs, the face and the movements of the entire body.[36] He also refers to śākhā, nṛtta and aṅkura as components of āṇgikābhinaya.[37] By śākhā he refers to āṅgika, which he does not elaborate upon. Abhinavagupta does not have any commentary on the topic. It seems that the term śākhā here refers to gesticulation that expresses meaning. Śārṅgadeva, the most influential author on dance and music of the medieval period, supports this view.[38] Nṛtta is again defined as the creation of beauty by means of the movements of the body, these movements being structured into karaṇa and aṅgahāra. Finally, the term aṅkura, that is, pantomiming through gestures, is mentioned as the other component.[39] Concerning that abhinaya which is created through facial movements Bharata discusses in detail the movements of the different parts of the face as well as the application of these movements in expressing feelings. Next he discusses the movements of the parts of the rest of the body. Among these, hand-movements are the most important. By moving the fingers in specific ways the meaning of words as well as emotions can be expressed and the movements and their application are discussed in detail. At the end of the discussion of nṛttahastas, that is, the hand-movements meant for nṛtta, he adds a verse:

> नृत्तेऽभिनययोगे च पाणिभिर्वर्तनाश्रयैः ।
> मुखभ्रूनेत्रयुक्तानि करणानि प्रयोजयेत् ॥
>
> (*NŚ*. 9.219)
>
> In nṛtta and in the discipline of abhinaya (=nāṭya), karaṇas should be applied with hands [moving] in

---

[36] *NŚ*. 8.12.

[37] *NŚ*. 8.15.

[38] *SR*. 7.35-8.

[39] Ghosh, 1951, p. 152.

vartanā along with [the movements] of the face, the eyebrows and the eyes.

To nṛtta, then, Bharata is adding the features of abhinaya, not in order to express meaning but to beautify the production. He directs the performer to use the same kinds of movements in both nṛtta and abhinaya. In abhinaya, facial action will express emotion while in nṛtta it will enhance beauty. That the technique of abhinaya is used for both purposes is asserted also in the discussion on hastapracāra in the ninth chapter, which deals with āṅgikābhinaya. Bharata calls the hastas nāṭyanṛttasamāśrayāḥ –dependent on nāṭya and nṛtta.[40] The association of techniques of abhinaya with nāṭya indicates that they express emotion, while their association with nṛtta indicates that they serve the needs of that art-form, that is, the creation of beauty by means of physical action. Bharata's view here is that abhinaya is differently used in different art-forms. In the body of a nāṭya abhinaya is of all four kinds, namely, āṇgika, vācika, sāttvika and āhārya, while in the pūrvaraṅga vācika is left out of the abhinaya performed by the dancer, who employs āṇgika, sāttvika and āhārya to express the meaning of the song as it is sung by the singers. In the pūrvaraṅga it is the singer who uses vācika–appropriately, since singing is verbal expression. Thus, abhinaya is an art that employs body movements to express meaning in nāṭya while it lends beauty to nṛtta. That is why Bharata defines abhinaya as an art which is so called because it "brings forward" the presentation:

अभिपूर्वस्तु णीञ्धातुराभिमुख्यार्थनिर्णये ।
यस्मात् प्रयोगं नयति तस्मादभिनयः स्मृतः ॥

(*NŚ*. 8. 7.)

---

40 *NŚ*. 9. 181.

> The root ṇīṅ is preceded by abhi in the sense of towards. Abhinaya is so called because it brings [forward] the presentation.

It seems that in the evolution of dancing abhinaya played a central role as the bridge between nāṭya and nṛtta. As we have seen above, Bharata recommends the use of abhinaya not only in nāṭya but also in nṛtta. He treats nāṭya and nṛtta as different but complementary art-forms, nāṭya being used as a term encompassing a larger area of presentation. In the early period, it seems, nāṭya included abhinaya, which was of four kinds, and āṅgika with its stylized movements was a necessary part of nāṭya. Nṛtta was a separate art-form employed to beautify the pūrvaraṅga of a drama. But it is doubtful whether nṛtta was ever used in a play towards the development of a theme. However, this is an entirely different issue which is beyond the scope of the present investigation. All we can say is that the concept of abhinaya provided a wide scope for interpretation and speculation in expressing new ideas.

It seems likely that it was due to the versatility of abhinaya that an entirely new art came into being, although it did so after Bharata's time. This was nṛtya, which evolved out of the synthesis of nṛtta and nāṭya. This mimetic dance form is not mentioned by Bharata, nor by his immediate follower, the author of *Viṣṇudharmottara Purāṇa.*[41] That the concept of dance was undergoing change is evident from the fact that although the *Viṣṇudharmottara Purāṇa* does not uses the term nṛtya it uses another term, lāsya, as one category of nṛtta. The absence of the term nṛtya in that work shows that mimetic dance developed even later. The term lāsya, as we shall see in our discussion in the next chapter, was used by Bharata to indicate a delicate style of dramatic presentation. But by the time the

41 *VDP.* 3.20.1.

Viṣṇudharmottara Purāṇa was written lāsya had come to be recognized as a form of nṛtta or dancing.

In earlier times, before nṛtya was established as a separate art form two terms, nṛtya and nāṭya may have been used interchangeably or synonymously, as it is evident in the *Amarakośa*.[42] In modern times we find the term Bharatanāṭyam, the classical dance of Tamilnadu, which includes both abstract and mimetic dance. The term nāṭya applied to dance is a perfect instance of equating nṛtya with nāṭya. Although the name Bharatanāṭyam was given only in the thirties of the present century, the usage is traditional. The word for nāṭya in Tamil is āṭṭa, which has always been used to mean dance and Bharatanāṭyam developed from Dāsīāṭṭam of Tamilnāḍu. Mohinīāṭṭam of Kerala is another dance style that uses āṭṭam to mean dance.

The category known as nṛtya or mimetic dance thus evolved from the concepts both of nṛtta and nāṭya in the *Nāṭyaśāstra*. Before we consider the process of that evolution, it will be useful to examine one of the most basic of these concepts, that of lāsya, because the various meanings attributed to the term in the post-Bharata śāstric tradition substantially influenced the understanding of the nature and technique of dancing.

---

42 *Amarakośa*, 1808, p. 42.

Chapter 4

LĀSYA: A DRAMATIC ART

In the critical literature of the performing arts of classical India, there is some confusion about what is meant by the term lāsya. It is usually regarded today as a feminine dance described by Bharata in the *Nāṭyaśāstra.*[1] There is, however, no authority for this view in the *Nāṭyaśāstra* which, on the contrary, compares lāsya with bhāṇa, that is, a form of drama:

> अन्यान्यपि लास्यविधावङ्गानि तु नाटकोपयोगीनि ।
> अस्माद्विनिःसृतानि तु भाण इवैकप्रयोज्यानि ॥
> भाणाकृतिवल्लास्यं विज्ञेयं त्वेकपात्रहार्यं च ।
> +प्रकरणवदूह्य कार्यसंस्तवयुक्तं विविधभावम्+॥ [2]
>
> (*NŚ*.19.117-18)

In the practice of lāsya,there are other elements [lit: limbs] that are suitable for nāṭaka. But when they have emerged from it, they, like the bhāṇa, are to be performed by one person. Lāsya is to be so defined as to have a form similar to that of bhāṇa and it is to be

---

[1] Chattopadhyaya, 1978, p. 56; Lath,1978, p. 32.

[2] "प्रकरणवदूह्य कार्यसंस्तवयुक्तं " This reading in the G.O.S. edition seems very obscure. The Kāśī edition gives a better reading: "प्रकरणवदूह्यकार्य संस्तवयुक्तं"..which was also independently suggested by S.J. Sanderson of Wolfson College, Oxford. The last two lines are found in the G.O.S. and Kāśī editions of the *Nāṭyaśāstra*; the Kāvyamālā edition does not have them, nor does Abhinavagupta have any commentary on them. I have followed the reading of the Kāśī edition in translating this line. However, the readings still remain unsatisfactory.

> acted by one person. As in prakaraṇa, its plot [lit:the function] is a conjectured one which relates to praising and a variety of emotions.

The emphasis here is on the dramatic quality of lāsya. It can be divided into parts that lend themselves to dramatic representation and constitute dramatic action. More than just a performing style, lāsya is compared in this passage to such dramatic genres as nāṭaka, bhāṇa and prakaraṇa. Its association with dancing is not evident from this passage, nor its identity – later taken for granted–as a feminine art.

The dramatic quality attributed by Bharata to lāsya excludes it from his definition of tāṇḍava, which is Bharata's term for dance because it was Taṇḍu who received the art of dancing from Śiva. As we have noticed in the previous chapter, the method of dancing that was created, Bharata says, is known as tāṇḍava: नृत्तप्रयोग: सृष्टो य: स ताण्डव इति स्मृत: (*NŚ.* 4. 261); here nṛttaprayoga is taken as a karmadhāraya samāsa. By this definition nothing that falls outside the category of tāṇḍava, that is, nṛtta, could be called a dance.

If lāsya is comparable to nāṭaka, bhāṇa and prakaraṇa, then it cannot be a component of nṛtta which is defined by Bharata as a non-referential art:

> अत्रोच्यते न खल्वर्थं कञ्चिन्नृत्तमपेक्षते ।
>
> (*NŚ.* 4. 263)
>
> Here, it is said that dance not require any [representational] meaning.

That Bharata regarded lāsya as a dramatic art becomes even clearer from his description of the ten forms of lāsya that he mentions:[3]

गेयपदं स्थितपाठ्यमासीनं पुष्पगण्डिका ।
प्रच्छेदकं त्रिमूढं च सैन्धवाख्यं द्विमूढकम् ॥
उत्तमोत्तमकं चैवमुक्तप्रत्युक्तमेव च ।
लास्ये दशविधं ह्येतदङ्गनिर्देशलक्षणम् ॥
आसनेषूपविष्टैर्यत्तन्त्रीभाण्डोपबृंहितम् ।
गायनैर्गीयते शुष्कं तद् गेयपदमुच्यते ॥
प्राकृतं यद्वियुक्ता तु पठेदात्तरसं स्थिता ।
मदनानलतप्ताङ्गी स्थितपाठ्यं तदुच्यते ॥
आसीनमास्यते यत्र सर्वातोद्यविवर्जितम् ।
अप्रसारितगात्रं च चिन्ताशोकसमन्वितम् ॥
वृत्तानि विविधानि स्युर्गेयं गाने च संश्रितम् ।
चेष्टाभिश्चाश्रयः पुंसां यत्र सा पुष्पगण्डिका ॥
प्रच्छेदकः स विज्ञेयो यत्र चन्द्रातपाहृताः ।
स्त्रियः प्रियेषु सज्जन्ते ह्यपि विप्रियकारिषु ॥
अनिष्ठुरश्लक्ष्णपदं समवृत्तैरलङ्कृतम् ।
नाट्यं पुरुषभावाढ्यं त्रिमूढकमिति स्मृतम् ॥
पात्रं विभ्रष्टसङ्केतं सुव्यक्तकरणान्वितम् ।
प्राकृतैर्वचनैर्युक्तं विदुः सैन्धवकं बुधाः ॥
मुखप्रतिमुखोपेतं चतुरश्रपदक्रमम् ।
श्लिष्टभावरसोपेतं वैचित्र्यार्थं द्विमूढके ॥
उत्तमोत्तमकं विद्यादनेकरससंश्रयम् ।
विचित्रैः श्लोकबन्धैश्च हेलाहावविचित्रितम् ॥
कोपप्रसादजनितं साधिक्षेपपदाश्रयम् ।
उक्तप्रत्युक्तमेवं स्याच्चित्रगीतार्थयोजितम् ॥(*NS.* 19. 121 -35)

[3]In his edition of the *Nāṭyśāstra,* Rāmakṛṣṇa Kavi includes two extra types of lāsya on the strength of Abhinavagupta's commentary. In view of Bharata's categorical statement that the number is ten, the addition seems to be an interpolation.

Geyapada, sthitapāṭhya, āsīna, puṣpagaṇḍikā, pracchedaka, trimūḍhaka, saindhava, dvimūḍhaka, uttamottamaka and uktapratyukta–these ten features characterise lāsya.

Where the male singers, being seated in the seats sing dryly [i.e., uttering meaningless syllables] being supported by stringed instruments and drums, it is known as geyapada.

Where a separated woman, her body burning with the fire of love, remains withdrawn and reads Prākṛt [verses], it is sthitapāṭhya.

When [a woman] sits, without any musical instrument around her, without stretching out her body and is overcome with anxiety and sorrow, it is Āsīna.

Where songs are sung in different metres, where geya [the composition to be sung] is dependent on gāna [the regional style, as opposed to traditional gāndharva style [4]] abounding in manly movements, it is puṣpagaṇḍikā.

That is known as Pracchedaka in which women, although wronged by lovers, are attached to their lovers, being struck by the moonlight [in love].

Trimūḍhaka is a nāṭya [performed by women] composed of gentle and tender words, adorned with even metres and abounding in manly emotions.

---

[4] Lath, 1978, pp. 183-4; *SR*. 4.3.

> Where a person has failed to keep a tryst, recites Prākṛt to the accompaniment of karaṇas, it is Saindhavaka.
>
> Where a song is presented with mukha and pratimukha [=exposition and progression] [sung] in a series of caturaśrapada adhering to bhāva and rasa and arriving at a different meaning, it is known as dvimūḍhaka.
>
> Uttamottamaka is known to be dependant on many rasas [expressed through] a variety of ślokas and is adorned with [feminine movements], such as helā and hāva.
>
> Uktapratyukta is derived from anger or pleasure and [often] contains words of censure. It [should also] contain a variety of expressive songs.

From these descriptions it seems that lāsya was the representation of brief segments of dramatic action which called for the expression of the softer emotions. It is to be noted that lāsya is discussed in connection with one kind of drama, not with dance. The dramatic nature of lāsya is further attested by Bharata's remark in a later chapter:

> लसनाल्लास्यमित्युक्तं स्त्रीपुम्भावसमाश्रयम् ।
>
> (*NŚ*. 31.333)
>
> Since it is playful [from the verbal root las] it is called lāsya. It is based on the emotional relations of men and women.

Yet, against Bharata's explicit statements, later authors categorized lāsya as a dance and a feminine one at that. The first work to include lāsya under dancing was the *Viṣṇudharmottara Purāṇa,* which, of the works that deal with dancing, seems to be chronologically the closest to the *Nāṭyaśāstra*.[5] This text states:

> नृत्तं तु द्विविधं प्रोक्तं नाट्यलास्याश्रयं सदा ।
>
> (*VDP*. 3. 20. 2.)
>
> *Nṛtta*, always based on nāṭya and lāsya, is known to be of two types.

This classification seems debatable in a work that follows the *Nāṭyaśāstra* so faithfully. Since nṛtta is agreed to be a non-referential dance form,[6] it is a contradiction in principle to state that it is always based on nāṭya and lāsya, which are specifically characterized by Bharata as containing plot elements. Evidently, by the time the *Viṣṇudharmottara Purāṇa* was written, lāsya had acquired a strong association with dancing. In part, the reason for this may be found in the *Nāṭyaśāstra*. Bharata states,

> रेचकैरङ्गहारैश्च नृत्यन्तं वीक्ष्य शङ्करम् ॥
> सुकुमारप्रयोगेन नृत्यन्तीं चैव पार्वतीम् ।
>
> (*NŚ*. 4. 249-50.)
>
> Seeing Śaṅkara dancing with recakas and aṅgahāras and seeing Pārvatī dancing with delicate movements.

---

[5] This text has been variously dated but its editor places it between the fifth and seventh centuries (P.Shah, ed. *Viṣṇudharmottara Purāṇa*, vol. I. Introduction, p. xxvi.). Pingree assigns this part of the text to the first half of the fifth century; Ludo Rocher has discussed the arguments for the different dates in detail in his volume on his history of Purāṇa literature. However, since the author of this text adds a ninth rasa, śānta, to the list of eight rasas in the *Nāṭyaśāstra*, there can be little doubt that at least this part of the text postdates the *Nāṭyaśāstra*.

[6] *NŚ*. 4. 263.

Sukumāraprayoga means the use of less strenuous aṅgahāras as opposed to the vigorous movements of Śiva. By associating Pārvatī with delicate movements, this passage provides authority for correlating feminine grace with a delicate style of dancing, although it does not call that style lāsya. The association between femininity and delicate movements is further reinforced by a later verse:

> देवस्तुत्याश्रयकृतं यदङ्गं तु भवेदथ ।
> माहेश्वरैरङ्गहारैरुद्धतैस्तत् प्रयोजयेत् ॥
> यत्तु शृङ्गारसम्बन्धं गानं स्त्रीपुरुषाश्रयम्।
> देवीकृतैरङ्गहारैर्ललितैस्तत् प्रयोजयेत् ॥
>
> (*NŚ.* 4. 311-12.)
>
> Whatever part [of a play, i.e., pūrvaraṅga] is for praising gods, that [one] should perform with the vigorous aṅgahāras created by Maheśvara, while a song related to erotic sentiment involving [lit:depending on] man and woman should be performed with the aṅgahāras created by Devī.

Abhinavagupta explains this passage as follows:

> ...उद्धतैरिति । विद्युद्भ्रान्तगरुडप्लुतकादिप्रधानैः। अत्र हेतुर्यतस्ते महेश्वरप्रयुक्ताः। . . . ललितैरिति । तलपुष्पपुटलीननितम्बाद्यारब्धैः। अत्र हेतुः यतस्ते देवीकृताः।
>
> (Abhinavagupta on the *Nāṭyaśāstra,* G.O.S. ed.,Vol.I, p. 180)
>
> . . . By uddhata [=energetic] is meant mainly by[the use of karaṇas such as] vidyudbhrānta or garuḍapluta. The reasoning here is that these are employed by Maheśvara. . . . By lalita [=delicate] is meant done by

> [karaṇas such as] talapuṣpapuṭa, līna and nitamba. The reasoning here is that these are created by Devī [Pārvatī].

While commenting on tāṇḍava and its connection with devastuti, Abhinavagupta says that whenever tāṇḍava is mentioned, lāsya has to be understood implicitly as its complement in the art of dance. To explain this complementarity and as a comparable instance he cites the maxim of गोबलीवर्दन्याय in which the correlation between the cow and the bull is derived from the logic of associative inference:

> ताण्डवमिति सर्वं नृत्तमुच्यते। लास्यशब्देन सन्निधौ गोबलीवर्दन्यायेन प्रवर्त्तते।
>
> (*NŚ.* G.O.S. ed.,1956,Vol. I, p. 180)
>
> Tāṇḍava is said to refer to [lit:to be] all nṛtta (=dancing). By proximity the word lāsya is taken as in the maxim of gobalīvarda.

Commenting on गोबलीवर्दन्याय the *Mīmāṁsākośa* says,

> गामानय बलीवर्दं चानय इत्यत्र गोपदेनैव बलीवर्दबोधसिद्धौ बलीवर्दपदं दुर्दम्यत्वज्ञापनपरत्वेन सफलमिति।
>
> (*Mīmāṁsākośa*, p. 1617)
>
> Bring a cow and bring a bull as well–here, although by using the word 'go' alone, the implication of 'balīvarda' is achieved [yet] the effectiveness of the word 'balīvarda' [consists] in indicating uncontrollability.

Even though the entire phrase gobalīvarda is needed for emphasis, the word go suffices on its own to express the totality of meaning. By analogy with this formula of reasoning, any reference to tāṇḍava may be taken to include lāsya as well. In the complementary relationship thus formed, tāṇḍava represents virility and energy while lāsya represents delicacy and grace. Given such characteristics, the categorization of tāṇḍava and lāsya as masculine and feminine, respectively, is not surprising. It is on this basis that Abhinavagupta takes lāsya as a style of dancing. As the evidence of the *Viṣṇudharmottara Purāṇa* suggests, after Bharata's time the term lāsya had generally come to mean a feminine style of dancing and Abhinavagupta was interpreting the *Nāṭyaśāstra* to provide support for current usage. The association of Pārvatī with lāsya is thus an outcome of her use of delicate aṅgahāras in the legend given in the *Nāṭyaśāstra* in which she is said to have used delicate aṅgahāras.[7]

The same view is repeated by other early writers. Nandīkeśvara reports in his *Abhinayadarpaṇa* that lāsya was taught by Pārvatī.[8] Whether he was the first author to ascribe lāsya specifically to Pārvatī cannot be ascertained since the date of the *Abhinayadarpaṇa* has not been put prior to Abhinavagutpta's commentary on the *Nāṭyaśāstra.* Nandīkeśvara may well have borrowed the idea from the existing literature on the subject. He has little to offer in the way of description or analysis, for he stops at including lāsya in a brief review of nāṭya, nṛtta and nṛtya, and stating merely that it was an art demonstrated by Pārvatī.[9] The *Saṅgītamakaranda* of Nārada talks about lāsyāṅgas, elements of lāsya, in connection with the qualities required in a dancer but does not describe the nature of these lāsyāṇgas.[10]

---

[7] Ibid. 4. 249-50.

[8] *ADar.*4.

[9] *Ibid.*5.

[10] *SMak.*2. 1. 54.

Among the early writers on alaṁkāraśāstra, Daṇḍin specifically mentions lāsya as a form of dance.[11] The dramatists, Kālidāsa, Bhavabhūti and Harṣadeva, have used lāsyāṅgas,that is, elements of lāsyas in their dramas. Abhinavagupta has cited them in in his commentary on lāsyāṅgas.[12] Another early text, the *Daśarupaka* of Dhanañjaya, calls lāsya one of the two major classes of dance styles, the other being tāṇḍava.[13]These works show that soon after the writing of the *Nāṭyaśāstra* tāṇḍava and lāsya came to be associated with masculine and feminine qualities, respectively, and with male and female dancers, a segregation that never appears in the *Nāṭyaśāstra.*

That lāsya was commonly recognized in the early period as an art lending feminine grace to stage actions is attested by the general literature of the period. Dāmodaragupta in his *Kuṭṭanīmatam* identifies lāsya as a form of movement related to a female performer, calling it strīlāsya.[14] Rājaśekhara in his *Karpūramañjarī* refers to lāsya without describing its nature.[15] Although it was so widely known, lāsya was never described in detail until much later. As we have seen, even Abhinavagupta does not provide descriptions. He refers to lāsya while commenting on lāsyāṅgas in the nineteenth chapter and also while discussing tāla in the thirty-first chapter, the tālādhyāya, refers to the style of lāsya; but does not tell us what this lāsya was like except that it used delicate movements.

In the medieval period lāsya continued to be discussed, and discussed at some length, but whether it should be regarded as dance or drama

---

[11] *K.A.* 1.39.

[12] Abhinavagupta on the *NŚ.* 1954, Vol. III, pp. 75-77.

[13] *DR.* 1.9-10.

[14] *Kuṭṭanīmatam*, 853. Dāmodaragupta lived in the eighth century. See Kṛṣṇamāchāriar, 1974, p.353.

[15] *Karpūramañjarī*, 4. 10. Rājaśekhara is believed to have lived in the last quarter of the ninth and the first quarter of the tenth century. See Poddar,1974, p. 174.

remained uncertain. Bhoja categorizes lāsya as a variety of nartanaka, an uparūpaka, which uses graceful and delicate movements to express bhāva (emotions).[16] The other three in this category are identified by Bhoja as śamyā, chalika and dvipadī:

> यत्र पदार्थाभिनयं ललितलयं सदसि नर्तकी कुरुते ।
> तन्नर्तनकं शम्यालास्यछलिकद्विपद्यादि ।
>
> (*Śr.P.* Vol. II, p. 468)
>
> Where in an assembly, a female dancer performs [in] a graceful tempo to act out the meaning of the word, it is nartanaka [which comprises] śamyā, lāsya, chalika and dvipadī etc.

Here the association between lāsya and drama seems strongly suggested. At the same time, Bhoja continues like others before him to emphasize the graceful quality of lāsya inherent in the erotic sentiment, stating, तदिदं शृङ्गारप्रधानत्वाल्लास्यमुक्त (It is [called] lāsya because it deals mainly with śṛṅgārarasa [erotic sentiment]). Since he also categorizes lāsya as a form of dṛśyakāvya (i.e., a poetic composition to be seen), another form being tāṇḍava, he is apparently attributing to it the qualities both of dance and drama. Its suitability as a vehicle of dramatic communication is further indicated in the śabdālaṁkāra section of Bhoja 's *Sarasvatīkaṇthābharaṇa*, where he divides compositions into prekṣya (to be viewed) and śravya (to be heard). Prekṣya is subdivided into lāsya, tāṇḍava, chalika, śamyā, hallīsaka and rāsaka, while lāsya is defined as one containing mainly śṛṅgārarasa.[17] The dramatic nature of lāsya is recognized by Bhoja also in his comments on piṇḍībandhas or group dances. In the *Śṛṅgāraprakāśa* he calls them necessary parts of the rāsaka and nāṭyarāsaka types of

---

16 *Śṛṅgāraprakāśa*, 1963, Vol. II, p. 468.

17 *SKA*. 1969, pp. 124-25.

uparūpakas rather than of lāsya.[18] Here Bhoja seems to be following traditional thinking; Abhinavagupta quotes Kohala and the cirantanas, that is, ancient authorities,[19] to explain that these two nṛtya types of uparūpakas contained both delicate and vigorous nṛtta movements but he mentions lāsya nowhere in the context.

The tradition of regarding lāsya as a dance form is carried on in a major work on music and dancing from the next century, the *Mānasollāsa* of Someśvara, which views lāsya as a dance consisting of aṅgahāras, specifically lalita aṅgahāras.[20] But this work provides no further information. A much fuller discussion appears in the *Bhāvaprakāśana* of Śāradātanaya, which discusses dramaturgy and allied arts. This compendium of critical works, extending from that of Bharata down to the writings of Kṣemendra in the eleventh century, was written before the *Saṅgītaratnākara* and the *Nṛttaratnāvalī*. Śāradātanaya's treatment of lāsya is rather confusing. He defines lāsya as a dance composed of delicate aṅgahāras:

> ललितैरङ्गहारैश्च निर्वर्त्यैर्ललितैर्लयैः ॥
> वृत्तिः स्यात्कैशिकी गीतिर्यत्र तल्लास्यमुच्यते ।
>
> (*Bh.P.* p. 296)
>
> That is known as lāsya in which the style is kaiśikī, [where] there is a song and which is composed of [lit: being done by] graceful aṅgahāras done to delicate layas.

According to him, lāsya is of four types, namely, sṛṅkhalā, latā, piṇḍī, and bhedyaka:

---

[18] *Śṛ.P.* 1963, Vol. II, p.468.

[19] *NŚ*.1956, Vol. I, p. 181-2.

20 *Mānas.* 16. 4. 962 - 63.

सुकुमारप्रयोगो यो नियतो लास्यमुच्यते ।
तच्छृङ्खलालतापिण्डीभेद्यकैः स्याच्चतुर्विधम् ॥

(*Bh.P.* p.297)

What is delicately applied is called lāsya, which can be of four varieties–śṛṅkhalā, latā, piṇḍī and bhedyaka.

Śāradātanaya goes on to enumerate further sub-divisions and describe the actual movements of these four types. These types, though not the identical terms, are taken from the *Nāṭyaśāstra*:

पिण्डीनां विधयश्चैव चत्वारः सम्प्रकीर्तिताः ॥
पिण्डी शृङ्खलिका चैव लताबन्धोऽथ भेद्यकः।

(*NŚ.* 4. 287-88)

The ways [of forming] piṇḍīs are known to be four: piṇḍī, śṛṇkhalikā, latābandha and bhedyaka.

Śaradātanaya's attempt, unsupported by the *Nāṭyaśāstra,* to include these movements under lāsya is inconsistent with his own statement earlier in the treatise:

अपरैर्नृत्यभेदास्तु गुल्मशृङ्खलितालताः।
भेद्यकश्चेति चत्वारः कथ्यन्तेऽत्र मनीषिभिः ।

. . . . .

पिण्डीबन्धश्च गुल्मश्च पर्यायाविति केचन ॥

(*Bh.P.*. p. 246)

Here, other experts have described four nṛtyabhedas [such as] gulma, śṛṅkhalitā, latā and bhedyaka. . . . Some say that piṇḍībandha and gulma are synonymous.

In this passage Śāradātanaya clearly identifies piṇḍībandhas as dramatic types, for nṛtyabhedas are varieties of dramatic action. It is possible that he took lāsya primarily as a dramatic art, for he states on the authority of Kohala that:

> कोहलादिभिराचार्यैरुक्तं भाणस्य लक्षणम् ।
> लास्याङ्गदशकोपेतं . . . ॥
>
> (*Bh.P.* p. 245)
>
> The characteristics of bhāṇa are described by experts [such as] Kohala and others as being arrived at by ten lāsyāṅgas . . .

By telling us that lāsya forms part of the presentation of bhāṇa, Śāradātanaya is again placing lāsya in the context of dramatic art. As subdivisions of that art, piṇḍībandhas would necessarily be dramatic pieces.

One of the first manuals on dancing to describe lāsya in detail is the *Nṛttaratnāvalī* of Jāya Senāpati. In the first chapter of the first section of the book he defines nṛtta and says that

> लास्यताण्डवभेदेन द्वयमेतद् द्विधा पुनः ।
> सुकुमारं तयोराद्यं भवेदपरमुद्धतम् ॥
>
> (*NR.*1. 1.56)
>
> By the distinction between tāṇḍava and lāsya this [dance] is again of two types. The first of the two is delicate and the other is energetic.

He then goes on to describe the parts of lāsya as they appear in the *Nāṭyaśāstra.* These lāsyāṅgas, according to him, are elements of traditional forms of dance (mārga). In expressing this opinion he is obviously not following Bharata, whose emphasis is on the dramatic nature of lāsya. The first section of the *Nṛttaratnāvalī* deals with mārga and the second with deśī. In the second section the author deals with deśīlāsya, that is, the regional variations of lāsya. He lists forty-six such deśīlāsyas.[21] Since these movements employ only āṅgika, not vācika abhinaya, they may be categorized as dance movements.

The *Saṅgītaratnākara* of Śārṅgadeva defines lāsya as a delicate dance that stimulates erotic sentiments:

> लास्यं तु सुकुमाराङ्गं मकरध्वजवर्धनम् ।
>
> (*SR.* 7.30)
>
> Lāsya has delicate features [lit: limbs] and arouses erotic [sentiments].

But Śārṅgadeva does not treat the subject in full, discussing only deśī lāsyāṅgas, that is, only the local or regional varieties of lāsya. He follows the *Nāṭyaśāstra* and Abhinavagupta's commentary in discussing and defining āṅgika abhinaya, that is, movements of the aṅga and upāṅga, cārī, sthāna, maṇḍala, karaṇa and aṅgahāra, but omitting from his discussion the forms of lāsya described by Bharata. This seems perfectly justifiable since those forms were specified by Bharata as dramatic actions, not dance movements. Śārṅgadeva seems to be the first author to realize that the elements of lāsyas described by Bharata are meant for dramatic actions. The deśī lāsyāṅgas he describes in detail are ten and they are dance movements requiring tāla (=rhythm) etc. Śārṅgadeva and Jāya were contemporaries, but *Saṅgītaratnākara* was written before the *Nṛttaratnāvalī*, and as V. K. Raghavan points out, there is internal evidence that Jāya knew about the existence of the *Saṅgītaratnākara* when he wrote his text.[22] However, that does not minimize the importance of Jāya's work, which deals with dance in even greater detail than Śārṅgadeva's, giving us a fuller picture of the deśī tradition, although in

---

[21] *NR.* 6. 117-73.

[22] *NR.* Introduction, pp. 73-77.

the later literature after the fifteenth century on dance we find the influence of Śārṅgadeva, not Jāya.

The meaning of lāsya has been further clouded by the use of the term lāsyāṅga in several of the texts that came after the *Nāṭyaśāstra*. The term was never used by Bharata in the *Nāṭyaśāstra* Abhinavagupta did so in his commentary on the *Nāṭyaśāstra* but he used it not to mean a class of movements distinct from lāsya but simply in the sense of the different components of lāsya. That the word lāsyāṅga was no more than a derivative of [the word] lāsya is clear from Abhinavagupta's commentary.[23] It is worth noting that the *Nāṭakalakṣaṇaratnakośa* of Sāgaranandin, the only work that faithfully follows the *Nāṭyaśāstra* directly rather than Abhinavagupta's commentary in describing the type of lāsya, does not use the term lāsyāṅga.[24] We must also remember that Bharata's discussion of lāsya and its aṅgas forms part of his description of the elements of a dramatic composition rather than a dance. This is a categorization also followed, among the later writers, by Viśvanātha who, in his *Sāhityadarpaṇa*, includes the aṅgas of lāsya among the elements of dramatic representations, such as sandhi etc., just as Bharata did.[25]

However, the term lāsyāṅga found general acceptance among the later authors, most of whom viewed lāsya and lāsyāṅga as different classes of movements, drawing a distinction that has caused some confusion. The confusion is worst in the *Bhāvaprakāśana*, which reproduces in chapter eight the same ten movements described in the *Nāṭyaśāstra* as parts of lāsya. Later, however, in chapter ten, the *Bhāvaprakāśana* divides dancing into tāṇḍava and lāsya, going on to enumerate four types of lāsya, two of which–sṛṅkhalā and bhedyaka–are divided each into ten lāsyāṅgas,

---

[23] Abhinavagupta on the *NŚ*. 1954, Vol. III, 19. 117-135.

[24] *NLRK*. pp. 270-76.

[25] *SD*. 6. 270.

which are the same ten movements previously specified as lāsya in chapter eight.[26]

We have noted before that *Saṅgītaratnākara* defines lāsya as a dance that arouses erotic sentiments. It also describes ten types of delicate movements, calling them lāsyāṅgas but not equating them with lāsya:

> लास्याङ्गानि दशैतानि देश्यां देशीविदो विदुः ।
> कोमलं सविलासं च मधुरं ताललास्ययुक् ॥
> नातिद्रुतं नातिमन्दं त्र्यश्रताप्रचुरं तथा ।
> पादोरु कटिबाहूनां यौगपद्येन चालनम् ॥
> चालिः सा शैघ्र्यसांमुख्यप्राया चालिवडो भवेत् ।
> सुकुमारं तिरश्चीनं विलासरसिकं च यत् ॥
> युगपत्कटिबाहूनां चालनं सा लढिर्मतः ।
> कर्णयोर्हावबहुलं लसल्लीलावतंसयोः ॥
> विलम्बेनाविलम्बेन सूकं तल्लयचालनम् ।
> विलम्बेनाविलम्बेन कुचयोर्भुजशीर्षयोः ॥
> ललितं चालनं तिर्यक् तज्ज्ञाः प्राहुरुरोङ्गणम् ।
> धसकः स्यात्सुललितं स्तनाधोनमनं लयात् ॥
> सतालललितोपेता क्रमात्कायार्धयोर्नतिः ।
> धनुर्वदङ्गहारः स्यादिति निःशङ्कभाषितम् ॥
> किञ्चित्तिर्यगधो मूर्ध्नो गतिरोयारको मतः ।
> स्मितं स्याद्विहसी यस्तु शृङ्गाररसनिर्भरः ॥
> अभ्यस्तादन्य एवातिसूक्ष्मप्रत्यग्रभङ्गिभाक् ।
> गीतादेरागतः स्थायस्तल्लयात्तन्मनो मतम् ॥
>
> (*SR*. 7. 1207- 15)

> These are ten lāsyāṅgas in the deśī [style] regarded by those who are knowledgeable in deśī. [They are] delicate, playful, attractive and [adorned]with tāla and lāsya [rhythm and grace].

---

26 *Bh.P.* p. 297.

Cāli is the simultaneous movement of the feet, hips, thighs and arms. It should be neither done too fast nor too slow, and [should be] full of oblique movements done in tāla.

The same action performed in a quick tempo, mainly facing the front, is known as cālibaḍa.

Laḍhi is known to be the simultaneous horizontal movements of the hips and arms which is soft and graceful.

Sūka is a rhythmic movement full of hāva [feminine gestures], of the ears shining with dangling earings and performed either slowly or quickly.

Uroṅgaṇa is known as a graceful and oblique movement, slow or fast, of the shoulders and the breasts.

Dhasaka is the graceful and rhythmic downward movement of the breast.

Aṅgahāra is the successive bending of the two halves of the body, slowly and gracefully to tāla, and in the likeness of a bow, so says the confident one [i.e., Śārngadeva].

Oyāraka is a slightly oblique and downward movement of the head.

Vihasi is a smile full of the sentiment of love different from a trained one. It has an extremely subtle and novel charm.

Mana is known [to be performed] to songs etc. set to rāga in the sthāya tempo.

These movements do not constitute lāsya as Bharata understood the term, for the *Saṅgītaratnākara* classifies them as deśī forms, that is, popular or regional as opposed to mārga or refined classical forms, while the *Nāṭyaśāstra* bypasses the whole subject of deśī forms. It is evident that scholarly opinion, presumably following performing practice, had changed considerably since the time of Bharata. An important point established by the description of lāsya movements in the *Saṅgītaratnākara* is that by the time that work was written, lāsya had definitely come to mean dancing and had a defined form. It is also evident that lāsyāṅgas had come to be regarded as deśī forms.

Pārśvadeva in his *Saṅgītasamayasāra* gives us a list of nineteen deśyaṅgas which, from their description, seem to be the same kind of movements as the lāsyāṅgas given in the *Saṅgītaratnākara.* This is supported by the fact that Jāya lists forty-six deśī lāsyas, which are similar in character to those described in the *Saṅgītaratnākara,* although only ten of them match Śārṅgadeva's list. The nineteen deśyaṅgas mentioned by Pārśvadeva and the ten lāsyāṅgas of the *Saṅgītaratnākara* are all included in Jāya's list of forty-six deśī lāsyāṅgas. Pārśvadeva is earlier than Jāya,[27] and it is possible that the latter has taken similar movements from the *Saṅgītasamayasāra* and the *Saṅgītaratnākara* and combined them into one category, calling them lāsyāṅgas of the deśī variety and adding others. In a similar way, the *Nṛtyādhyāya* of Aśokamalla and the *Nṛttaratnakośa* of Mahārāṇā Kumbha give lists of thirty-six deśī lāsyāṅgas, again a combination of the deśyaṅgas and the lāsyāṅgas described respectively by Parśvadeva and Śārṅgadeva. Śubhaṅkara's *Saṅgītadāmodara* describes the ten categories of movements included under lāsya in the *Nāṭyaśāstra,* but calls them lāsyāṅgas which, according to the author, are necessary to bhāṇa.[28] Śubhaṅkara later defines lāsya as: ...स्त्रीनृत्यं लास्यमुच्यते। [29]–feminine dancing is known as lāsya–which he calls a deśī form of dancing.

---

27 See *NR.* 1965, Introduction, pp. 79-80.

28 *SDām.*. pp. 73-4.

29 Ibid. pp.69.

When we examine the dance-sequences described by the medieval authors, those who came after Kumbha, we again find the use of these deśī lāsyāṅgas.

On reviewing these texts it seems that from the time of the *Bhāvaprakāśana* lāsya and lāsyāṅga begin to be considered as two different types. These later texts also state that lāsyāṅgas form a part of bhāṇa. But this position is not entirely satisfactory. Bharata, as we have seen above, says that lāsya is suitable for dramatic performances. In that connection he refers to bhāṇa, a type of drama which is performed by only one person. Lāsya is similar to it because this too is done by one person. But mere similarity does not mean that bhāṇa may include any form of lāsya. Bharata never claims anything of the sort when he describes bhāṇa in chapter nineteen of the *Nāṭyaśāstra*.[30] On the other hand, he says specifically that kaiśikī vṛtti should not be applied to bhāṇa:

> उत्सृष्टिकाङ्को व्यायोगो भाणः प्रहसनं डिमः ।
> कैशिकीवृत्तिहीनानि रूपाण्येतानि कारयेत् ॥
>
> (*NŚ*.18. 8-9)
>
> Utsṛṣṭikāṅka, vyāyoga, bhāṇa, prahasana and ḍima– these rūpas are to be performed without the kaiśikīvṛtti [the delicate and graceful style].

This excludes delicate movements from bhāṇa. Since both lāsya and bhāṇa involve one performer, and since in the *Nāṭyaśāstra* the ślokas about lāsya occur just after the passage on bhāṇa, some relation between lāsya and bhāṇa may be conjectured. But no relationship is actually established by Bharata. The proximity of the ślokas in the *Nāṭyaśāstra* was probably the reason why later authors were led to think that lāsya or its aṅgas were auxiliary to bhāṇa.

---

30 *NŚ*. 18. 108-10.

In his commentary on bhāṇa, Abhinavagupta states that bhāṇas are chronicles of prostitutes and men who live by their wits.[31] But the *Nāṭyaśāstra* does not mention any such thing. Later treatises, however, seem to accept Abhinavagupta's view. They may have also tried to connect bhāṇa with lāsyāṅga because a lāsyāṅga, being a delicate movement, might pertain to the arts as they were practised by prostitutes. The *Daśarūpaka* prescribes vīra and śṛṅgārarasa for bhāṅa.[32] The *Bhāvaprakāśana* mentions Kohala's view and says that bhāṇa should only have śṛṅgārarasa.[33] The *Nāṭyadarpaṇa* of Rāmacandra and Guṇacandra states that śṛṅgāra should be predominant in bhāṇa.[34] The *Nāṭakalakṣanaratnakośa* does not say that the various forms of lāsya are necessary to bhāṇa, though according to it bhāṇa can also be performed by a woman; when it is so performed, aṅgahāras must be used. In this text, the description of ten lāsyāṅgas follows its account of bhāṅa, because a lāsyāṅga, like a bhāṇa, is performed by a single actor.[35]

The history of lāsya makes the evolution of the performing arts of India particularly complex. As we have seen in the foregoing survey, the term lāsya is never used in the *Nāṭyaśāstra* to denote dancing of any kind. Instead, that text accords lāsya the same status as a performing art as it gives to bhāṇa, although it does not equate them. For later authors, by contrast, lāsya is a style of dancing distinguished by its feminine qualities, while tāṇḍava appears in their works as a virile style embodying masculine qualities. This recognition of lāsya as an independent style of dancing and its separation from tāṇḍava is not found in the *Nāṭyaśāstra* but in all likelihood came about in the following way: Bharata's description of

---

31 Abhinavagupta on the *NŚ.*, 1954. Vol. III, 18. 109-10.

32 *DR.* 3.50.

33 *Bh.P.* p. 245.

34 *ND.* p.127.

35 *NLRK.* pp. 270-71.

lāsya movements shows them to be delicate and graceful; elsewhere in the text he mentions that Pārvatī adorned her dance with "sukumāraprayoga," that is, with delicate grace.[36] When the *Saṅgītaratnākara* or the *Abhinayadarpaṇa* attributed lāsya to Pārvatī, they did so, presumably, because of the delicacy and grace of her movements, and gave it the status of proper dance, a status not conferred by Bharata himself. The association of erotic sentiments with lāsya may thus be seen as a result of its association with Pārvatī. It was evidently because of that association and also because of its essentially gentle grace, that lāsya was considered to be suitable for female performers. Tāṇḍava, on the other hand, appears from all descriptions to be a strenuous, physically demanding style of dancing. That is why it seemed to call for male performers.

But, again, such a division of labour is not authorized by the *Nāṭyaśāstra*. Whenever Bharata talks about a dancer, he uses the feminine noun nartakī.[37] He could, then, hardly exclude female dancers from performing tāṇḍava, the form of dancing on which he focuses his attention. Iconographic support for this may be found in the Cidambaram temple sculptures depicting the compositions described in the *Nāṭyaśāstra*.[38] Bharata states that uddhata or vigorous aṅgahāras are suitable for devastuti, or praise-offerings to gods, while lalita, or graceful aṅgahāras are best suited to the depiction of erotic sentiments.[39] This distinction may have given later authors yet another reason for correlating tāṅḍava and lāsya respectively with men and women. Lāsya, however, does not necessarily involve erotic sentiments and can also be used in devastuti.[40] Abhinavagupta supports this view when he says that lāsya is meant to

---

36 *NŚ*. 4.250.

37 *NŚ*. 4. 118-20.

38 Naidu, V., Naidu, S. and Pantulu, V.R., 1971.

39 *NŚ*. 4. 268-69 and 4. 311-12.

40 *NŚ*. 4.302.

please the gods or kings.[41] In the context, therefore, of the earliest source of the Indian tradition of the performing arts, it seems likely that any allocation of tāṇḍava and lāsya separately to men and women would be a matter of convenience rather than of principle.

The evidence of the *Nāṭyaśāstra* clarifies the meaning of lāsya in two important ways. First, lāsya–as originally practised–was neither nṛtta, the pure form of dancing, nor was it bhāṇa. Instead, it was an art form possessing qualities of both and was a wholly independent art bridging dance and drama. Secondly, lāsya was not necessarily an art reserved for female performers, although it could be the representation of feminine moods. Despite the various–and often confusing–opinions of Bharata's successors regarding lāsya, the continued acknowledgement of its suitability for representing emotional status reflects a growing trend towards recognizing the dramatic potentiality of dancing. In the following chapter we shall examine the connection between forms of dancing and of drama perceived in musicological literature.

---

[41] *A.B.* on the *NŚ.* 1956, Vol. I, 4. 268, p. 180-81.

Chapter 5

NṚTYA AND UPARŪPAKA

In the last two chapters we have seen how dance was conceived in the literature of the earliest period, especially in the *Nāṭyaśāstra*. It is important to bear in mind that Bharata describes dance mainly in the context of the preliminaries of a play. He also recommends the use of the karaṇas (components of nṛtta) in the body of the drama, for scenes of battle or for gaits which he mentions only once (*NŚ*. 4. 56). Finally he describes the karaṇas, but does not specify which karaṇas are to be used for which purpose. However, in his commentary on the *Nāṭyaśāstra* Abhinavagupta correlates some of the karaṇas with particular dramatic characters (*A.B.*Vol.I, p.206). Bharata's own interests seem to have been in the broader principles of stage presentation, which included elements of dance.

Bharata classifies dancing by using comparatively few terms. These were, as we have seen in chapter 3, nṛtta, tāṇḍava, abhinaya, piṇḍībandha and sukumāraprayoga. Nṛtta and tāṇḍava are used synonymously to mean abstract dance, that is, compositions of movements that please the senses but carry no meaning (*NŚ*. 4. 261). Abhinaya, in the context of the preliminaries of a play, is the art of miming the meaning of a song through gestures and body movements (*NŚ*. 4. 283). Piṇḍībandhas are group dances forming different emblems to represent different gods for the purpose of showing reverence to them (*NŚ*.4. 252-59; 4. 287-90). Sukumāraprayoga is the graceful and delicate way of presenting dance movements (*NŚ*.4. 250). To these terms he adds lāsya, which he applies to a form of dramatic art. However, as we have seen in chapter 4, the meaning of lāsya became much more complex after Bharata's time.

That this growing complexity was not restricted to the understanding only of lāsya but extended to the whole art of dancing is shown by the persistent attempts to expand its classification by adding new terms to its conceptual vocabulary. With the *Nāṭyaśāstra* as its starting point, the discourse on dancing began to widen its scope and soon after the *Nāṭyaśāstra*, new terms that represented the proliferation of conceptual classification began to appear in dramatic as well as other literature.[1] The literature of the early period used these terms extensively, but later, in the medieval period, most of these terms were absorbed in more general terms that represented broader concepts. To set the later, broader terms in their historical context, it is necessary first to consider the earlier terms, although the focus of the present chapter will be on the two terms into which most of them were assimilated, namely, nṛtya and uparūpaka.

Nṛtya and uparūpaka do not appear before the tenth and the fourteenth centuries, respectively.[2] That does not, of course, mean that the art forms represented by these terms were not known before the medieval period, but rather that they were not important or popular enough to be the subject of serious discussion. They might have been simply left undescribed, just as regional varieties of dancing were ignored by Bharata even while he acknowledged their existence (*NŚ.* 9. 164). Their evolution becomes clearer when we examine other terms that appear in the early literature where they are used for various art forms involving dancing. They are never defined in any work but what they stood for may usually be conjectured from the content of the discussion if we consider the contexts in which they appear. The descriptions are often cryptic and brief but in the absence of any detailed discussion, we may form a picture from the

---

1 *Mālavikāgnimitra, Vikramorvaśīya* of Kālidāsa, *Ratnāvalī* of Harṣa, *Kuṭṭanīmata* of Dāmodaragupta and *Arthaśāstra* of Kauṭilya are some of the relevant texts.

2 The term nṛtya first appears in the Daśarūpaka and uparūpaka appears first in the *Sāhityadarpaṇa.*

little information we have before we examine the meaning of nṛtya and uparūpaka.

The terms we examine here are eight: dvipadī, śamyā, rāsaka, skandhaka, chalika, carcarī, lāsya and saṅgītaka. Most of these terms disappeared from dance literature after the early period. One that remains well-known is lāsya, which, as we have seen already, was treated as a separate, special category denoting both movements that conveyed meaning and those that did not. Rāsaka is another that has survived and is now applied to a group dance mostly connected with religious festivals in different regions of India and depicts episodes from legends of Kṛṣṇa, Rādhā and the gopīs.

When they first appeared, each of the eight terms had different connotations in different works but they all signified dance presentations. They have been examined by D. R. Mankad in his study of drama.[3] The occurrence of these terms in various textual sources, excepting that of saṅgītaka, has been noted by V. Raghavan. He has also described the characteristics of the dances represented by these terms while discussing minor plays in his study of the *Śṛṅgāraprakāśa* of Bhoja.[4] A. K. Warder has discussed them at length, giving instances from different texts in which they occur.[5] To avoid duplicating these studies, the present work will deal very briefly with the use of these terms in the early texts. These terms stand for short dance pieces in which the emphasis falls on portraying an emotion (bhāva) or creating an aesthetic affect (rasa).[6] Not surprisingly, these terms were mostly used in the kāvya and alaṁkāra literature, although references are found in other literature as well, but they are never clearly defined.

---

[3] Mankad,1936, pp. 91-144.

[4] Raghavan, 1963, pp. 545-74.

[5] Warder,1972,Vol. I, pp.138-68.

[6] Raghavan,1978, p. 539.

Dvipadī literally means a composition of two metres or two verses. In Bhāmaha's *Kāvyālaṁkāra* this term represents a mimetic presentation: abhineyārtham (*KAlaṁ.*1.24). However, in other works the term appears to have different meanings. For instance, in the *Vikromorvaśīya* of Kālidāsa, it is taken as a graceful body movement. In Act IV, Citralekhā moves about in dvipadikā while looking at different directions and getting up from a reclining position (Act IV, prose passages following verses 1, 5 and 7). The directions are: प्रवेशान्तरे द्विपदिकया दिशोऽवलोक्य (after entering looks in all directions in dvipadī); अनन्तरे द्विपदिकया दिशोऽवलोक्य (afterwards looks in all directions in dvipadī) and द्विपदिकयोत्थाय निःश्वस्य (after getting up in dvipadī and sighing).[7] Each of these stage directions is followed by a verse. It is perhaps the presence of verse passages that has prompted Raghavan to take dvipadikā as a laya.[8] But again on the same page we find the stage direction: द्विपदिकया दिशोऽवलोक्य। निःश्वस्य । सास्रम्। (afterwards looking in all directions in dvipadī and sighing with tears). A prose line follows which also refers to body movements. In his commentary on the *Mālatīmādhava* Jagaddhara refers to Mādhava's entrance in dvipadikā as described in the text: ततः प्रविशति यथानिर्दिष्टरूपो माधवः (then Mādhava enters in the manner indicated) and Jagaddhara comments: माधवप्रवेश इह द्विपदिकया (Mādhava here enters in dvipadikā),[9] which indicates a slow movement (गमनमलसम्. . .). Rāghavabhaṭṭa takes dvipadikā as a laya or tempo: अयं . . . द्विपदीनामा लयभेदः (here . . . dvipadī is a division of tempo).[10] Raghavan says that "from the laya to the song and from the song to the dance, the name Dvipadī has had its semantic extension." Raghavan also

---

[7] *Vikromorvaśīya*, Velankar ed. 1961, pp. 61, 65, 66.

[8] Raghavan, 1963, p. 560.

[9] शोकविभ्रमयुक्ते तु व्याधिचिन्तासमाश्रिते ।
श्रुतवार्तादिवैरूप्ये योज्या द्विपदिका बुधैः ॥ Bhandarkar edition, 1876, p.36.

[10] Rāghavabhaṭṭa's commentary on *Abhijñānaśakuntalā*, Kale edition, 1902, p. 8.

refers to a dvipadikā metre and a dvipadikā song still current in Telugu and Tamil.[11] Warder refers to dvipadīkhaṇḍa as a sub-variety of dvipadī and cites Harṣa's *Ratnāvalī* where two actresses are directed to act and sing a dvipadīkhaṇḍa.[12] In his *Śṛṅgāraprakāśa,* Bhoja refers to dvipadī as one of the features of nartanaka, a minor drama (padārthābhinayātmaka prekṣyaprabandha, that is, a composition which is to be seen and which expresses the meaning of the words).[13] Śārṅgadeva defines dvipadī as a musical composition sung to karuṇa tāla in the *Saṅgītaratnākara,* and in the *Nāṭyadarpaṇa* Rāmacandra and Guṇacandra take it as a metre. Dvipadī is described as a laya by Dāmodaragupta in his *Kuṭṭanīmata.*[14] In the *Nartananirṇaya* Puṇḍarīka merely follows Śārṅgadeva in defining dvipadī (*NN.* 39b). According to K. S. Upadhyaya, dvipadī is still used in yakṣagāna, one of the folk dance-dramas of Andhra.[15] We find no instance of dvipadī as a drama or a dance in late medieval literature. Therefore, it seems that although Bhāmaha defines it as a dramatic presentation, in later times it was identified with musical composition, metre and tempo, to which a delicate dance was sometimes performed.

Another term from early times is śamyā, which literally means a stick. In the *Nāṭyaśāstra* śamyā is described as a time-beat (*NŚ.*31.36-7). The *Hṛdayaṁgamā* on the *Kāvyādarśa* of Daṇḍin describes a dance so named, which involves the use of a coloured stick (*Hṛdayaṁgamā* on the *Kāvyādarśa.*1. 39). It developed as a group dance which can be identified with daṇḍarāsaka (rāsa dance with coloured sticks). Daṇḍarāsaka is still practised in Gujarat. Bhāmaha refers to śamyā as a form to be acted

---

[11] Raghavan, 1963, p. 561.

[12] *Ratnāvalī,* Shastri edition,1978, p.6; Warder, Vol.I, 1972, p.153.

[13] Raghavan, 1963, p. 555.

[14] *SR.* 4. 213-19; *ND.* 1929, p. 214; *Kuṭṭanīmata,* Kāvyamālā ed.,Vol. III, 338, 858.

[15] Upadhyaya, *Sangeet Natak,* No.11, p. 39.

(abhineyārtha) and Daṇḍin as one to be seen (prekṣyārtha).[16] In the *Svarasvatīkaṇṭhābharaṇa*, Bhoja describes śamyā as one of six kinds of dramatic presentations, others being tāṇḍava, lāsya, chalika, hallīsaka and rāsa (*SKA*. 1969, p.124) and he says that chalika becomes śamyā when it relates to kinnara (तदिदं छलिकमेव किन्नरविषयं शम्या – *SKA*. 1969, p.125). In the *Śṛṅgāraprakāśa,* it is described as a feature of the nartanaka type of minor drama (*ŚrP*. 1963, Vol. II, p. 468). In the latter instance lāsya and śamyā both appear as features of nartanaka. The authors of the *Nāṭyadarpaṇa* refer to śamyā as a lāsyanṛtta pertaining to the kinnaras (किन्नरविषयं लास्यं नृत्तं शम्या – *ND*. 1959, p.191). Raghavan has cited many instances from the *Nāṭyaśāstra,* the *Amarakośa* and the *Rāmāyaṇa* as evidence that the term means a time-beat, an opinion in which Warder concurs.[17] In the *Saṅgītaratnākara* śamyā is used as a time-beat (*SR*.5.6; 9). M. Lath quotes Dattila and says that śamyā was a concept central to the gāndharva tāla.[18] Except for Bhāmaha, then, śamyā is not described by any other writer primarily as a dramatic presentation and Daṇḍin merely mentions it as a visual presentation. However, in later times the writers followed the interpretation of the *Nāṭyaśāstra* and in medieval works on saṅgīta śamyā is described as a tāla.

The definition of rāsaka first appears in Bhāmaha who lists it as a dramatic presentation. It is generally described as an elaborate dance in a number of early texts. Daṇḍin does not mention the term but Kohala (quoted in the commentary on *Haravijaya*)[19] describes it as a play. Abhinavagupta quotes authorities who treat it primarily as a dance which is performed by a number of women and is full of a variety of rhythm and tempo. Since he states this while describing nṛttātmakaprabandhas,

---

[16] *Kāvyālaṁkāra,* 1. 24; *Kāvyādarśa,* 1. 39.

[17] Raghavan, 1963, pp. 561, Warder, Vol. I, 1974, p.152.

[18] Lath, 1978, p.101; *Dattilam,* 1930, 110.

[19] Commentary on *Haravijayam,* XVII, p.108.; Warder, Vol. I, 1974, p.145.

rāgakāvyas and gīyamānarūpakas,[20] it would seem that he himself did not think of rāsaka exclusively as a dance but as a dramatic composition presented through music and dance movements. A similar term used by Abhinavagupta is rāsakāṅka (an example being the *Rādhāvipralambha* by Bhejjala),[21] which means a play in a regional language depicting Kṛṣṇa and Rādhā. Rāsaka, according to Bhoja, is a padārthābhinayātmaka prekṣyaprabandha or minor drama (*ŚṛP.* Vol.II, pp. 468-69) and Bhoja says that in rāsaka, piṇḍībandhas or group dances forming different patterns were performed. In his *Sarasvatīkaṇṭhābharaṇa* and *Śṛṅgāraprakāśa* Bhoja says that hallīsaka becomes rāsaka when danced to definite tālas.[22] This comment suggests that rāsaka was primarily a dance. The *Nāṭakalakṣaṇaratnakośa* (*NLRK.* 3205-9) describes rāsaka as a one-act play using a variety of languages and five characters, etc. This text prescribes delicate and forceful emotions (masṛṇodāttabhāvabhūṣitam) for rāsaka but does not mention any tāla and laya. It seems that the author of this work, Sāgaranandin, takes it primarily as a drama. In his *Nartananirṇaya,* Puṇḍarīka describes rāsaka as a composition employing rāsatāla that had four different varieties (*NN.* A Soc. Ms. 46b).

Rāsaka is an important term which appears to have come down from an early period and it represents a dance-drama or a dance with dramatic overtones. In two of the present-day classical styles of India, Manipuri and Kathak, it is still a major part of the repertoire. In folk-dances in several regions of India rāsa continues to be performed in some form or other. Gujarat, Tamilnad and Andhra, for instance, have their individual regional versions of rāsa.

Skandhaka appears as a dramatic presentation in Bhāmaha who considers its use to be abhineyārtha: to be acted (*KAlaṁ.*1.24). However,

---

[20] *NŚ.* Vol. I, 1956, p.181.

[21] *NŚ.* Vol. III, 1954, pp. 63, 72.

[22] *SKA.* p. 125; *ŚṛP.* Vol. II, p. 468; Raghavan, 1963, p.562.

Daṇḍin refers to it as a metre (*KĀ*.1. 37). Bhoja says that it was composed in Prākṛt (*ŚṛP.* 1963, Vol. II. p. 480). Very little information can be gathered about it "beyond the fact that it is the Prākrit name for the metre āryāgīti, a form of gaṇachandas (musical 'bar' metre)."[23] It seems to have been used for a performance that included songs and dances. Warder describes it as a single musical strophe used in Mahārāśṭrī.[24]

Chalika or chalita appears in Kālidāsa's *Mālavikāgnimitra* as a dance composition that forms part of a drama (छलितं नाम नाट्यम् –Act I, prose passage following the prastāvanā). Mālavikā dances to a song in prākṛt, expressing the emotion of love.[25] Daṇḍin refers to this form as a prekṣyārtha kāvya (*KĀ*.1. 39). Somadeva in his *Kathāsaritsāgara* describes chalita as a dance performed by Rambhā in heaven (*KSS.* Vol.III, iii. 20). In the *Svarasvatīkaṇṭhābharaṇa,* Bhoja describes chalika as one of six dramatic presentations and states that it creates both vīra and śṛṅgārarasa (*SKA*. p. 124-25). In the *Śṛṅgāraprakāśa,* he describes it as a part of the minor dramatic type called nartanaka (*Śṛ.P.* Vol.II, p. 468). The *Hṛdayaṁgamā* on the *Kāvyādarśa* follows Kāṭayavema (Raghavan, 1963, p.556) in interpreting chalika but adds that instrumental music is a feature of chalika (*Hṛdayaṁgamā* on *KĀ*.1.39). In the *Bhāvaprakāśana* it is described as an element of prekṣaṇaka, a minor dramatic type (*Bh.P.* p. 263). Raghavan takes chalika, not chalita, to be the correct older form of the term (Raghavan, 1963, p. 557). A similar variant of the term occurs in the *Harivaṁśa* (II, chapters 88, 89, 93) which mentions chālikya; chapter 89 of the work is called chālikyakrīḍā and relates how at the request of Kṛṣṇa and Balarāma apsarases dance to vocal and instrumental music (Harivaṁśa, II, 89.5). The dancers use gestures and dance rāsa

---

[23] Warder, Vol. I, 1954, p.153.

[24] Ibid. p.176.

[25] Kāṭayavema, the commentator on *Mālavikāgnimitra* explains it as a piece based on chala or deceit; Raghavan, 1963, p.556.

(*Harivaṁśa,* II, 89.24, 30) singing songs in different local dialects and keeping rhythm by the beats of the palms and wearing regional costumes. The songs tell legends of Kṛṣṇa. Chālikya is also referred to as a song (*Harivaṁśa,* II, 89.67). There are more instances of such uses of the term chālikya.[26] The authors of the *Nāṭyadarpaṇa* refer to chalita, which they say delineates vīra, śṛṅgāra and raudrarasa (*ND.*1959, p.191). In his study of minor dramas, Warder describes chalika as a form containing four strophe, called vastu.[27] However, the descriptions in the relevant literature do not warrant the view that chalika was taken as a minor drama; rather, it was considered to be a performance featuring songs and delicate body movements that created rasa.

Carcarī is yet another term that appears in a variety of meanings in different texts. In a number of dramas it appears in stage directions that seem to indicate body movements as well as singing. In the *Vikramorvaśīya* of Kālidāsa, for instance, a stage direction indicates: चर्चरीकया विचिन्त्य (thinking with [movements in] carcarī), and a prose passage follows which represents what the king is supposed to say while seated. From this position he gets up and again the stage direction states: अनन्तरे चर्चरी (afterwards carcarī), and a verse follows which is either to be recited or sung, accompanied by some body movements.[28] In the *Ratnāvalī* (Act I, pp. 4, 5-6) carcarī appears in a spring festival as a piece of music with a dance performed to suit it.[29] The *Karpūramañjarī* of Rājaśekhara describes carcarī as a dance (*Karpūramañjarī* 4. 9). The *Kuvalayamālā* of Udyotana does the same.[30] Bhoja equates carcarī with

---

26 *Ibid.* pp.556-58.

27 Warder, Vol. I,1972, p. 151. चतुष्पादोद्भवं छलितम्.... (*Mālavikāgnimitra,* Karmakar ed. 1950, p. 22).

28 *Vikramorvaśīya,* Velankar ed.1961, Act. IV, p. 67.

29 Prabhā on *Ratnāvalī,* 1978, describes it as a song (Act. I, pp. 22, 30.).

30 Warder, Vol.I, 1972, p.147.

nāṭyarāsaka and describes it as a dance performed in springtime in which dancers perform in pairs and groups (*ŚṛP.* Vol.II, pp. 468-69). The *Bhāvaprakāśana* follows Bhoja (*Bh.P.* pp. 264-66). In *Kuṭṭanīmata,* Dāmodaragupta speaks of carcarī performed in a spring festival (886) and later refers to it as a song (904). Raghavan describes carcarī as a laya and later, following Bhoja, he equates carcarī with nāṭyarāsaka.[31] Ajay Mitra Śāstrī has given an extensive account of carcarī, its meaning and incidence in various places. He equates it with staff-dance and calli dance (merry making in general).[32] Calli or cilli appears in Abhinavagupta's commentary and in Hemacandra's work but its nature is not clear from the references. The confusion regarding carcarī is further compounded later by its use in saṅgīta literature as a tāla.[33] However, from the various references and discussions mentioned here one may conclude that carcarī was taken as a song performed during festive occasions, particularly in spring, when not only music but dance was often performed as well.

Lāsya is a term that appears in the earlier literature in very many different connotations, as we have seen in the extensive discussion in chapter 4. But it may be briefly noted again in the present context that initially the term lāsya signified a general rather than a specific class of movements, movements that were associated with emotion and delicacy. Among the eight terms discussed here, this is the only one that developed into a distinct category and was not absorbed in either nṛtya or uparūpaka. Lāsya, as we have noted before, appeared in the *Nāṭyaśāstra* as a delicate movement used in dramatic presentations, and later became identified as a dance presentation, delicate, graceful and at times erotic as well, which has survived as a major feature of dancing till the present time.

---

31 Raghavan, 1963, pp.562-65.

32 Śāstrī, 1975, p. 160.

33 *SR.* 5.241; 5.266.

Saṅgītaka, the last term in this group, seems to refer to a mimetic dance. However, when Vararuci refers to saṅgītaka he means a dramatic presentation involving dance, music and acting performed during the spring festival: भगवतो नारायणस्य भवने मदनसेनया मदनाराधने संगीतके यथारसमभिनीयमाने (in acting out the saṅgītaka named *Madanārādhanā* with appropriate rasa in the house of Lord Nārāyaṇa –*Ubhayābhisārikā,* 1959, 3. 9; pp. 122-23) and कुसुमपुरपुरन्दरस्य भवने पुरन्दरविजयं नाम संगीतकमभिनेतव्यम् (the saṅgītaka named *Purandaravijaya* is to be enacted in the house of Purandara of Kusumapura –*Ubhayābhisārikā* 28.7; p.134). In both instances the author seems to have taken saṅgītaka as a dance-drama. By contrast, in two other instances the term saṅgītaka may have been used by the same author to mean a song or a mimetic dance, but the passages are not clear enough to indicate what the author specifically meant by the term (*Ubhayābhisārikā,* 28.7, pp.134, 141). In the *Mālavikāgnimitra* of Kālidāsa saṅgītaka is used as a dance-piece: प्रवृत्तं संगीतकम् (the saṅgītaka has begun –*Mālavikāgnimitra,* 1950, p. 24) and a verse follows, to the accompaniment of which Mālavikā performs. It seems that Mālavikā sang and mimed to that verse. In Harṣa's *Ratnāvalī* (Act I, after verse 5) and in Śūdraka's *Mṛcchakaṭika* (Act I, after verse 8) we find the use of saṅgītaka, which in these instances seems to mean mimetic dancing. Bhoja seems to refer to a dramatic presentation when he says that saṅgītaka should be performed by women (*Śṛ.P.* Vol.II, p. 466). Śāradātanaya refers to saṅgītaka as a metre (*Bh.P.* p.295). According to Katz, "The post *Nāṭyaśāstra* term itself suggests a concerted form. The word saṅgītaka mentioned in the *Ubhayābhisārikā* of Vararuci and once in Śrīharṣa's *Ratnāvalī* was a form of music in which all three elements were present. It is possible that the term saṅgīta came into use alongside or even after this theatrical form."[34] From the early medieval period on, saṅgīta is defined in saṅgīta literature as an art composed of three arts: vocal and

---

[34] Katz, 1987, Vol. II, note on verse 22, p. 9.

instrumental music (gīta and vādya) and dance (nṛtta and nṛtya).[35] It is possible that the saṅgītaka mentioned by Vararuci was not a full-fledged drama but a long piece with song and dance as part of it which required the performer to mime a story. Warder and Raghavan offer no explanation but Mankad takes it as a dramatic presentation.[36] Since we do not have any instance of saṅgītaka as a dramatic presentation other than Vararuci's unclear references, Katz's view seems justified.

From the early medieval period onwards, six of these eight terms disappeared from the literature of dance, with the exception of lāsya and rāsaka. It is worth considering briefly what happened to the others. We have seen that all of these terms represented performances that used body movements set to rhythm and tempo, but with this additional feature in common, that all of them mimed emotional states or presented stories. It was this mimetic character that differentiated them from Bharata's nṛtta. They were presumably different also from abhinaya performed in the pūrvaraṅga as Bharata describes it, because they followed rhythmic beats as opposed to the abhinaya portion of the pūrvaraṅga, which could not have been set to rhythm since Bharata prohibited musical accompaniment for it (*NŚ.* 4.276).

It is likely that the performances denoted by the terms discussed above were developments after Bharata. It is important to remember that for Bharata nṛtta was the only art form that depended upon both body movements and tāla and laya, and that nṛtta was expressly defined by Bharata as a non-representational art. Yet later we find an art called nṛtya which, like nṛtta, is an art of body movements to the accompaniment of tāla and laya but, unlike nṛtta, has referential meaning. No doubt it was to fit this art into Bharata's conception of the performing arts that Kohala

---

35 *SR.* 1.21.

36 Mankad, 1936, p.35.

(if we place him after Bharata) added in his account the following explanation, reported by Abhinavagupta, of the origin of nṛtya:

> सन्ध्यायां नृत्यतः शम्भोर्भक्त्याद्री नारदः पुरा ।
> गीतवांस्त्रिपुरोन्माथं तच्चित्तस्त्वथ गीतके ।
> चकाराभिनयं प्रीतस्ततस्तण्डुं च सोऽब्रवीत् ।
> नाट्योक्त्याभिनयेनेदं वत्स योजय ताण्डवम् ।
>
> (*A.B.*on *NŚ*.Vol.I, p.180)
>
> In time past, while Śambhu was dancing in the evening, Nārada sang, immersed in devotion, a song about [Śiva's] victory over Tripura, and setting his mind in the song. He [=Śiva] mimed it [i.e., the content of the song]. Being pleased [with this, He] said, Taṇḍu, my boy! Please add this tāṇḍava to acting as described in the *Nāṭya [Śāstra].*

Evidently, an expansion of Bharata's conception of dancing was in progress in the thought of his followers, and the eight terms examined here marked that process. They denoted minor art forms used in a drama, not as a part of the pūrvaraṅga, but as modes of graceful miming in the main body of the drama. That the stage directions call for rhythm, tempo and presumably songs to accompany body movements in various situations, suggests that abhinaya and nṛtta, variously combined into a new type of presentation element, became part of a dramatic performance. The terms chalika, śamyā, dvipadī, skandhaka and carcarī seem to have been associated more with tempo and singing, while rāsaka, as found in the early works, began as a dance-drama and later on became identified in medieval texts as a dance and is still performed as a dance in various parts of India. Lāsya, the graceful dramatic presentation mentioned by Bharata, later became a graceful and delicate style of dance and the term came to be used generally to denote all forms of performance which were particularly known for their delicacy and grace. Such forms included many that had been earlier denoted by some of the eight terms discussed here. The term saṅgītaka seems gradually to have evolved into the term saṅgīta which came to denote the three allied arts of vocal and instrumental music and dance taken together. This change took place in medieval times and saṅgītaka ceased to be used in the narrower sense of a dance-drama or dramatic presentation.

Raghavan's view of the history of these terms is worth noting here. According to him, the terms that were associated entirely with laya and metre gradually became associated with songs and then with dances, which were set to those songs.[37] Later, only the term lāsya came to used generally for all dance movements that were particularly graceful and delicate. From the tenth century onwards nṛtya appears in the literature first as a term for minor drama[38] and then, from the thirteenth century, as mimetic dance.[39] Since nṛtya could have two variations, lāsya and tāṇḍava, if a dance had qualities of lāsya and/or nṛtya, that is, delicate and/or mimetic features, any other term became unnecessary to denote them, and the terms carcarī, chalika, śamyā, dvipadī and skandhaka became obsolete in dance literature even though they continued to be used in the literature of music. Rāsaka remained a variety of group dance. It is interesting to note that from the time the terms lāsya and nṛtya begin to appear in dance literature, carcarī, chalika, śamyā, dvipadī and skandhaka are no longer found in association with dancing.

The growing importance of the broad genre known as nṛtya is first seen in the *Daśarūpaka* of Dhanañjaya in the tenth century. Dhanañjaya describes nṛtya as: भावाश्रयं नृत्यम् (nṛtya is dependent on emotion -*DR*.1. 9). But then he adds that it is padārthābhinaya, which means that nṛtya

---

[37] Raghavan, 1963, p.561.

[38] *DR*. 1.9.

[39] *SR*. 7.26-7.

calls for mimimg the meaning of words (*DR*.1. 9). What, then, did the term nṛtya exactly mean in the *Daśarūpaka*? If we are to judge by Dhanika's commentary on the *Daśarūpaka*, nṛtya was an art that had some features of drama without being drama proper. Dhanika mentions seven divisions of nṛtya: ḍombī, śrīgadita, bhāṇa, bhāṇī, prasthāna, rāsaka and kāvya (*DR* p. 8), all of which are known from other texts to be minor types of drama. Since Dhanika takes them to be varieties of nṛtya, he evidently understands Dhanañjaya to take nṛtya as an art with dramatic overtones. We may note in passing that Abhinavagupta never uses the term nṛtya.[40] Bhoja does not use the term nṛtya but he does provide support for defining nṛtya as a dramatic art. He places all dramatic representations under one term, prekṣyaprabandhas (compositions to be seen) which he divides into two classes, padārthābhinaya (i. e., one that expresses the meaning of a word) and vākyārthābhinaya (i. e., one that expresses the meaning of an entire sentence – *Śṛ.P.* Vol.II, pp. 461, 466). If, then, he takes all padārthābhinaya to be dramatic, he must take Dhanañjaya's nṛtya as dramatic as well because it is padārthābhinaya (*DR*. 1.9). That here he does have in mind the same types of composition as those in Dhanañjaya's conception of nṛtya is proved by the fact that his own list of types of padārthābhinayātmaka prekṣyaprabandhas –twelve in all– includes the seven mentioned by Dhanañjaya's commentator Dhanika. While nṛtya was considered to be a dramatic art, it was clearly not drama proper. This becomes evident from Dhanañjaya again, for he distinguishes nṛtya from rūpaka-which was synonymous with drama-by calling nṛtya bhāvāśraya and rūpaka rasāśraya. Dhanika strengthens the distinction by commenting that rūpaka is vākyārthābhinaya. Since nṛtya is padārthābhinaya it has a

40 One may well ask why, if nṛtya was at all a valid category for Dhanañjaya, it is not mentioned by his contemporary Abhinavagupta. The answer is that Abhinavagupta was commenting on Bharata's views and since Bharata does not speak of nṛtya, there was no occasion for Abhinavagupta to include it in his commentrary.

narrower scope of dramatic expression than rūpakas and hence could be no more than minor dramatic presentation. That rasa was a broader category than bhāva was of course a principle established by Bharata himself: नानाभावोपगमाद् रसनिष्पत्तिः (*NŚ.* Vol.I, p. 287). Vākya has a broader scope inasmuch as it is a compound of many bhāvas, while padārthābhinaya is a representation of only one bhāva.

That Dhanañjaya was using nṛtya to denote minor dramatic types is supported also by Śāradātanaya's use of the derivative word, nṛtyabheda, to signify types of minor dramas that he classifies under padārthābhinayātmaka rūpakas (*Bh.P.* 255). He also refers to them as the "other" rūpakas,that is, other types of dramatic presentation. The same use also occurs in the *Nāṭyadarpaṇa* (अन्यान्यपि च रूपकाणि – 1959, pp. 190-92) of Rāmacandra and Guṇacandra. The list of rūpakas in the *Nāṭyadarpaṇa* matches the list given by Bhoja. Sāgaranandin, another author who discusses minor dramas, has no name for the class but gives the same names of the individual types. Nṛtya and nāṭya are used synonymously in the *Amarakoṣa,* which shows that at some point in the development of the performing arts in India nṛtya was equated with nāṭya.[41] The association continues today in the terms Bharatanāṭyam and Mohiniāṭṭam ('āṭṭam' being the Tamil for the Sanskrit nāṭya).

It was not till the 13th century that the term nṛtya came to be dissociated from nāṭya and to be used exclusively for the art of dancing. The first work to define nṛtya categorically as dance was the *Saṅgītaratnākara* (*SR.* 7.26-7). From that time on saṅgīta literature also began to divide dancing into two types, nṛtta and nṛtya, the former being abstract dancing and the latter mimetic dancing (*SR.* 7.26-8). By the 14th century the sister arts of dance and drama had become clearly separated as different genres and dance was no longer considered to be a kind of minor drama. The term used from this time on for minor dramatic types

---

[41] Colebrooke, 1808, p. 42.

was uparūpaka, a term first used by Viśvanātha (*SD.* 6.6). The later medieval texts all followed Śārṅgadeva in using nṛtya for mimetic dance while they followed Viśvanātha in using uparūpaka for drama.

To sum up, then, in alaṁkāra literature, such influential authors as Dhanañjaya, Dhanika and Śāradātanaya use the term nṛtya to mean minor types of drama. Bhoja does not use the term nṛtya at all, but it is clear that he does recognize a dramatic type of performing art as a definite category which expresses meaning. He draws a distinction between two types of prekṣyaprabandhas (compositions to be seen) by designating one as vākyārthābhinaya (acting that brings out the sense of entire sentences) and padārthābhinaya (acting that brings out the sense of words). Bhoja's concept of this second type of composition parallels Dhanañjaya's definition of nṛtya as an art that employs padārthābhinaya. Further, Bhoja lists the same nṛtyabhedas those we find in Dhanika and Śāradātanaya, thus tacitly endorsing the categorization of nṛtya as a dramatic type.

Turning to saṅgīta literature, that is,works on dance and music, we find that *Mānasollāsa* is the first work of this kind to mention nṛtya, which forms the title of an entire section called Nṛtyavinoda. The author, Someśvara, uses the terms nṛtya and nartana synonymously (16.4.950) and includes nāṭya among the six varieties of nartana (16.4.959-60). Stating: साम्प्रतं वर्णयिष्यामि नृत्यं लक्षणसंयुतम्: (I shall now describe nṛtya with its characteristics – 16.4.950), Someśvara describes nartana as:

> नाट्यं लास्यं ताण्डवं च लाघवं विषमं तथा ।
> विकटं चेति निर्दिष्टं नर्तकं(नं) षट्प्रकारम् ॥
>
> (*Mānas.* 16.4.959-60)
>
> Nartaka(na) is said to be of six kinds: nāṭya, lāsya, tāṇḍava, lāghava, viṣama and vikaṭa.

Throughout this work he uses nṛtya as a generic term for dancing.

The sense of nṛtya is more restricted in the *Saṅgītasamayasāra* of Pārśvadeva, which seems to take nṛtya as a deśī or regional form of dancing (*S.Sam.* 7.130-32), although it gives no precise definition. The first definition of nṛtya in saṅgīta literature came from the *Saṅgītaratnākara* of Śārṅgadeva, according to whom nṛtya is one of three divisions of nartana, a term he uses in the general sense of stage presentation. Here he differs from Someśvara in taking nartana as the broader term, not nṛtya, which he considers to be one of the divisions of nartana, the other two being nāṭya and nṛtta (*SR.* 7.2-3). He states that nāṭya is both vākyārthābhinayātmaka and padārthābhinayātmaka, although it employs all four types of abhinaya, and that it creates rasa and bhāva (*SR.* 7.33-4). Nṛtya is defined as body movements that express emotion: आङ्गिकाभिनयैरेव भावानेव व्यनक्ति यत् । तन्नृत्यं (that is nṛtya which expresses emotion by miming through body movements – *SR.* 7.26-7). It is interesting too that about the same time Jāya, the author of *Nṛttaratnāvalī*, defines nṛtya as bhāvāśraya and padārthābhinayātmaka (*NR.*1.50) and cites examples of nṛtya as: नृत्यं श्रीगदितादि स्यात् (nṛtya is [represented by]śrīgadita etc. – *NR.*1.52). As in the *Saṅgītaratnākara*, here the emphasis on bhāva and padārthābhinaya suggests that at this stage nṛtya was viewed as a mode of dramatic expression distinguished by singing and dancing, although it was no longer thought of as a category of drama. From this time on, almost all the works that are concerned with music consider nṛtya primarily as a form of dancing. The only exception is the *Saṅgītadāmodara* which at one point classifies as nṛtya all twenty-seven types of drama recognized by it (*SDām.* p. 79). However, when the author defines the minor dramatic types, he calls them uparūpakas rather than nṛtya. Moreover, when he comes to describe dance movements, he classifies them under aṅgahāra and nṛtya, taking nṛtya as regional dance forms. *Saṅgītopaniṣatsāroddhāra* gives an unusual definition of nṛtya by identifying it as a dance danced only by women (*SUS.* 5.8), although the author uses the term as a generic label for the art of dancing (*SUS.* 5, 6).

In the *Saṅgītacandra* nṛtya is again taken to represent the art of dancing in general (*SC.* 389). Similarly, Mahārāṇā Kumbhā in his *Nṛtyaratnakośa* discusses nṛtya as a form of dancing and refers to it as a mārga form although he does not define it (*NRK.*1.1.291). Moreover, he uses the term nṛtyabheda to indicate different varieties of dance (*NRK.*1.1.466; 4.3.106). We may recall that the term nṛtyabheda was earlier used by Dhanika and Śāradātanaya to denote minor types of drama. The change in the meaning of nṛtyabheda thus shows that by Mahārāṇā Kumbhā's time nṛtya had come to be identified as a form of dancing. It would seem that to begin with, nṛtya was regarded as part of a dramatic presentation, but later it moved away from the domain of drama, and though it retained its mimetic character, it no longer employed speech and evolved into a dance form.

Closely associated with nṛtya is the term uparūpaka, which is a category of major significance in dance literature. We have already noted that the term came into existence fairly late, at the very end of the śāstric tradition of alaṁkāra. In these later works it denotes certain types of drama but it is not clear precisely which types. We may recall that Bharata himself deals only with the major types of drama. But that there were others is clear from the *Nāṭyaśāstra,* which contains a reference to a treatise that Kohala was supposed to be writing, presumably covering grounds untrodden by Bharata.[42] That these included the minor types of drama left out of his description by Bharata is evident from the commentary of Abhinavagupta who mentions these types under various class names when speaking of Kohala. Abhinavagupta further cites other authorities who evidently dealt with minor types of drama.[43] Since we have none of these texts, we have no knowledge of the dramatic types they discussed. We do know that they existed but it is often hard to distinguish them from the nṛtya forms on the basis of their treatment in the texts.

---

[42] *NŚ* 36.65 (Kaśī), *NŚ* 37.18 (G.O.S.), *NŚ* 37.18 (Kāvyamālā).

[43] *NŚ* Vol. I, pp. 171, 181, 182

Bhāmaha is the earliest extant writer of alaṁkāra literature to name some of the types of stage presentations of a dramatic character. As already pointed out, although these types (dvipadī, śamyā, rāsaka and skandhaka) are stated to be abhineyārtha, that is, to be acted and in that sense similar to major drama, they are in fact not even minor dramatic forms but mimetic dance pieces. Daṇḍin, the next writer on alaṁkāra, defines the terms lāsya, chalika and śamyā as prekṣyārtha (i.e., meant to be seen), which again seems to indicate that these were mimetic dances, although neither Bhāmaha nor Daṇḍin describes the dances. The minor dramatic types are named by Abhinavagupta, who quotes various authorities to list the names as well as their characteristics. He lists ten types in all: ḍombikā, bhāṇa, prasthāna, ṣidgaka, bhāṇikā, preraṇa, rāmākrīḍa, hallīsaka, rāsaka (all these being taken from older authorities) and kāvya (from Kohala). Even from Abhinavagupta's brief discussion of these types it is evident that they were short dramatic pieces that presented emotional situations by miming short stories and required at least one, sometimes several female dancers, their dances being set to particular tāla and laya. In some of these presentations male performers also took part.

Abhinavagupta was not the only early writer to refer to these types of stage presentations. Vātsyāyana (believed to be from the 3rd century A.D.)[44] in his *Kāmasūtra* mentions hallīsaka, nāṭyarāsaka, prekṣaṇaka and goṣṭhī.[45] Kumārila (believed to have lived between 590-650 A.D.)[46] in his *Tantravārtika* mentions dvipadī and rāsaka.[47] Since both Vātsyāyana and Kumārila pre-date Abhinavagupta, the latter's references show a continuing tradition of recognizing minor dramatic

[44] Warder, Vol. I, 1972, p. 11.

[45] *KS.*; I.6, II.10.25.

[46] Krishnamachariar, 1974, p. 618

[47] *Tantravārtika*, Chowkhamba edition, p. 279.

types, although we have no detailed characteristics since neither Vātsyāyana nor Kumārila elaborate on them. The *Agnipurāṇa*[48] lists 27 such varieties of dramatic presentation but does not give them a class name. From the names given we can identify the first ten as belonging to the class of rūpakas or major types of drama. The other seventeen are minor dramas (*AP.* 338.2-4). All of these are presumably the abhineya kāvyas mentioned in the preceding chapter of the text (*AP.* 337.1, 39) but they are not defined anywhere. We have noted that Dhanika's avaloka on the *Daśarūpaka* names seven classes of nṛtya (*DR.* p. 8), but he does not explain what they are. Abhinavagupta's brief discussion of ten minor dramatic types remains the only descriptive account of these little known forms till the time of Bhoja, from whom we get a fuller picture. He lists twelve types. He further mentions dombalikā, which may be the same as the dombikā mentioned in the *Abhinavabhāratī*.[49] The *Nāṭyadarpaṇa* describes fourteen such types, calling them 'other' kinds of rūpakas and following Bhoja in describing them.

A different approach is taken by Hemacandra, who places minor dramas under the class geya (*KAnu.H.* pp.327-29). In this he is closely followed by Vāgbhaṭa (*KAnu.V.* p.18). In his commentary on his own work Vāgbhaṭa uses the term geyarūpaka as the class name. Both Hemacandra and Vāgbhaṭa quote the *Abhinavabhāratī* for the views of the cirantanas; they also quote Bhoja's lines on goṣṭhī. Their lists include śrīgadita, to define which they add the following lines:

यस्मिन् कुलाङ्गना पत्युः सख्यग्रे वर्णयेद् गुणम् ।
उपालम्भं च कुरुते गेये श्रीगदितं तु तत् ।

(*KAnu.H.* p.446;*K.Anu.V.* p.18)

That geya in which a virtuous woman

---

[48]De, 1960, p. 99

[49] Raghavan, 1963, p. 567.

> describes the qualities of her husband and
> censures him as well in front of her friend, is
> known as śrīgadita.

The *Nāṭakalakṣaṇaratnakoṣa* lists fifteen minor types of drama and describes them briefly (pp. 126-34). The author includes two types called nāṭikā and toṭaka which, however, he does not place in any particular category. Śāradātanaya provides the longest list by far of minor dramatic types, all twenty of which he describes (*Bh.P.* p. 255). The *Sāhitya Darpaṇa* lists eighteen, calling them uparūpakas and describing them in detail (*SD.* 6.6).

The nature of uparūpakas, their names and their numbers have been discussed by several modern scholars. Mankad made the first detailed study of minor types of drama that involved dancing, comparing their characteristics in tabular form.[50] However, he had insufficient data and occasionally arrived at observations that have since proven to be incorrect. That lacunae, it is hoped, will be remedied by the comparative descriptions provided in the present chapter, based on additional material. It will also help to distinguish the two genres that we are considering here: one that employed only body movements and carried dramatic overtones; and a second which used both body movements and speech as in drama proper, though forms of this genre were narrower in scope than major dramatic types. The first kind consisted of mimetic dances and, from the time of Śārṅgadeva, were designated as nṛtya. The second kind were minor types of drama which were distinguished from the nṛtya forms by being termed uparūpakas.

Besides Mankad two other modern scholars have dealt with uparūpakas extensively. V. Raghavan has discussed them at several

---

[50] Mankad, 1936, pp. 129-31.

places,[51] most exhaustively in his study of Bhoja's *Śṛṅgāraprakāśa*. Bhoja lists twelve types of major dramas, of which two, nāṭikā and saṭṭaka, are regarded as minor types by other early writers. Raghavan's discussion of uparūpakas includes the twelve minor types termed padārthābhinayātmaka prekṣyaprabandha by Bhoja. In course of his discussion Raghavan also cites the views of other writers on these types.

The other important work in which minor types of drama are studied is by Warder (1972, Vol. I, pp. 137-68). He takes each type of minor drama and dance mentioned in alaṁkāra literature and lists what the different authorities have said about it, thus offering an invaluable compendium of the material available. It is unnecessary to duplicate here the information given by Warder but since he restricts himself to alaṁkāra literature for descriptions of the types, it is necessary to draw material from dance and music manuals. This has been attempted here in two parts. First, the references to minor dramatic types in all relevant sources–from both alaṁkāra and saṅgīta literature–have been tabulated, with the sources arranged chronologically. Second, the descriptions of each type as they appear in the sources have been summarized, noting in particular the major differences if any. This survey will thus help in discovering how the understanding of the minor dramatic types evolved through time.

Before going on to the descriptions of nṛtya and uparūpaka, which included musical plays, dance dramas, dramatic dances and mimetic dances, we may briefly note the many terms used by the early authors for this broad spectrum of dramatic presentation, which often confuse by their variety. Abhinavagupta uses the following terms in the *Abhinavabhāratī:* rāgakāvya [a musical play] (*NŚ*.Vol. I, pp. 172, 174,181,182), nṛttakāvya [a dance drama] (pp. 175, 177), rāgadarśanīya [a musical (play), to be seen] (p.172), gīyamānarūpaka [a play to be sung] (pp. 171, 175, 176, 180) and nṛtyapradhānarāgakāvya [a musical play presented principally

[51] Raghavan, 1964-5, 1966-7, pp. 31-54; 1963, pp. 545-74.

through dance] (p.180). Dhanika uses the term nṛtyabheda for minor dramatic presentations (*DR.* p. 8). Śāradātanaya refers to minor dramatic presentations both as rūpakas [dramas] (*Bh.P.* p. 221) and nṛtyabhedas (*Bh.P.* p.181, 255). Bhoja calls them padārthābhinayātmaka prekṣyaprabandhas [a composition to be seen that expresses the meaning of words] (*Śṛ.P.*Vol.II, pp. 466-69). Both Vāgbhaṭa and Hemacandra refer to them as geya [to be sung] (*K.Anu.H.* pp.327-29;*K.Anu.V.* p.18). Rāmacandra and Guṇacandra call them simply the other rūpakas [plays] (*ND.* p. 190). Sāgaranandin lists the types without placing them under any class (*NLRK.* pp. 113-14, 126-34) and Viśvanātha calls all of them uparūpakas [minor dramas] (*SD.*6.6). The following list shows which types appear in what sources. The types will then be taken individually and their descriptions summarized.

MINOR DRAMATIC TYPES

Source	*Types*
Abhinavagupta	ḍombikā, bhāṇa, prasthāna, ṣidgaka, bhāṇikā, preraṇa, rāmākrīḍa, hallīsaka, rāsaka and kāvya (*A.B.* on *NŚ.* Vol. I, pp.171, 181-2).
Vātsyāyana	hallīsaka, nāṭyarāsaka, prekṣaṇaka, goṣṭhī (*Kāmasūtra,* II.10. 25, p.154).
Kumārila	dvipadī, rāsaka (*Tantravārtika,* p. 279).
Bhāmaha	dvipadī, rāsaka, śamyā, skandhaka (*KAlam.* 1. 24).
Daṇḍin	lāsya, chalita, śamyā (*KĀ.*1. 39).
Agnipurāṇa	troṭaka, nāṭikā, saṭṭaka, śilpaka, karṇa, durmallikā, prasthāna, bhāṇikā, bhāṇī, goṣṭhī, hallīsaka, kāvya, śrīgadina(ta), nāṭyarāsaka, rāsaka, ullāpyaka, preṅkhaṇa (*AP.* 338.2-4).

Dhanika	ḍombī, śrīgadita, bhāṇa, bhāṇī, prasthāna, rāsaka, kāvya (*DR.* p.8).
Bhoja	śrīgadita, durmilitā, prasthāna, kāvya (citrakāvya), bhāṇa (śuddha, citra, saṁkīrṇa), bhāṇikā, goṣṭhī, hallīsaka, nartanaka, prekṣaṇaka, rāsaka, nāṭyarāsaka.(*Śṛ.P.* Vol. II, pp. 466-69).
Rāmacandra and Guṇacandra	saṭṭaka, śrīgadita, durmilitā, prasthāna, goṣṭhī, hallīsaka, nartanaka, prekṣaṇaka, rāsaka, nāṭyarāsaka, kāvya, bhāṇaka, bhāṇikā (*ND.* 1959, pp.191-92).
Hemacandra	ḍombikā, bhāṇa, prasthāna, śiṅga, bhāṇikā, preraṇa, rāmākrīḍa, hallīsaka, rāsaka, goṣṭhī, śrīgadita (*KAnu.H.*p.327-29).
Vāgbhaṭa	ḍombikā, bhāṇa, prasthāna, bhāṇikā, preraṇa, śiṅgaka, rāmākrīḍa, hallīsaka, śrīgadita, rāsaka, goṣṭhī (*KAnu.V.* p.18).
Sāgaranandin	goṣṭhī, saṁlāpa, śilpaka, prasthāna, kāvya, hallīśaka, śrīgadita, bhāṇikā, bhāṇī, durmallikā, prekṣaṇaka, saṭṭaka, rāsaka, nāṭyarāsaka, ullāpyaka (*NLRK.* pp.126-34: 3026-3216).
Śāradātanaya	toṭaka, nāṭikā, goṣṭhī, sallāpa, śilpaka, ḍombī, śrīgadita, bhāṇa, bhāṇī, prasthāna, kāvya, prekṣaṇaka, nāṭyarāsaka, rāsaka, ullopyaka, hallīśa, durmallikā, kalpavallī, mallikā, pārijātaka (*Bh.P.* p. 255).
Viśvanātha	nāṭikā, troṭaka, goṣṭhī, saṭṭaka, nāṭyarāsaka, prasthānaka, ullāpya, kāvya, preṅkhaṇa, rāsaka, saṁlāpaka, śrīgadita, śilpaka, vilāsikā, hallīśa, durmallikā, prakaraṇī, bhāṇikā (*SD.* 6.6).

Śubhaṅkara	nāṭikā, prekṣaṇa, toṭaka, śāṭaka, goṣṭhī, saṁlāpa, śilpa, bhāṇī, hallīśa, rāsaka, ullāpaka, śrīgadita, prasthāna, nāṭyarāsaka, durmallikā, lāsikā, kāvya (*SDām.* p. 79-80).

In performing most of the types listed above the style of presentation employed is the one known as kaiśikīvṛtti, which Bharata defines in the following verse:

या श्लक्ष्णनैपथ्यविशेषचित्रा
स्त्रीसंयुता या बहुनृत्तगीता ।
कामोपभोगप्रभवप्रचारा
तां कैशिकीं वृत्तिमुदाहरन्ति ॥

(*NŚ.* 20. 54-55)

That which is graceful, varied with special costume and make-up, performed by [lit:added with] women, which [contains] a lot of dance and song [and is] prominent in the enjoyment of passion is known as kaiśikīvṛtti.

This suggests that when a dramatic type calls for kaiśikīvṛtti it also requires singing and dancing. But the descriptions in the texts show that not all minor dramatic types could be called musical plays that used dancing, nor did they use all the features of kaiśikīvṛtti. The features of these types are summarized here from the sources; only those sources have been mentioned that either give the representative view or markedly differ from other sources.

DESCRIPTIONS OF MINOR DRAMATIC TYPES

1. Ullāpyaka: This term is variantly spelt ullāpaka, ullopyaka, ullāpya etc. It is first mentioned in the *Agnipurāṇa* as a minor drama. But, as Warder points out, it is understood in the *NŚ* as a kind of song (*NŚ.* Vol.

IV, 31.194, 221) and Abhinavagupta does not connect it with a musical play (Warder, 1972, Vol. I, p.165). Sāgaranandin states that it includes songs, the hāsya, śṛṅgāra and karuṇa rasas, a three-act structure and is similar to śilpaka, an example being *Devīmahādevam (NLRK.* 3213-16). *Bh.P.* has a definition similar to the *NLRK,* citing the *Gāndharvanirṇaya,* and gives two examples of the type, *Devīmahādevam,* and *Udāttakuñjaram* (*Bh.P.* p.266). *SDām.* gives a similar definition but emphasizes the need for a great number of songs (p. 95). From this it would seem that by Śubhaṇkara's time the type had evolved into a rāgakāvya.

2. Kalpavallī: This is described in the *Bh.P.* (p. 268) as a form that arouses the śṛṅgāra and hāsya rasas, has an exalted hero and a supporting hero (udāttanāyaka and pīṭhamarda upanāyaka). The situation it portrays is that of the heroine waiting for the hero or going to meet the hero. It is characterized by the use of dvipadīkhaṇḍa, rathyātāla, vāsakatāla, three layas, ten lāsyas and sandhis. The example given of this form is *Māṇikyavallikā.*
3. Karṇa: *Agnipurāṇa* (*AP.*338.3) is the only text to mention the name giving no description.
4. Kāvya: Abhinavagupta quotes Kohala (*NŚ.*Vol. I, p.182) on rāgakāvya or kāvya and treats it separately, distinguishing from other types of minor dramas that are basically mimetic dance pieces (*NŚ.* Vol. I, p.181). According to Abhinavagupta, a kāvya should be presented in a variety of tempi to the accompaniment of rāgas and should have a well-constructed plot, as exemplified by *Rāghavavijaya* or *Mārīcavadha,* which are performed, respectively, to the ṭhakka and kakubha rāgas. Dhanika includes kāvya in his list of nṛtyas, which suggests that he associated it with music and dance although he does not define it. Bhoja refers to kāvya and citrakāvya in his list of minor plays. He differs from Abhinavagupta in stating that kāvya is set to one rāga but citrakāvya to several. Bhoja also gives technical details regarding the

tāla and mātrā of the rāgas. The same information is repeated in the *Nāṭyadarpaṇa* (*ND.* 1959, p. 191). Sāgaranandin suggests more technical details of tāla, vṛtti, rasa and sandhi in this minor play and cites *Utkaṇṭhitamādhavam* as an example (*NLRK.*3151). The author of the *Bh.P.* gives the longest description of kāvya. The description is similar to that by Sāgaranandin but mentions in addition the use of dvipadīkhaṅḍa and, occasionally, of lāsya, as seen in *Gauḍavijaya.* Another work mentioned in the same context is *Sugrīvakelana,* which exemplifies a variant of the type, one that has a brilliant hero, a young heroine and employs joyful speeches (*Bh.P.* pp. 262-3). The author also includes in his description of rāsaka two lines from Bhoja's definition of kāvya (*Bh.P.* p. 265). Viśvanātha prescribes lāsya and śṛṅgārarasa for kāvya, which he considers to be a type of one-act play in which khaṇḍamātrā, dvipadī and bhagnatāla should be used but not the ārabhaṭīvṛtti. An example is *Yādavodaya* (*SD.* 6.284-85). Śubhankara's description is similar to Viśvanātha's (*SDām.*p. 96).

5. Goṣṭhī: This does not appear in Abhinavagupta's account, nor in Dhanika's. Bhoja was the first writer to include it in his list of minor dramas. According to him, the purpose of goṣṭhī is to show the young Kṛṣna sporting with cowherds and milkmaids (*ŚṛP.*Vol. II, p. 468). This view is repeated in the *ND* (1959,p. 191). The author of the *NLRK* calls goṣṭhī a one-act play that lacks garbha and avamarśasandhi and is performed in the kaiśikīvṛtti (*NLRK.* 3026-27). Śāradātanaya's description is quite elaborate: goṣṭhī is a one-act play, it is performed in the kaiśikīvṛtti, and it celebrates the deeds of Kṛṣna, particularly his killing of demons (*Bh.P.*p. 256). A similar definition is given by the *SD,* which mentions the one-act structure, kaiśikīvṛtti and śṛṅgārarasa (*SD.* 6. 274-75). Kaiśikīvṛtti is mentioned also in the *SDām* (p. 93). All of these accounts agree that these performances involve a number of performers both male and female and employ numerous songs and dances.

6. Ḍombī, ḍombikā: Abhinavagupta makes several references to this type as a nṛtyakāvya (*NŚ*.Vol.I, pp. 166, 180, 181, to cite a few). According to the ancient authorities he quotes, it is a dramatic dance composition in four scenes, intended to please the king (*NŚ*.Vol.I, pp. 175,181,188). Abhinavagupta gives two examples: *Guṇamālā* and *Cūḍāmaṇi* (*NŚ*.Vol.I, pp.171,175; Vol. IV, p. 271). The *Bh.P.* (p. 257-58) repeats *AB* as do Hemacandra and Vāgbhaṭa (*KAnuH.* pp.327-29; *KAnuV.* p.18) and Dhanika mentions the type without providing much information. Warder has a detailed discussion on ḍombī (Warder, 1972, Vol. I, pp.156-7).
7. Toṭaka, troṭaka: This is a variety of nāṭaka (*NLRK.* 2766, *BhP.*.238; *SD.*6.273). Although this is not a musical piece, nor a dance type, and although the writers do not prescribe dance and music for it, the example they give of the form is *Vikramorvaśīya,* which does include dance and music. The *Agnipurāṇa* includes the form in its list of dramatic types (*AP.* 338.2) and *SDām.* describes it as a primarily verbal drama (*SDām.* p. 92).
8. Durmallikā, durmilitā: This is mentioned in *AP* (338. 2), *Śṛ.P.* (Vol. II, p. 466) *ND* (p. 191), *NLRK* (3187), *SD* (6. 303) and *SDām.* (p. 69). This is a humorous play in four acts which employs kaiśikīvṛtti. The story involves a 'stolen love' and a deceitful female messenger whose function is interpreted by Raghavan as blackmail. According to Raghavan this is a vulgar performance. No author has cited any example. The reason, according to Warder, may be that this kind of performance did not attract scholarly attention. Raghavan and Warder discuss this form in detail (Raghavan, 1963, p. 547; Warder, 1972, Vol. I, pp. 142-3).
9. Nartanaka: This seems to be a mimetic dance in which the dancer mimes, through graceful movements, the meaning of the words of a song. According to the *Śṛṅgāraprakāśa,* it has four varieties, namely, śamyā, lāsya, chalika and dvipadī (*Śṛ.P.* Vol. II, p.468; Raghavan, 1963,

pp.555-56). The same description is repeated in the *Nāṭyadarpaṇa* (1959, p.191). Raghavan calls it a nautch danee (Raghavan, 1963, p. 555).

10. Nāṭikā: This is similar to nāṭaka and employs songs and dances (*A.B.* on the *NŚ.* 1956,Vol.I, p. 436). Examples can be taken from all periods, such as *Pratijñāyaugandhārāyaṇa, Ratnāvalī* (*SD.* 6.269-72, *AP.*338.2, *Bh.P.* p. 243-4, *SDām.* p. 91). A variant form of the term is nāṭī, which appears in the list of twelve rūpakas in *ND* (1959, p. 7).
11. Nāṭyarāsaka: This is mentioned in the *Agnipurāṇa* and described in *Śṛ.P,* which is followed by *ND.* Śāradātanaya, Sāgaranandin, and Viśvanātha treat it as a one-act play. According to Bhoja nāṭyarāsaka is also known as carcarī. Nāṭyarāsaka is described as a springtime dance performed by a group of female dancers (Raghavan, 1963, pp. 562-67), requiring formation dancing or piṇḍībandhas. Warder points out that Bhoja may have confused rāsaka and nāṭyarāsaka: "he inserts the description of the nāṭyarāsaka into the middle of that of the rāsaka, but this may be the result of manuscript corruption" (Warder 1972, Vol. I, p.146). The term nāṭyarāsaka suggests some kind of dramatic content but the description shows it as a dance form. *Bh.P.* has a long description (pp. 263-65) following Bhoja which includes formation dancing or piṇḍībandhas. It also gives carcarī as an alternative name for the type. Rāmacandra and Guṇacandra describe it as dance danced by women to the rāga vasanta (*ND.*1959, p. 192). Sāgaranandin says that this form employs a number of lāsyāṅgas and a variety of rhythm and tempo, as for instance in the composition *Vilāsavatī* (*NLRK.* 3210-12). Viśvanātha similarly suggests the use of ten lāsyāṅgas and a variety of rhythm and tempo (*SD.* 6. 277-9), as in *Narmavatī* and *Vilāsavatī*. *SDām.* follows the definition of *SD.* (*SDām.* pp. 95-6).
12. Pārijātaka, pārijātalatā: This is a one-act play mentioned only by Śāradātanaya (*Bh.P.* p. 268) who says that it requires a number of female dancers and the performance of daṇḍarāsaka, citing as

example of the type *Gaṅgātaraṅgikā.* Warder thinks there may have been some confusion between pārijātaka and daṇḍarāsaka.

13. Prakaraṇikā, prakaraṇī: This is a species of prakaraṇa (*A.B.* on the *NŚ.*Vol. II, p. 436). No examples are given or found. *ND.*, which is followed by *SD.*(6.306), says that it is similar to nāṭī but the hero should be as in Prakaraṇa, including including the form in its list of rūpakas (*ND.* p. 7).

14. Prasthānaka: This type is characterized by descriptive gestures. It is in two acts divided into four scenes. It mainly uses delicate movements, with occasional vigorous passages, such as the gait of an elephant, which stands for the idea of journeying abroad (*NŚ.* Vol. I, pp. 166, 181). It is listed in the *Agni Purāṇa* and described by Abhinavagupta, Dhanika, Bhoja, Rāmacandra and Guṇacandra, Hemacandra, Vāgbhaṭa (who like Hemacandra simply reproduces Abhinavagupta), Sāgaranandin, Śāradātanaya, Viśvanātha and Śubhaṅkara. In their detailed descriptions Abhinavagupta and Bhoja mention apasāra, that is, exit, as one of its features. *ND.* defines apasāra as interludes between dances (p. 191). *Bh.P.* defines it as a musical performance set to rhythm and tempo and performed in kaiśikīvṛtti (p. 262). As example it mentions *Śṛṅgāratilaka. SD.* suggests rhythm, tempo and both kaiśikīvṛtti and bhāratīvṛtti (6. 280-81). *SDām* 's definition is similar to *SD.* 's (*SDām.* p. 95). *NLRK* says that it requires many rhythm and tempo arrangements (*NLRK.* 3147-50). Both Raghavan and Warder have extensive discussions on this type (Raghavan, 1963, pp. 548-49; Warder, 1972, Vol. I, pp. 160-61).

15. Prekṣaṇaka, preṅkhaṇaka: The term prekṣaṇaka appears in Bhāsa's *Bālacarita* and, as Warder points out, may simply mean drama (Warder, 1972, Vol. I, p. 139). The *Kāmasūtra* refers to it as a one-act play (*KS.* II.10.25). The *AP* mentions preṅkhaṇa. No similar term appears in the *A.B.* but Bhoja, Rāmacandra and Guṇacandra, Sāgaranandin, Śāradātanaya and Viśvanātha all list this type. Bhoja

says that spectacles like the immolation of Eros are characteristic of the type, and this view is repeated in *ND* (1959, p. 191). *SD* states that all the vṛttis are to be used in this type which it calls preṅkhaṇa (6. 286-87). *SD* 's description follows that of Sāgaranandin (*NLRK.* 3192-7) and both texts cite *Bālivadha* as an example. *Bh.P.* has a confused view because it uses the account of nartanaka in Bhoja to define prekṣaṇaka (p.263). *SDām* describes the type as a play that uses all vernaculars but Śaurasenī in the main (p. 92). It is discussed in detail by Raghavan and Warder (Raghavan, 1963, p. 561; Warder, 1972, Vol. I, p. 144).

16. Preraṇa: This is a one-act play featuring comic action and characters. Abhinavagupta describes it as full of laughter and riddles (Abhinavagupta on the *NŚ.*1956,Vol. I, pp. 172, 181). Among writers on alaṁkāra Abhinavagupta alone discusses it but in saṅgīta literature preraṇa (or its variants, peraṇa or peraṇī) appears in almost every work as a form dancing (*SR.* 7.46, 1316-25; *NR.* 7. 34-58; *SSam.* 7. 217-22). The form is discussed in both Mankad and Warder (Mankad, 1936, pp.127-28; Warder, 1972, Vol. I, p.144). It will be discussed in detail later in the present study in course of examining the dance forms that developed from the time of the *SR* through the medieval period.

17. Bhāṇa, bhāṇaka: This term represents both a major and a minor dramatic type. The term has caused considerable confusion in the literature of dance and drama. Its importance to the understanding of the evolution of dancing lies in the fact that though it is a type of drama it employs bold, vigorous body movements and instrumental music. As a minor dramatic type it first appears in the *A.B.* (*NŚ.* 1956, Vol, I, .p.181) which distinguishes it from the bhāṇa that appears in the list of major dramatic types. The major type is a satirical monologue but the minor type is a presentation that calls for vigorous body movements (*NŚ.*1956,Vol. I, p.181) and a great deal of instrumental music (*NŚ* 1956,Vol. I, p.166) with irregular beats. Bhoja has a long discussion on this type (Raghavan, 1963, pp. 451-54) which he divides into three

varieties, namely, śuddha, saṅkīrṇa and citra. According to him it requires dancing. *ND* closely follows Bhoja and like Bhoja states that it is difficult to perform (*ND.* p. 191). It is said to be of three varieties: uddhata, lalita, and lalitoddhata. *Bh.P.*'s description of the minor type known as bhāṇa is very long, running from page 258 to 262. It says that lāsyāṅgas form part of bhāṇaka. Later in the text (p. 266), Abhinavagupta's definition of the term is given in the middle of discussing rāsaka. Abhinavagupta's definition is reproduced also by Hemacandra and Vāgbhaṭa. Dhanika offers no definition. A variety of bhāṇaka is known as nandimālī (*BhP,* p.261, *ŚṛP.* Vol. II, p. 467). Both Raghavan and Warder have substantial discussions on bhāṇa (Raghavan, 1963, pp. 551-54; Warder, 1972, Vol. I, pp.158-59). A detailed study has been made by S. S. Janaki in her dissertation (1971).

18. Bhāṇikā: Bhāṇikā is mentioned in the *Abhinavabhāratī, Agni Purāṇa, Śṛṅgāraprakāśa, Nāṭyadarpaṇa, Kāvyānuśāsana* (of Hemacandra), *Kāvyānuśāsana* (of Vāgbhaṭa), *Nāṭakalakṣaṇaratnakośa* and *Sāhityadarpaṇa.* Abhinavagupta refers to the enactment of bālakrīḍā (presumably of Kṛṣṇa) in bhāṇikā (*NŚ.* 1956, Vol. I, p. 181). Bhoja says that bhāṇikā is similar to bhāṇa but that the movements are delicate (*Śṛ.P.*Vol II, p.467). Śāradātanaya considers lāsyāṅgas as necessary in bhāṇikā as in bhāṇa and states that the minor dramatic type known as bhāṇa has the features of bhāṇarūpaka, of which *Vīṇāvatī* is an example (*Bh.P.* p. 262). *NLRK* prescribes both bhāratī and kaiśikīvṛtti for bhāṇikā (3160-63). *SD* gives a similar account of the type and cites *Kāmadattā* as an example (6. 308-13). Vāgbhaṭa and Hemacandra follow Abhinavagupta, quoting him. Raghavan and Warder discuss it in detail (Raghavan, 1963, pp. 551-5; Warder, 1972, Vol.I, pp.159-60).

19. Bhāṇī: This type is mentioned in the *AP,* the avaloka of Dhanika, *NLRK,* and *Bh.P.* In the *AP* and *NLRK* both bhāṇī and bhāṇika are discussed. *AP* offers no definition of bhāṇī but *NLRK* distinguishes it from bhāṇikā by saying that bhāṇī contains lāsyāṅgas and arouses

śṛṅgārarasa, offering as example *Vīṇāvatī* (*NLRK.* 3184-6). Śāradātanaya lists bhāṇī as one of the nṛtyabhedas (*Bh.P.* p. 255) but in describing it he equates it with bhāṇikā(p. 262). Śubhaṅkara (*SDām.* p.94) follows *NLRK* and *Bh.P.*

20. Mallikā: This is mentioned only by Śāradātanaya (*Bh.P.* pp. 267-8) who identifies it as the same as maṇikulyā, a mystery story. The description is unclear but seems similar to that of durmallikā. It includes a jester or parasite among its characters and is in two acts. Warder discusses it in some detail (Warder, 1972, Vol. I, pp.144-5).

21. Rāmākrīḍa: Abhinavagupta briefly discusses this type which is characterized by the description of the seasons (*NŚ.*Vol. I, p. 181). *BhP.*, the *Kāvyānuśāsana* of Hemacandra (*KAnu.H.*p. 327-29) and the *Kāvyānuśāsana* of Vāgbhaṭa (*KAnu.V.* p. 18) mention this type of minor drama, *Bh.P.* repeating a line from its discussion on rāsaka (p. 266). No other text mentions rāmākrīḍa.

22. Rāsaka: This is mentioned in almost every early text. It is found in Abhinavagupta, Kumārila, Bhāmaha, Dhanika, Bhoja, Rāmacandra and Guṇacandra, Hemacandra, Vāgbhaṭa and appears in the *AP, NLRK, BhP, SD.* and *SDām.* As noted earlier in this chapter (pp. 159-60), it is treated both as a drama and as a dance in the literature. Abhinavagupta identifies it as a dramatic dance (*NŚ.* Vol. I. p. 181). Kumārila, Bhāmaha, Dhanika and the *AP* offer no definition. According to Bhoja hallīsaka becomes rāsa when it is performed to certain defined tālas. In his detailed discussion he states that piṇḍībandhas or group dances are a feature of this type and describes them (*ŚṛP.*Vol. II, p. 468; *SKA.* p.125). Evidently, Bhoja sees it primarily as a dance, although he places it under padārthābhinayātmaka prekṣyaprabandhas. Rāmacandra follows Bhoja (*ND.*1959, p. 191). Hemacandra and Vāgbhaṭa quote Abhinavagupta's view. The *Harivaṁśa* has references to rāsa (2.89.67; 93.24). *NLRK*'s definition implies the importance of verbal acting

(sakalabhāṣāvibhāṣāśobhitam) but does not include dance or music (3205-9). As example it cites *Madanikākāmūka*. *Bh.P.* gives a highly confusing description (pp. 265-66). Śāradātanaya reproduces Abhinavagupta's quotation from the cirantanas in the middle of his own definition. From the discussion in *SD* it seems that rāsaka is a minor drama characterized by verbal acting but employing singing and dancing as well (6. 288-90). *SDām.* follows *SD* but adds that the type is also known as the krīdārāsaka of the gopīs (*SDām.* p. 95). Both Warder and Raghavan have long discussions on rāsaka that attempt to resolve the confusion in the texts (Raghavan, 1963, pp. 561-67; Warder, 1972, Vol. I, pp. 145, 148).

The dance called daṇḍarāsaka perhaps evolved out of śamyā, as Warder has suggested (Warder, 1972, Vol. I, p. 152). It is a group dance performed with sticks, as we find in *Karpūramañjarī* (4.10-11). This is a feature of pārijātaka as described in *Bh.P.* (p. 268), which suggests that daṇḍarāsaka and pārijātaka are one and the same. However, *Bh.P.* later (p. 297) equates rāsaka with latā, a variety of lāsya, and divides rāsaka into three classes, daṇḍarāsaka, maṇḍalarāsaka, and nāṭyarāsaka. A saṅgīta text, *Saṅgītasamayasāra,* describes it as a dance that requires various tālavādyas and is performed with sticks (*SSam.*6. 240-45). *NR.* describes rāsaka primarily as a piṇḍībandha, (7. 84-97); nāṭyarāsaka as mime to a song (7. 100) and daṇḍarāsaka as a group dance performed with coloured sticks(7.101-7). All three are described as deśīnṛttas danced to music. The *Nartananirṇaya* describes rāsa and daṇḍarāsa in the similar manner putting them under the anibandha category of deśī dancing (*NN.* 53a). This type of performance has survived into our times, especially in Gujarat (Raghavan, 1963, pp. 561-2).

23. Vāra: Bodhāyana (*Bhagavadajjukīya,* 1925, p. 4) mentions this but offers no definition. *Bh.P.* (p. 241) refers to a form of nāṭaka it calls nṛtyacāra (vāra being an alternative reading). Abhinavagupta

mentions nāṭyadhāra (*NŚ*.Vol. III, p.172), which, Warder suggests, may be a scribal error. He conjectures that vāra was an ancient and obsolete type of drama which was not recorded by later writers (Warder, 1972,Vol. I, p.141). None of the available references is clear enough to indicate the nature of vāra.

24. Vilāsikā: This appears only in the *SD* which describes it as employing ten lāsyāṅgas and arousing śṛṅgārarasa. This type was evidently also known as vināyikā (*SD*. 6. 301-2, p.106, comm.). In his discussion of vilāsikā (Warder, 1972, Vol. I, pp.162-3) Warder derives the term from lāsikā, which he considers to be an alternate form of lāsya. He further states that lāsikā, which appears in the *Alaṅkārasaṁgraha* of Amṛtānanda, is the same as the bhāṇī of Sāgaranandin. In *SDām.* lāsikā has the same meaning as vilāsikā mentioned in *SD* (*SDām.* p.96).

25. Śilpaka: This term appears in *AP, NLRK, BhP, SD* and *SDām. NLRK* says that it consists of four vṛttis and twenty-seven aṅgas (*NLRK* 3029-46). *BhP* (p. 257) and *SD* (6. 296-300) agree with *NLRK*'s description. All of them cite *Kanakāvatīmādhava* as an example. Śubhaṅkara follows them (*SDām.* p. 94).

26. Śrīgadita: This term appears in the *AP* and in Dhanika, Bhoja, Rāmacandra, Hemacandra, Vāgbhaṭa, Śāradātanaya, Viśvanātha and Śubhaṅkara, but the *AP* and Dhanika do not describe it. Bhoja says that it depicts through songs and recitations the state of separation in love. *ND* follows Bhoja (1959, p.191) as do *SDām.* (p. 95) and *NLRK* except that *NLRK* says that the performance involves mainly verbal acting and does not call for songs, an example being *Krīḍārasātala* (*NLRK.* 3157-59). *Bh.P.* agrees that śrīgadita should mainly employ verbal acting but recommends some singing and lalita movements (p. 258). *SD* gives a definition similar to Bhoja's but adds that the presentation should frequently use the word "śrī," as in *Krīḍārasātala.* Raghavan compares śrīgadita with the Tamil kuruvañci and with the varṇam and padam of Bharatanāṭyam (Raghavan, 1963, pp. 546-7).

27. Ṣidgaka, śiṅgaka: This type is termed ṣidgaka by Abhinavagupta (*NŚ*.Vol. I, p. 181), and śiṅgaka by Hemacandra (*KAnuH.* p.327) and Vāgbhaṭa (*KAnuV.* p.18), but has the same definition in all three. Abhinavagupta says that it is a musical play full of songs ("gīyamānarūpaka"-*NŚ*.Vol. I, p.166) and that although it is a delicate form, it makes extensive use of vigorous movements. He later quotes the cirantanas (*NŚ*.Vol. I, p.181) who describe it as a delicate form. The type described as śrīgadita by Bhoja seems to be similar to ṣidgaka. Hemacandra refers to śrīgadita and śiṅgaka (a variant spelling of ṣidgaka) as different types but defines śiṅgaka similarly as Bhoja's śrīgadita. Abhinavagupta's definition of ṣidgaka is quoted in *Bh.P.* (p. 266) to form the definition of śilpaka, although a few pages earlier *Bh.P.* describes śilpaka as in *NLRK* (*Bh.P.* p. 257; *NLRK* 3029-46). Raghavan compares ṣidgaka with śrīgadita (Raghavan, 1963, pp. 546-7). Warder has a long discussion (Warder, 1972, Vol I, pp. 161-62) on the possible connection between this and other types of minor drama.

28. Śāṭaka, saṭṭaka: This is mentioned in the *AP*, in Hemacandra, *NLRK*, *BhP.*, *SD* and *SDām.* Hemacandra, who includes it in the class of rūpakas, says that it is performed in prākṛta and is similar to a nāṭikā (*KAnuH.* p.317). The *NLRK* recommends kaiśikīvṛtti for this type which it calls similar to nāṭikā, citing as example *Karpūramañjarī* (*NLRK*.3198-3204). *Karpūramañjarī* uses śāṭaka, the prākṛt form of the term. Śāradātanaya agrees that the type is similar to nāṭikā but does not include it in the list of minor dramas or recommend kaiśikīvṛtti (*Bh.P.* p. 244). Both *NLRK* and Śāradātanaya suggest the use of prākṛta. *SD* agrees with *Bh.P.* and cites *Karpūramañjarī* as an example (6. 276-7). The edited text of *SDām.* refers to śāṭaka (pp. 79, 92-3) as a type of minor drama and defines it in the same way as saṭṭaka, which is found in *Bh.P.* and *SD.* This text also gives (*SDām.* p. 93) śaṭaka as a reading from the India Office Library manuscript, which suggests that the two terms are alternate spellings of the same term. The term is

listed by Bhoja as a rūpaka (*Śṛ.P.*Vol. II, p. 466) and is so defined by him. In *Karpūramañjarī* (Act IV, 10-11) there is a description of the dance called daṇḍarāsa which is introduced by the stage direction "tataḥ praviśati carcarī." This suggests that while śāṭaka was not a dance drama, it used dance and music. Except for *NLRK* no text prescribes kaiśikīvṛtti as such but the common view that the type resembles nāṭikā implies the use of songs and dances as found in *Karpūramañjarī.*

29. Sallāpa, saṁlāpa: *NLRK, Bh.P, SD* and *SDām.* describe this as a minor drama that does not use the kaiśikī and bhāratī vṛttis. *NLRK* suggests the sāttvatī and ārabhaṭī vṛttis as essential to the type (*NLRK.* 3028). *Bh.P.* gives a similar definition at greater length (p. 256). *SD* (6. 291-92) agrees with *NLRK* and *Bh.P.*, as does *SDām.* (p. 93). The example cited by *NLRK, SD* and *SDām.* is *Māyākāpālika.*

30. Hallīśaka, hallīsaka: This is a group dance resembling rāsaka and is mentioned by Vātsyāyana (*KS.* II.10.2, p.154), by Bhāsa in the *Bālacarita* (Act 3), and in *AP* (338.3), *Harivaṁśa* (89.68), *A.B.* (*NŚ.* Vol. I, p. 181), *Śṛ.P* (Vol. II, p. 468), *ND* (1959, p. 191), Hemacandra (*KAnuH.*p.327), Vāgbhaṭa (*KAnuV.* p.18), *NLRK* (3154-6), *Bh.P.* (pp. 266-7), *SD* (6. 307), and *SDām* (p. 94). Abhinavagupta describes it as a dance and places it under musical or dance dramas. *Śṛ.P.* considers it to be a minor dramatic type but defines it after *A.B.*, which is quoted by Hemacandra and Vāgbhaṭa. *ND.* reproduces Bhoja's account. *NLRK* follows Abhinavagupta and Bhoja and cites *Keliraivataka* as an example. The same example is given by *BhP* which treats hallīśaka at some length, calling it a dramatic type that employs geyalāsya and some of the technical features of drama. The technical features of drama are mentioned also by *SD,* which gives a shorter account, stating that the type calls for kaiśikīvṛtti and the use of a variety of rhythm and tempo. The example given is again *Keliraivataka.*

Raghavan (1963, pp. 554-5) and Warder (1972, Vol. I, pp.139,152) have long discussions on the type.

These, then, are the thirty types of minor dramatic performances which came to be known as uparūpakas. We find them in alaṁkāra literature as well as in related works. Some of these types involve dance and music, and these are found in the works on saṅgīta that begin to appear around the 13th century. Of these, only those are relevant to the present study that employ dancing, some being primarily dance forms while some are dance dramas. Minor dramatic types may thus be classified into three broad categories: first, those that use no music or dance; second, those that use music and dance; third, those that are primarily dance dramas, or musical plays, or dance performances. In the first category we may include the following: durmallikā, prekṣaṇaka, mallikā, preraṇa,[52] śilpaka and saṁlāpa. The second category includes the following: nāṭikā, troṭaka, kalpavallī, prakaraṇa and saṭṭaka. The third category has two subdivisions: musical plays and dance dramas. The following types of musical plays are mentioned: kāvya, prasthānaka, rāmākrīḍa (this may be included in the first type but its definition is not clear), ullāpyaka and ṣidgaka. The other sub-category, that of dance drama, includes the following: goṣṭhī, ḍombī, nartanaka, nāṭyarāsaka, pārijātaka, vāra, vilāsikā, bhāṇaka, bhāṇikā, bhāṇī, rāsaka and hallīsaka. Of these, the following may be considered as a separate group, for they are exclusively dance compositions: goṣṭhī, ḍombī, rāsaka, nāṭyarāsaka and hallīsaka. To this group belongs one of the few surviving forms from this period, namely, rāsaka or rāsa, which is still practised in Gujarat and Manipur.

The use of the term uparūpaka thus reflects a gradually coalescing view of those forms of performing arts which required body movements

---

[52] A term very likely derived from this later came to denote a different presentation; see p. 185 *supra* and pp. 232-33 *infra*.

that were aesthetically pleasing as well as representational. In other words, these forms possessed characteristics of both dance and drama, though some were more dance than drama and some the other way about. As our survey here shows, till the early medieval period there was a great variety of such forms, not always clearly distinguished from one another and even when so distinguished, not greatly differing from one another. With the passage of time it became evident that these forms fell into two broad divisions, both mimetic in nature but one achieving its effect primarily by the representational functions of body movements, the other by their form, one emphasizing the verbal representation of events and character, the other appealing to the senses through physical action. Art forms of the first kind were considered to belong to a sub-category of drama proper, hence the term uparūpaka, while the other forms were placed under nṛtya, or mimetic dance. Thus, the development of the two broad categories marked a progressively clearer conception of the characteristics of dance as well as drama. It also meant that the classification of the performing arts was simplified, whereby the class names used earlier, except for lāsya, became part of the terminology of music rather than of drama.

The attempt to classify categories was, however, not restricted to the use of the terms nṛtya and uparūpaka. A similar trend towards definitive classification may be seen also in the attempt to distinguish the tradition of dancing described first by Bharata from the later, more broad-based and popular forms of the art. The next two chapters will examine how this distinction came about and what it meant in terms of the content and style of performance.

Chapter 6

BANDHA AND ANIBANDHA

During the period that started with Someśvara in the eleventh century and ended with Mahārāṇā Kumbhā in the fifteenth, that is, the second period of the evolution of the concept of dance, we find that the thought of these authors focused on the division of dance into two traditions, a division that was firmly entrenched by the end of this period. One tradition was termed mārga, and regarded as the central tradition established by Bharata, and the other deśī, the tradition which represented local and popular forms of dancing and which Bharata left out of his account. In this second period the most influential of all the authors was Śārṅgadeva who discussed deśī and continued to influence the authors in the third period of development.

In the third period, however, we find another development–a different kind of categorization of dancing. At least one author, Puṇḍarīka Viṭṭhala, draws our attention to another major development while describing dance traditions of different regions of his time.[1] In his work on dancing and dramaturgy, the *Nartananirṇaya,* written in the sixteenth century, he does not merely divide dance into the two traditions, but gives a full account of the deśī tradition, presenting material he evidently collected from different regions, showing the varieties of dancing that existed in his time. Quite often these descriptions offer full identifications of different styles.

[1]Puṇḍarīka Viṭṭhala is better known in the field of music and although his work on dancing, the *Nartananirṇaya,* has been known by name, neither a critical edition nor a critical study of this work has been done so far. An account of its content has been given by the present writer in her B. Litt. thesis and her book (Bose, 1964, 1970).

Information is given about which part of India the particular style came from, what language was used in the accompanying songs, and, at times, modes of presentation. By comparing his accounts of those styles with the styles practised today, it is possible to establish links between these styles. This text thus offers us a major breakthrough in understanding both the evolution and the continuity of the art of dance because it enables us to reconstruct the styles prevalent at a transitional period in the cultural history of India.

One important contribution of the *Nartananirṇaya* is the evidence we may draw from it to establish firmly the time of the origin of two major styles of India today, namely, Kathak and Odissi. There has always been some controversy about the evolution of these two styles. Dance historians in general are agreed that while the roots of Kathak go back to ancient Hindu culture, its present form is derived from dancing styles imported by Mughal rulers. There is no doubt that Kathak did absorb some Persian influence, but the case for that influence is overstated. This can be easily seen by comparing the detailed descriptions found in the *Nartananirṇaya* with the movements of Kathak. The style described in the *Nartananirṇaya* is, of course, not termed Kathak, a name that came into use much later, but the descriptions clearly show it to be the same as what we know today as Kathak.

The same historical perspective is lent by the *Nartananirṇaya* to the Odissi style. Odissi was in oblivion for a long time. Even during the renaissance of the dance, when Bharatanatyam was rediscovered and hailed as the true core of the authentic tradition of the art, Odissi remained unknown to the general public and even to many dancers and dance scholars. When eventually Odissi began to be performed in the early 1950s, its authenticity was called into question, some critics suggesting that it had been concocted by some interested performing artists of

Orissa.[2] But the *Nartananirṇaya* provides incontrovertible proof that as a distinct style Odissi goes back at least four centuries, although it was not then known as Odissi, a name that came into use much later, just as we find in the case of Kathak. Puṇḍarīka's discussion of these and other styles show a high degree of correspondence with present-day styles. The *Nartananirṇaya* thus marks a definite terminal point in the ancestry of today's classical Indian dancing.

The historic importance of the *Nartananirṇaya* has remained unacknowledged for two reasons: first, Puṇḍarīka has been traditionally known as an expert in music rather than dancing; secondly and surprisingly, most of the other texts of this third period, although written after the *Nartananirṇaya,* have followed the *Saṅgītaratnākara* in the main. As a result, the detailed information available in the *Nartananirṇaya* has remained unexamined.[3]

Before we examine the technical details of the styles described in the *Nartananirṇaya,* we must consider the categorization attempted in it. Throughout the history and evolution of dancing, its literature has been given to categorizing the art in many ways. Many of the categories used at one time or another seem of doubtful use since they overlap with others or are not distinct enough to be taken as individual categories. It is for this reason, no doubt, that most of such categories have disappeared from accepted usage and have no relevance to the art as it is practised today. However, the readiness of the authors of Sanskrit dance manuals to formulate categories indicates a sustained attempt to systematize the study of dancing by classifying its forms. One such attempt of particular historical significance is seen in the use of the terms bandha and

---

[2]Bose, N. "Odissi Dance today and its Exponents," *Classical and Folk Dances of India,* part iv,'Odissi,' p. 51.

[3]A critical edition is under preparation by the present writer.

anibandha. Applied to dancing, these terms appear first in the *Nartananirṇaya.* The author describes the two categories thus:

> कार्यं तत्र द्विधा नृत्तं बन्धकं चानिबन्धकम्
> गत्यादिनियमैर्युक्तं बन्धकं नृत्तमुच्यते
> अनिबन्धं त्वनियमाद . . . ॥
>
> (*NN.*39b)[4]
>
> Nṛtta can be of two kinds: bandha and anibandha. Bandhanṛtta is structured with gati etc. while anibandha comes from following no rule.

How these categories came into existence must be considered in the context of how dancing and its literature evolved. As we have seen in the previous chapters, in the earliest works the categories are few; it is in the later works that categories begin to multiply. The *Nāṭyaśāstra* of Bharata, the first and most influential of the texts on dance, drama and music, does not divide dancing into any categories. Bharata recorded only one kind of dancing: nṛtta, the kind that later came to be known as mārga or classical. He mentions the existence of popular, regional dance forms, forms later categorized as deśī.[5] Bharata obviously did not find them important enough to be included in his treatise. For several centuries after Bharata, manuals on music and dancing were virtual copies of the *Nāṭyaśāstra* and described nothing that was substantially new. However, as time went on, the manuals began to extend their accounts to include new forms and techniques of dancing. The texts began to include the deśī style as an individual, descriptive category around the seventh and eighth centuries

[4]Textual references are to the India Office Library Manuscript, London, unless otherwise noted.

[5]*NŚ.* 9. 163-64.

A.D. The *Bṛhaddeśī* by Mataṅga, written in the eighth century,[6] was the first text to deal with the deśī style in the field of music.[7] In the field of dance too deśī styles began to be mentioned around this time. And although Someśvara, from the eleventh century, was the first writer to give us a brief account of the deśī style, it is not until we arrive at the *Saṅgītaratnākara* by Śārṅgadeva that we find a systematic study of both mārga and deśī dance styles as separate categories.[8] The *Saṅgītamakaranda,* which also gives an account of one deśī style, may have been earlier but with a corrupt and undependably edited text we hardly get a picture clear enough to identify that style as a separate deśī style. However, from the description that it gives it seems likely that the style was a regional one that was practiced by prostitutes.[9]

A further subdivision occurred later when the terms bandha and anibandha were applied to types of dancing. Parallel terms with similar meanings but different forms–nibaddha and anibaddha–had already been in use in music to denote two parts of a musical composition, or prabandha. While both parts followed certain rules of structure and of development, anibaddha was comparatively loose in its structure since it was free of the regimen of tāla. By contrast, baddha was more rigorously constructed, bound as it was by the constraining patterns of tāla. These musical terms were first used in the *Nāṭyaśāstra* :

निबद्धं चानिबद्धं च येन तेन द्विधा स्मृतम् ॥

(*NŚ*.32. 28)

Nibaddha and anibaddha can be of two kinds.

---

[6]Katz, 1983, p. 59.

[7]अवालगोपालैः क्षितिपालैर्निजेच्छया ।
गीयते सानुरागेन स्वदेशे देशिरुच्यते ॥ (*Bṛhaddeśī*. 13.)

[8]*SR*. 7. 26-7; 749-50; 1207; 1278.

[9]*SMak*.4.

Later the *Bṛhaddeśī* and the *Saṅgītaratnākara* used them and the distinction was clearly drawn in both:

> निबद्धश्चानिबद्धश्च मार्गोऽयं द्विविधो मत:।
> आप्लापादि(?)निबद्धो य: स च मार्ग: प्रकीर्त्तित:॥
>
> (*Brhaddeśī.* 14)
>
> This mārga is said to be of two kinds, namely, nibaddha and anibaddha. That which is structured by ālāpa (?) etc.is called mārga.
>
> बद्धं धातुभिरङ्गैश्च निबद्धमभिधीयते।
> आलप्तिबन्धहीनत्वादनिबद्धमितीरिता॥
>
> (*SR.* 4. 5)
>
> Nibaddha is known by being structured with dhātus and [other] aṅgas. Anibaddha is so called because it is not structured with ālapti.

The distinction between nibaddha and anibaddha clearly represents one of the important principles by which ways of composing music may be differentiated. It is to this categorization that we owe the term ālāpa, which still carries the connotation of free improvisation within the given framework of a rāga.

Almost 1500 years after these terms came into use in music, Puṇḍarīka Viṭṭhala's work on dancing applied the terms bandha and anibandha to dancing,[10] attempting to draw a distinction between categories of dancing that reflected the spirit of the distinction made in music, though the terms did not exactly correspond in form or meaning to those used in music.

Before examining Puṇḍarīka Viṭṭhala's use of these terms it is necessary to note that the bulk of his work was in music. It is, therefore,

---

[10]Bose, 1970, p. 5.

not surprising that when he tried to distinguish categories of dancing by using as the differentiating principle the degree of improvisation permissible, he should have borrowed terms from his primary expertise, even though the parallel was not exact and the forms of the words were different.[11] It would seem that this is the sense in which this distinction came to be understood after Puṇḍarīka, for the only substantial work on dancing to be written after the *Nartananirṇaya*, the *Saṅgītadarpaṇa* by Dāmodara, repeats the usage and reproduces the discussion of the terms as in Puṇḍarīka's work.[12]

Puṇḍarīka uses the terms unambiguously. Bandhanṛttas are set pieces with every movement in their structured sequences clearly specified for the dancer. Given such detailed descriptions, a dancer trained in the appropriate style of dancing could reconstruct a composition perfectly, executing all the movements down to the minutest detail in precisely the sequence prescribed. The bandhnṛttas are, then, fully structured compositions that the dancer is required to reproduce unaltered, with no variations, no straying from the set choreography. Herein lies the significance of the term bandha, that is, a "closed" composition.

By contrast, anibandhanṛttas are flexible in both form and content within broadly specified frameworks of aesthetic purpose. The *Nartananirṇaya* does not describe any of the anibandhanṛttas in sufficient detail to allow us to reconstruct a full composition. What then was this anibandhanṛtta? On the basis of the scanty descriptions in *Nartananirṇaya*, anibandhanṛttas seem to be short dance-sequences, using which a dancer can choreograph her own piece. Thus, they have the same

---

[11] कार्यं तत्र द्विधा नृत्तं बन्धकं चानिबन्धकम् । (*NN.* 40a).
निबद्धश्चानिबद्धश्च मार्गोऽयं द्विविधो मतः । (*Bṛhaddeśī.* 14)
निबद्धमनिबद्धं च तद् द्वेधा निगदितं बुधैः । (*SR.* 4.4.).

[12] Dāmodara is believed to have been a court poet of Jahangir, which places him in the 17th century; see Krishnamachariar, 1974, p. 806.

function in the dancer's choreographic design as the karaṇas of the mārga tradition. But their structural principle is entirely different from that of karaṇas in that they are entirely flexible as to their components and structure while karaṇas are of course rigidly set structures. The *Nartananirṇaya* does not give details about the movements constituting the anibandhanṛttas but only discusses the movements in broad, general terms.

It would seem that the anibandhanṛttas were unlike any other dance pieces described in the literature before the *Nartananirṇaya*. Did they then represent a new, hitherto unrecorded style of dancing that differed from other post-mārga styles in being still uncodified and therefore allowing the dancer a far greater measure of freedom? Was the author trying to create for this new style a new category since it could not be fitted into any other, inasmuch as even the relatively new, deśī styles adhered to the accepted principle of prescriptive design and this new style did not? Evidently, the author was recording two different classes of dancing, the distinction between which demanded the use of two different terms. This hypothesis, and perhaps only this would explain the use of the terms bandha and anibandha and clarify their meaning as categories, bandhanṛttas denoting dances for which there already were prescribed rules, and anibandhanṛttas denoting dances for which there were none.

That this is more than mere speculation is suggested by the history of dancing. We find that a new style of dance, still unnamed but later to be known as Kathak, was indeed taking shape at this time, and that this style placed a greater emphasis on creating dances within the general structure of movements than on following a set regimen of technical details. This new style offered a new approach to dancing and appeared on the dance scene precisely at the time when the *Nartananirṇaya* was written.

On its part the *Nartananirṇaya* describes several entirely new dances, all of them deśī and all previously unreported, although it follows the *Saṅgītaratnākara* in describing some other deśī dances. When we look closely at the technique of the dance described under the anibandha category, we begin to see certain striking similarities with the technique of Kathak. One cannot say that the style described in the *Narananirṇaya* matches Kathak in every detail, but one may certainly view that style as the precursor to Kathak.

The historical context of the *Nartananirṇaya* makes this connection highly plausible. The text was part of the same cultural world of the Mughal court that nurtured Kathak. Indeed, the colophon states that the work was written by Puṇḍarīka Viṭṭhala for the delectation of the Emperor Akbar, the Mughal ruler :

> अकबरनृपरुच्यर्थं भूलोके सरलसङ्गीतम् ।
> कृतमिदं बहुतरभेदं सुहृदां हृदये सुखं भूयात् ॥
>
> (*NN.* 53b)

> In [this] world this simple saṅgīta is created [with] a lot of varieties in order to please the king Akbar. May it please the heart of the good-hearted ones.

By Akbar's time the ideals and techniques of Persian art were firmly entrenched in the cultural life of India, co-existing with varied native traditions. Puṇḍarīka declares that along with the regional styles of dancing he is describing the dance of the yavanas, in this case, the Persians:

> यत्नचेष्टाविरहितं तन्नृत्यं जक्कडी मतम् ।
> पारसीकैः पण्डितैस्तूद्ग्राहादिस्वरभाषया ।
> यद् गीतं जक्कडीसंज्ञं यवनानामतिप्रियम् ॥
>
> (*NN.* 53a)

> That dance is known as jakkaḍī which is devoid of effort and action. The song sung by the experts from Persia using udgrāha, svaras etc. and vernacular is known as jakkaḍī which is the favourite of the yavanas.

Since modern scholars believe that Kathak is influenced by Persian dance-forms, Puṇḍarīka's statement provides a strong argument to trace the ancestry of Kathak to the style he describes. The *Nartananirṇaya* seems, thus, to be the proper textual source for Kathak. This claim becomes stronger still on examining points of technique, as I shall shortly attempt.

Two arguments help to validate the hypothesis that Puṇḍarīka Viṭṭhala devised the anibandha category to classify the kinds of dances that eventually evolved as Kathak. First, what we now call Kathak represented in its early days a new principle of design, because as a style largely moulded by the Persian influence it was certainly outside the framework provided by Bharata. Thus, even though it could be viewed as a regional or deśī form, it had to be distinguished by being put into a special category.

Secondly, the similarities between the techniques of Kathak and anibandhanṛttas are most suggestive. Unlike other styles, Kathak does not prescribe in detail the movements it employs. This does not mean that Kathak does not use the movements that we find in other styles. It uses all the minor movements prescribed for the different parts of the body in the *Nāṭyaśāstra* just as the other styles do. But unlike the other styles Kathak does not have set compositions consisting of body movements, which are to be rigidly followed by the dancer. In Kathak, for instance, descriptions of dances do not identify particular constituent movements by name; rather, the descriptions identify general types of movements. The parallel with the anibandhanrttas found in the *Nartananirṇaya* is obvious. Even a brief comparison of the respective techniques and requirements of Kathak and anibandhanṛtta underscores the parallel.

The *Nartananirṇaya* has four chapters, one each on rhythm, drum, song and dance. In the chapter on rhythm, when the author specifies the tālas appropriate to the dance he describes, the technical terms that he uses, sādhanās in particular, match those used in Kathak today and listed by

Nirmala Joshi in her article, "Technical terms pertaining to Dance in general and used in Kathak."[13] These terms, which Joshi calls prāṇas, or the life of tālas, are almost identical with the different sādhanās mentioned in the chapter on tāla in the *Nartananirṇaya.* For instance, in Kathak, yati or the rhythmic arrrangement of the tempo is divided into five categories, samā, srotagatā, gopucchikā, pipīlikā and mṛdaṅgī. The *Nartananirṇaya* lists the same types of yatis similar in every detail, although it includes a sixth type, kharjurikā. Another term, kuvāḍa, used in Kathak to denote the climax of a complex rhythmic pattern is also found in the *Nartananirṇaya.*

This similarity offers good reason to believe that the style described in the *Nartananirṇaya* was something very much like Kathak, since it required musical elements similar to those needed for Kathak. The argument becomes even more persuasive when we examine the specifics of the dance technique. But first let us briefly consider the typical characteristics of Kathak as known today.

A major characteristic of Kathak is that although like other forms of classical dancing it follows the same basic rules for the movements of the individual parts of the body, it expects the dancer to find his or her individual way to elaborate those movements within certain aesthetic condition given. A good example may be taken from Maya Rao's article, "The Hastas in Kathak": "In Kathak the body as a whole is visualised as the prime medium of expression. . . . For instance, if the dancer intends to represent the moon, not only will his hands show the Ardha-chandra Hasta, but his body will also bend in an arch to suggest the idea of a crescent moon."[14] The same approach to elaborating and dramatizing

---

[13]Joshi, 1963."Technical terms pertaining to Dance in general and used in Kathak," *Classical and Folk Dances of India,* part. iii, 'Kathak,' pp. 8-9.

[14]Rao, 1963. "Hastas in Kathak," *Classical and Folk Dances of India,* part. iii, 'Kathak,' p. 45.

basic movements is found in the *Nartananirṇaya.* The description of a dance called lāvaṇī includes an almost identical movement in which the dancer bends her body from her waist in ardhacandra :

> समपादे स्थितं पात्रं कटिन्यस्तार्धचन्द्रकम् ।
> कटेरुपरि तत् कायं भ्रामयेल्लावणी तदा ॥
>
> (*NN.* 52b-53a)
>
> [When] the performer stands in samapāda with her waist bent in [the shape of] half-moon and she rotates her body [lit : upper part from her waist], it is lāvaṇī.

The description of nāmāvalī, an anibandhanṛtya, strongly supports the contention that in this kind of dancing only a general guideline was provided for the dancer:

> यथाभिनयसम्पन्नं विचित्रगतिसुन्दरम् ।
> तीवटिग्रहभेदेन लयतालसमन्वितम् ।
> नामावलीनृत्तमिदं नृत्येज्जनमनोहरम् ॥
>
> (*NN.* 51b-52a)
>
> Created with proper abhinaya, beautified with various gaits and distinguishing between tīvaṭī and graha [which are] filled with laya and tāla, this nāmāvalīnṛtya, which is pleasing to people should be danced.

This description, which gives the dancer broad, general directions rather than detailed, specific instructions, is typical of Kathak, in which the dancer is similarly guided. The striking feature of such a description is its lack of detail; but that is precisely the feature that makes the dance form flexible and permits the dancer the freedom to make creative choices in building an individual choreography.

Maya Rao also mentions a composition by Shambhu Maharaj, called "rang-manch ka tukra," which is performed to invoke the blessings of the presiding deity of the stage. Rao finds striking resemblance between this composition and the invocatory dance described in the *Saṅgītadarpaṇa.* [15] As a matter of fact, the dance first appeared in the *Nartananirṇaya,* from which the *Saṅgītadarpaṇa* has merely copied the description.

Two of the most distinctive movements of Kathak are chakkars and tatkars. A chakkar is a rapidly spinning movement while a tatkar means to stamp on the ground with one foot or both, and marking the rhythm with ankle bells. Chakkar can be identified as the chakrabhramarī mentioned in the *Nartananirṇaya,* which describes it as a spinning movement:

> चक्रभ्रमरिकाखण्डसूच्यर्धे चक्रवद् भ्रमात् ।
>
> (*NN.* 47b)
>
> Cakrabhramarī [is performed] by spinning [lit: moving round] like a wheel in the middle of khaṇḍasūcī.

It is true that the bhramarīs were known long before the time of the *Nartananirṇaya*–Bharata refers to them–but they were not given the prominence that they receive in the *Nartananirṇaya.* Revolving movements are of course integral to all dance styles, but in classical styles other than Kathak the movements are never fast enough, nor sustained enough to achieve the aesthetic form that a chakkar creates in Kathak. It is the speed of revolution that sets it apart and it is precisely this element of fast spinning, comparable to that of the pirouette, that we find in the description of chakrabhramarīs in the *Nartananirṇaya.*

In its discussion of revolving movements the *Nartananirṇaya* also describes tirapabhramarī:

---

[15] *Ibid.*

> तिरपभ्रमरी तिर्यक् द्वावंघ्री स्वस्तिकात् परम् ।
>
> (*NN.* 47b)
>
> [Revolving] obliquely with both the legs after crossing them is tirapabhramarī.

A similar movement termed as tirapa is found in Kathak as well.[16]

As for the tatkār, it clearly corresponds with the gharghara, of which details are given in both *Nartananirṇaya* and *Saṅgītaratnākara.* It was first mentioned in *Saṅgītaratnākara* as a feature of the deśī dance called peraṇī. A reference to it is also made in the *Nṛttaratnāvalī,* which refers to this movement as a feature of the deśī dance named preraṇa but gives no detail. In the *Nartananirṇaya* it is a part of cindunṛtta which is identified as a dance from the south.

> देशी द्राविडदेशस्य चिन्दुरित्यभिधीयते ।
>
> (*NN.* 49a)
>
> The deśi [dance] from the country of the Drāviḍas is known as cindu.

The *Saṅgītaratnākara* gives the distinctive feature of gharghara as:

> तत्र घर्घरिकावाद्ये वह्निर्घर्घरो मतः ॥
>
> (*SR.* 7. 1304)
>
> Of these, gharghara is known to be the special practice in making the sound of ankle-bells.

The action is further clarified in the *Nartananirṇaya*:

> यत्र किंकिणीकावाद्यैराहतिर्घर्घरो मतः । (*NN.* 50a)

---

[16] Vyas, 1963, "The Background of Kathak" *Classical and Folk Dances of India*, part. iii, 'Kathak,' p. 6.

> Where striking [the ground] to make [lit: with] the sound of the ankle bells [is done] it is known as gharghara.

Six varieties of ghargharas are described in the *Saṅgītaratnākara* and the *Nartananirṇaya.* These descriptions show that ghargharas closely resemble the tatkārs practised by Kathak dancers.[17]

Two more examples will strengthen the relationship between Kathak and anibandhanṛtta. The *Nartananirṇaya* abounds in descriptions of anibandhanṛtta that fit Kathak. A particularly persuasive example is the following:

> यावनीभाषया युक्तं यत्र गीतं धृताञ्चलम् ।
> कल्लादिगजराद्युक्तं त्वाहङ्गेन विभूषितम् ॥
> विदध्यान्नर्त्तनं नानालयत्रयविचित्रितम् ।
> कोमलाङ्गैर्यदा नृत्तं भ्रमर्यादिविराजितम् ॥
> सशब्दा च क्रिया यत्र ध्रुवशम्यादिभेदतः ।
> यत्नचेष्टाविरहितं तन्नृत्यं जक्कडी मतम् ॥
> पारसीकैः पण्डितैस्तूद्ग्राहादिस्वरभाषया ।
> यद् गीतं जक्कडीसंज्ञं यवनानामतिप्रियम् ॥
>
> (*NN.*52b-53a)

> Where the song is [sung by the dancer] in the language of the yavana, holding her veil, [words] uttered with kalla etc. and gajara etc.[18] and beautified with āhaṅga, the dance should be performed being adorned with various three layas. When [this] dance is

---

[17] *NN.* 49b-50a. Kalyanpurkar, 1963, "The Techniques of Kathak" *Classical and Folk Dances of India,* part. iii 'Kathak,' pp. 25-27.

[18] The technical terms are not clear here. They occur in no other text, nor has there been any light shed on them by musicolgists.

> performed with soft movements adorned by bhramarīs, where the kriyā (keeping time with hands) is done with sounded beat in accordance with the difference between dhruva and śamyā, that dance, which is devoid of effort and action, is known as jakkaḍī. The song sung by the experts from Persia using udgrāha,svaras etc. and vernacular is known as jakkaḍī which is the favourite of the yavanas.

This is an almost exact description of the ghungat gat, one of the best known compositions in Kathak.[19]

The *Nartananirṇaya* describes a certain anibandhanṛtta as follows:

> कुञ्चिताङ्गुलिना यत्र प्रसृताङ्गुष्ठकेन चेत् ।
> प्रसार्य जङ्घिकाकम्पं विचित्रद्रुतमाचरेत् ॥
> घर्घरीभिः समायुक्तं तदैतत् कुडुपं मतम् ।
>
> (*NN.* 52b)
>
> Where [the dancer] contracts her toes [lit: one of her toes] with the big toe extended, shakes her shank after extending it with various quick [movements] and with ghargharīs [that is, tinkling her ankle bells]it is known as kuḍupa.

Precisely this action can be recognized today in Kathak when the dancer beats a fast tattoo on the ground to create rhythmic sounds with her ankle-bells.

The correspondence between Kathak and anibandhanṛtta is important not only for discovering the roots of Kathak but also for understanding the value that came to be attached to improvisation in medieval times. In

---

[19] Rao,1963, "The Hastas in Kathak" *Classical and Folk Dances of India*, part. iii, 'Kathak,' p. 47.

contrast with the prescriptive nature of the descriptions found in the earlier texts, those in the *Nartananirṇaya* and its contemporaries allow the dancer more structural flexibility while retaining the basic movements described by Bharata and his successors. This difference in the approach to choreography is most strikingly shown in the use of the contrasted categories, bandha and anibandha. The descriptions of the anibandhanṛttas give us a general sense of the choreography but leaves the specific movements largely to the discretion of the dancer. In contrast, Puṇḍarīka Viṭṭhala describes the bandhanṛttas exhaustively, specifying every movement required as well as the sequence of the movements. Allowing–indeed encouraging–the dancer to choreograph parts of a recital according to personal choice was a new approach to dancing.

There can be little doubt that the categories bandha and anibandha mark a historical point in the evolution of Indian dancing at which established traditions and new forms existed side by side. The bandha category encompassed the styles that had been firmly defined and codified by long usage. Other styles, still fluid and evolving, were placed within the anibandha category. With the passing of time, as all styles lost their unfamiliarity and became more firmly entrenched in the corpus of Indian dancing, the distinction between the categories faded, eventually making them obsolete. However, the term bandha is still in use in a very limited way and later in this chapter we shall examine the dances to which it is applied.

The term anibandhanṛtta has gone entirely out of use. Why it has disappeared from the vocabulary of dancing while the term bandha still has a limited use needs to be considered. Undoubtedly, the main reason is historical, as explained above, but there may also be a reason related to the very nature of dancing as an art form. We noted earlier that both in music and dancing similar categories, anibaddha in music and anibandha in dancing, were formulated to denote forms that allowed the artist wide choices and architectonic individuality within broad guidelines. Such a form is entirely appropriate for music, which permits–indeed demands–a vast range of permutations of notes and improvised structures. That is why the anibaddha category has survived in music as has the term itself, though in popular use it is known as ālāpa.

But dancing is an art in which, once certain structural guidelines are accepted, the dancer cannot have anything like the degree of freedom in composing a dance that a musician has with a musical composition. A dancer may still show her creativeness in a composition by combining different sets of movements in a variety of ways or by exploring the emotional content of the composition but not with the degree of freedom that a singer or an instrumentalist enjoys. The concept of anibandha in dance, therefore, can not be equated with anibaddha in music. The creativity of a dancer is shown on an entirely different level. The frameworks of music and dance are so different that a parallel categorization is not possible. Hence the term anibandha became redundant in the field of dance and we find the term neither in theory nor in practice any longer.

When the term anibandha disappeared from the theory and practice of dance, the need for its converse, the category bandha, became meaningless. In most styles of dancing the term bandha is no longer found. Nevertheless, there are two present-day styles in which this term is used. These are Odissi and Manipuri. In Manipuri the term has very little significance and according to one of the most eminent teachers of this style, guru Bipin Singh, bandha is just another dance-sequence in the Manipuri repertoire, which calls for greater technical virtuosity than other sequences. Odissi is the only style today in which practising artists still use the term to mean a separate category of dance sequences. These follow the strictest possible rules of movements, sometimes producing acrobatic postures.

When we compare the bandhanṛtta found in the *Nartananirṇaya* with the bandhanṛtta as practised in the Odissi style, we find striking similarities. The bandhanṛtta of the *Nartananirṇaya* requires combinations created out of a base of sixteen karaṇas or short dance sequences;[20] the bandhanṛtta of Odissi requires seventeen.[21]

In Orissa the bandhanṛttas have been kept alive only by the goṭipuas (goṭi=one, pua=putra) or boy-dancers attached to some of the temples, whose numbers are rapidly dwindling. The few who are taught bandhanṛtta start their extremely rigorous training at the age of seven and perform till they are eighteen, after which their muscles no longer remain flexible enough to be able to do such acrobatic movements. The goṭipuas are dressed as girls and perform in religious festivals, though not inside the temples. These dances are generally quite acrobatic. The most famous Odissi guru of the present time, Kelucharan Mahapatra, is one of the very few living artists trained as a goṭipua. When in the course of an interview with the present author he was shown line drawings of the bandhanṛttas described in the *Nartananirṇaya,* Mr. Mahapatra confirmed that these were indeed the sequences he was taught. According to him, these dances are physically so difficult that girls are not trained in them and that they are seldom performed even by men, the more acrobatic of the dances being performed now mainly by the Chau dancers of Mayurbhanj in Orissa. The difficulty inherent in these dances was further confirmed for by another leading dancer of the Odissi style, Rani Karnaa,who said that as a female she was not trained in the bandhanṛtta by her guru.

A comparison of the technique of the bandhanṛtta of the *Nartananirṇaya* with the bandhanṛtta of the Odissi style suggests a close relationship between the two. In particular, there are remarkable similarities in the standing postures prescribed in the *Nartananirṇaya* with the basic standing postures used in the Odissi style: chaukā and tribhaṅgī in

---

[20]*NN.* 32a-33b.

[21]Khokar,1963, " Technique and Repertory," *Classical and Folk Dances of India,* part. iii, 'Kathak,' pp. 28-31.

Odissi are comparable to vaiśākha-sthāna and agratalasañcara-pada as described in the *Nartananirṇaya.* Some of the acrobatic postures found in the *Nartananirṇaya* are still in use: daṇḍapakṣam, lalāṭatilakam and niśumbhitam and several others are found both in Odissi and in Chau.

To the evidence taken from bandhanṛtta I may add three particularly telling examples of correspondence between Odissi and the movements described in the *Nartananirṇaya.* The text describes the use of hand gestures to express seven principal musical notes. Each note, according to the author, is a correlative of a bird or an animal, which is represented by hand gestures, as the following passage explains:

> मयूरचातकछागक्रौञ्चकोकिलदर्दूराः।
> गजश्च सप्त षड्जादीन् क्रमादुच्चारन्त्यमी॥
>
> (*NN.* 20b)[22]
>
> Peacock, rainbird, goat, heron, cuckoo, frog and elephant are the seven (notes starting with) ṣaḍja etc that should be recited in order. [सा=मयूर: peacock; रे=चातक: rainbird; गा=छाग: goat; मा=क्रौञ्च: heron; पा= कोकिल: cuckoo; धा=दर्दूर: frog and नि=गज: elephant.].

Secondly, there is a dance called baṭunṛtta, a particularly difficult dance in the repertory of Odissi, that involves both non-representational dance and mimetic dance. In the *Nartananirṇaya* we come across the description of a dance called baṭu. Although it is a brief description, one can see how difficult it is. It can not be a mere coincidence that the same term should not only occur both in the *Nartananirṇaya* and in Odissi but

---

[22] Reference to this verse is to the Ms. in the Asiatic Society Library Manuscript, Calcutta.

designate dances involving similarly difficult poses. The brief description in the*Nartananirṇaya* is as follows:

> जानुभ्यां भूमिलग्नाभ्यां पद्भ्यां वा मण्डलाकृतिः ॥
> नम्रपृष्ठं लताहस्तौ पात्रं भ्रमणमाचरेत् ।
> तदासौ बटुरित्युक्तः सूर्यमण्डलवद् गतिः ॥
>
> (*NN.* 53a)

> When the performer revolves touching the ground either with both the knees or with both the legs describing a circle [while her] back is bent [backwards] with her hands in latā then it is known as baṭu [and its] movement is like [moving] in the orbit of the sun.

This description, insufficient as it is, corresponds to the pattern of movements in the baṭu dance of Odissi. Further evidence is provided by the following description of a bandhanṛtta in the *Nartananirṇaya,* a karaṇaneri:

> झम्पातालः सगोपुच्छः हस्तकोऽप्यलपल्लवः ।
> पार्श्वोर्ध्वजानुनी दण्डपक्षं तलविलासितम् ॥
> विद्युद्भ्रान्तं ततश्चन्द्रावर्त्तनामं निशुम्भितम् ।
> ललाटतिलकं पश्चाल्लतावृश्चिकसंज्ञकम् ॥
> नवभिः करणैरेभिः क्रमात् सव्यापसव्यतः ।
> कृत्वालीढे स्थितिर्यत्र नेरिः करणपूर्वकः ॥
>
> (*NN.* 43b-44a)

> [The dancer dances] in jhampātāla in gopucchayati. One of her hands is in alapallava. Pārśvajānu, ūrdhvajānu, daṇḍapakṣa, talavilāsita, vidyudbhrānta, candrāvarta, niśumbhita, lalaṭatilaka and latāvṛścika: where these nine karaṇas are performed one after the other facing the left and then the right in order and she

finishes off standing in the ālīḍha sthāna, it is Karaṇaneri.

This sequence is one of the twelve ūrupas described in the *Nartananirṇaya.* Ūrupas are sequences formed with the karaṇas prescribed for bandhanṛtta and are danced to specified varieties of yati, tāla and laya. Specific sthāna, cārī and hand gestures characterize them. Using these twelve ūrupas a dancer can reconstruct a composition as described in the *Nartananirṇaya,* which will not be far from what we see being performed by artists today. In Odissi we do find similar compositions. Such close correspondences are now proving to be of particular interest to many dancers and teachers who are trying to reconstruct older dance forms by following the Sanskrit manuals. In Tamilnadu and Orissa, eminent dancers and teachers such as Padma Subrahmanyam and Kelucharan Mahapatra are drawing upon the śāstras to choreograph their dance pieces. Dharu, a type of bandha dance from Andhra described in the *Nartananirṇaya* is being reconstructed by the famous dancer Guru Chinnasatyam in Mysore. The term dharu is used by Kuchipudi dancers of Andhra.

The categories known as bandha and anibandha therefore remain relevant not only to the dance scholar but to the practising dancer. As functional terms they may be of little use, since the distinction between codified and uncodified dance forms has largely disappeared. But the categorization attempted by Puṇḍarīka Viṭṭhala affords scholars valuable knowledge about a vital stage in the evolution of dancing in India, a stage which was marked by the infusion of new styles and techniques that characterized the deśī tradition.

Chapter 7

THE DEŚĪ TRADITION

The deśī tradition was first recorded in detail by Someśvara in his *Mānasollāsa.* As a separate, distinct tradition deśī is mentioned earlier in the *Daśarūpaka* but no details are given there. Earlier still, Bharata recognized in his *Nāṭyaśāstra* the existence of regional variations but he neither described them nor referred to them as belonging to a separate tradition called deśī.[1] In the entire period between the *Nāṭyaśāstra* and the *Mānasollāsa* we come across only one other manual on dancing, the *Viṣṇudharmottara Purāṇa,* and this too does not record or refer to any deśī tradition. Similarly, Abhinavagupta is silent about the deśī tradition. As we have noted earlier in the fourth and fifth chapters of the present study, many works of the classical period, from manuals to literary compositions, refer to a number of mimetic dances but no detailed description of a dance presentation ever appears in any of these works.

This picture changes around the eleventh and twelfth centuries when scholars begin to include the deśī tradition along with the older tradition in their manuals on dancing. With the growth of the popularity of dancing and the inclusion of the deśī as a tradition in the early medieval literature on poetics and musicology, that is, between the tenth and the fifteenth centuries, a number of manuals appear on the subject when art was flourishing in all of its branches, in music, dance, sculpture, architecture and painting. This interest in recording the later styles of dancing continued through the succeeding centuries into the nineteenth.

---

[1] *NŚ.* 9. 163-4

The description of the regional tradition differs from the mārga tradition in two ways: first, by putting its emphasis on the style of presentation rather than on the content of the composition, and second, by concentrating on the use of more acrobatic movements. As for the content, in structuring a dance piece the deśī tradition had very little to offer that was new. Mārga and deśī cannot, therefore, be judged to be exclusive of one another in terms of their components. They should rather be seen as different stylistic approaches that grew through time into separate traditions of the same basic art form. This relationship is clearly seen in the descriptions of the two traditions in the dance manuals of the medieval period.

In the first manual of this period, the *Mānasollāsa* (early 12th century), the deśī tradition is described only briefly, but a fuller picture appears a century later in the *Saṅgītasamayasāra.* An even more elaborate description of deśī appears still later, in the *Saṅgītaratnākara,* which was written in the late thirteenth century. The *Nṛttaratnāvalī,* which came a few years after the *Saṅgītaratnākara* and which deals only with dance, provides the most elaborate description of both the mārga or classical and the deśī or regional traditions of dancing. These four texts give us the first introduction to the deśī dance tradition. The deśī dance they describe is based on the framework of the tradition of Bharata, which is constructed first by laying down the groundwork of dance compositions with smaller movements and gradually progressing to build up the whole composition by forming small units consisting of individual movements and moving on to the large units of a composition. In deśī, this basic method of constructing a composition did not change, nor–generally speaking–did the stock of body movements, but the larger units of movements included more varieties of smaller movements in the deśī tradition and these varieties of smaller movements were more acrobatic in general. Structurally, this is what changed in the appearance of a deśī dance, as we shall find in the four early works mentioned above.

To begin with, these four texts will be examined to trace the progression in the content, in the styles of presentation, and in the treatment of the subject by the authors who wrote on deśī. With the exception of the *Bharatārṇava*, the later texts of this period more or less follow the same pattern. Not all the manuals on deśī record a full dance presentation. The *Mānasollāsa,* for instance, does not give us any description of a composed dance piece. The *Saṅgītasamayasāra* is the first text to describe deśī dance pieces. Its descriptions of the dances include references to music, rhythm, tempo and styles of presentation but no detailed description of individual movements. This text introduces a new class of features of the presentation, calling them elements of deśī, which are absent in the Bharata tradition. The later texts also describe this new element in their description of the deśī tradition. The *Saṅgītaratnākara* describes dances in a similar manner with further details of the musical accompaniment. The *Nṛttaratnāvalī* 's more elaborate descriptions have more information on the technical details of presentation but not on individual movements and it repeats the emphasis on the musical accompaniment along with the rhythm and tempo employed. The component movements of a composition, however, hardly ever appear in the descriptions of the deśī tradition found in this period of our study. The task of comparing the movements constituting the mārga and deśī styles is thus a difficult one.

This difficulty is further compounded by the fact that not all the details of the mārga style are known. By the early medieval period the tradition recorded by Bharata, was established and recognized as mārga, a term first used by Dhanañjaya to distinguish between two traditions. Beside Bharata's account of the older tradition we have the only other extant record in the *Viṣṇudharmottara Purāṇa.* In contrast, regional styles, termed as deśī, have been recorded by a number of authors who give us a varied picture of the deśī styles. These authors also describe the mārga tradition but in doing so merely follow the *Nāṭyaśāstra*. The earliest record of a dance presentation appears in the fourth chapter of the *Nāṭyaśāstra* which forms the preliminary part of a dramatic presentation, that is, the part in which the gods are invoked. It includes nṛtta and abhinaya. Unfortunately, even Bharata does not give detailed descriptions of the movements to be employed in the presentation, nor does he record any specific rhythm and tempo to be used in this presentation. Nevertheless, the basic difference between the descriptions of the presentations of the two traditions, I believe, becomes apparent when we closely compare them. Bharata describes the structure of the presentation but is silent about the presentation technique or specific music. Also, he speaks only briefly on the aesthetic aspects of a presentation. On the contrary, discussing these seems to be a growing concern of the writers on deśī.

To understand Bharata's view of dancing we shall first examine how he describes the presentation in the fourth chapter of the *Nāṭyaśāstra,* a performance meant for the offering of flowers, that is, puṣpāñjali, at the beginning of a play in order to please and invoke the gods. This presentation involves both abstract dance movements (that is, non-mimetic movements) with drum accompaniment, and mimetic action set to songs. Bharata describes no presentation that is constituted exclusively of the abstract movements known as karaṇas and aṅgahāras. In describing this preliminary presentation he does not specify the names of movements to be employed. The only specific name given by Bharata is that of a posture, vaiśākha sthāna, mentioned in this context as the opening posture of this presentation.[2] He does not specify any music for the presentation as do the works on deśī while describing the dance presentations. Bharata leaves the actual choreography of a dance piece as well as the accompanying music to the imagination of a dancer or a choreographer. The presentation is described in the following manner: a female dancer performs nṛtta to the playing of drums, offers flowers, moves around,

[2] Vaiśākha sthāna happens to be the basic posture of the Odissi style of today.

bows to the gods and mimes the meaning of a song without the accompaniment of drums. After this, she goes out and a group of dancers enter and perform various formations resembling the emblems of various gods, after which they make their exit. The main dancer enters again and repeats her performance of nṛtta and abhinaya and exits. The others again enter in the same manner as before and repeat their dance. Their performance is devoid of miming.[3] All of this is repeated again. The entire presentation is a repetition of nṛtta and abhinaya by one female dancer followed by the performance of nṛtta by a group of female dancers.[4] This presentation seems to be similar to what we see in the varṇam of the bharatanāṭyam style of today except for the part played by the group of dancers.[5] However, since the description of puṣpāñjali lacks specific instructions for the movements or the music, we do not know which movements constituted the nṛtta portion, nor do we have any idea of the specific music or rhythm used. All that we can say is that it seems to indicate that a scope for improvisation was permitted within the prescribed framework even in Bharata's time but, as we shall see when we examine the deśī tradition, such improvisation was acceptable here in a more restricted sense than in the deśī tradition.

The analysis of the contents of the dance presentations described in the later texts seems to indicate that the dancers had greater freedom to improvise, because they were allowed to begin improvising at an earlier stage of composition than in the mārga tradition. Apart from this greater freedom, the emphasis on one other aspect of presentation gradually becomes more and more apparent. Not only do these authors of the early

---

3 paryastaka or abhinayaśūnya (non-representational) dance is recommended. *NŚ*. 4. 280; *AB*. 1956, Vol. I, p. 188.

4 *NŚ*. 4. 272-291.

5 Padma Subrahmanyam, the noted performer and scholar of the Bharatanāṭyam style, is experimenting with Bharatanāṭyam danced by groups of dancers.

medieval period often emphasize the mimetic aspect of the presentation, they also describe the accompanying songs and music, often even specifying the tāla. The overall presentation technique, especially its aesthetic aspects, seems to be of greater concern for the writers on deśī. This approach is different from the way Bharata describes dancing. When we take a closer look at the specific dance pieces described in the later texts it seems that those who developed regional variations based their repertoire on the movements recorded in the *Nāṭyaśāstra* but combined the movements in their own ways rather than in a set pattern when forming dance units (or karaṇas) and dance-sequences (or aṅgahāras). Bharata gave directions that guided the dancer to the stage of the formation of the basic dance-units as well as the basic dance-sequences. His approach permitted the dancer only the permutation and combination of a number of the basic dance-sequences. Creativity was based on the use of such groups of basic dance sequences. However, while describing the presentation mentioned above, Bharata does not specify any dance unit, movement or sequence except for the introductory posture of the performance. The presentation is neither described as a dance piece nor is it described as a mimed piece but as a combination of both. Nor does Bharata offer any detailed guidelines to the aesthetic qualities of the presentation, which are of far greater concern to the later authors of the early medieval period. Their interest in these qualities is seen, for instance, in their use of a variety of terms to describe this aspect of presentations, whereby they attempt to specify the aestheic impact. Bharata does mention sauṣṭhava or grace and pramāṇa or harmony in a presentation, but he devotes little time to it. By contrast, the later authors emphasize the aesthetics of a presentation and the greater number of terms they use testifies to the rise of a more elaborate set of ideas in the field.[6]

---

[6] See Bose, 1970, pp. 165-66.

We may now attempt to examine these later texts chronologically to see the evolution of dance-movements in the tradition as recorded by the writers on deśī. The *Mānasollāsa,* the earliest text on deśī, shows us that it follows the basic framework laid down by Bharata and this seems to be an accepted pattern through the entire history of the writings on dancing. Although Someśvara's description of the deśī tradition is comparatively brief, his contribution in defining the parts of the body is important. To the existing division of the body into aṅgas and the upāṅgas, he adds one more division, the pratyaṅgas. We find that after this text appeared, all the authors of the medieval period, except for Pārśvadeva in his *Saṅgītasamayasāra* and Rāmacandra and Guṇacandra in their *Nāṭyadarpaṇa,* began to describe the body parts under these three divisions. However, this was only a reclassification: it did not materially change the movements. The movements of the smaller body parts, previously known as the upāṅgas, now came to be placed under two categories, the upāṅgas and the pratyaṅgas, while the category of major limbs, the aṅgas, remained unaltered. The descriptions of the smaller units of movements by Someśvara show us that new movements were added to the same class-name found in the *Nāṭyaśāstra.* but under deśī heading. For instance, in describing the basic movements of cārī and sthāna, the later authors added more varieties to the tradition recorded by Bharata.

Can we not say, then, that these later authors merely added to the tradition of Bharata rather than branching out from it? In what way did they differ then and why was the tradition they described termed deśī? The answer is that the difference was on the emphasis: the deśī tradition differed from the tradition of Bharata because the deśī dances involved more leaping and acrobatic movements and the writers describing them insisted on greater attention to aesthetic qualities. No new categories were created for these acrobatic movements, although new–one might say enhanced–varieties of sthānas, cārīs and even a few karaṇas of the deśī type involving leaps and acrobatic movements appeared in the *Mānasollāsa.* The writers on deśī dances remained content with the established class-names for such movements, namely, sthānas, cārīs and karaṇas.

The texts of our period seem to have been mainly interested in recording the movements of the parts of the body and their smaller units in course of describing the new regional varieties. The descriptions of the deśī cārī, sthāna and maṇḍala occur in all the later texts but the basic dance-units or karaṇas of the deśī variety are not. As for the aṅgahāras or basic dance-sequences of the deśī variety, they are described only in the *Bharatārṇava,* being absent in the other texts even when a composed dance-piece is described with the accompanying music. However, this approach of not describing the dance movements in a choreographed piece is not much different from what we find in the description of the puṣpāñjali of Bharata. Still, the consistent absence of descriptions of the entire set of aṅgahāras in the deśī tradition tells us that the regional varieties may not have used the aṅgahāras recorded in the *Nāṭyaśāstra.* Instead, the deśī tradition grew in a different direction where the choreography depended less on set units of movements taken from Bharata's tradition.

The interest in acrobatic compositions that characterized the deśī tradition grew through time. We find that in later medieval times the authors attempted to describe dance pieces that often required new combinations of smaller movements to produce new varieties of dance-units or karaṇas, often involving leaps and acrobatic movements. Such dance-units are called deśī karaṇas, or quite often, utplutikaraṇas, a name that indicates that they involve leaps. The *Mānasollāsa,* the *Saṅgītasamayasāra,* the *Saṅgītaratnākara* and the *Nṛttaratnāvalī,* all describe these deśī karaṇas. However, the *Mānasollāsa* describes only a few, whereas the later texts record a great many more.

The distinctive features of the deśī varieties of movements involving jumps and acrobatic movements become clear when the movements described in these texts are examined. To begin with, we shall take a few instances from the *Mānasollāsa* of Someśvara to describe them and compare them with the tradition of Bharata. Someśvara describes the deśī karaṇa named eṇapluta where the dancer jumps and performs sūcī in the air (*Mānas.*16.4.1396-97). Again, in the deśī añcita karaṇa the dancer stands in sama and then jumps straight up (*Mānas.*16.4.1384), and in the deśī antarālaga karaṇa the dancer jumps while arching her back and keeping her head between her shanks (*Mānas.* 16. 4. 1388). In the tradition of Bharata there are some difficult and acrobatic karaṇas like gaṅgāvataraṇa where the feet are raised with the soles turned up and the hands turned down in tripatākā while the head is bent. The whole body rests on the hands (*NŚ.* 4. 168-69). Or, we may take the vidyudbhrānta karaṇa, where one foot is moved in an arc backward and then extended and arched to touch the head and the dancer revolves. (*NŚ.* 4. 125-26). Thus, some acrobatic karaṇas can be cited from the *Nāṭyaśāstra* but few karaṇas in it involve such difficult movements. Besides, they seldom involve leaps which seems to be the most important feature of the deśī. On the other hand, the deśī karaṇas always contain acrobatic and leaping movements. Even in the descriptions of the sthānas and cārīs we find that the deśī varieties use more jumps and acrobatic movements compared to those in Bharata's tradition.[7]

We must also note that the *Mānasollāsa* is concerned only with the basic movements and a few deśī karaṇas, that is, the components of larger dance units and not with dances in their entirety. Because its interest lies in recording the smaller units of movement, it describes the deśī varieties of sthāna, cārī and karaṇa. But large compositions of any kind using these movements are not its concern.

It is not until the *Saṇgītasamayasāra* of the fourteenth century that we find any description of a complete dance. This text not only describes

---

7 *Ibid.* chapters 5 and 6.

specific dance pieces but adds a number of new movements of the cārī, the sthāna and the karaṇas of the deśī variety, all of which involve complicated leaping movements.[8] In the beginning of his chapter on dancing, the author Pārśvadeva mentions two kinds of presentation, nṛtta and nāṭya. He states that he is going to describe only āṅgīka or body movements, a class of movements that is of particular relevance for nṛtta. When he finishes describing these movements he proceeds to describe modes of presentation and finally to fully composed dance pieces. Such pieces he calls deśīnṛtya and not deśīnṛtta. The four complete compositions which he describes, calling them deśīnṛtyas, are peraṇa, pekkhaṇa, guṇḍalī and daṇḍarāsa (*SSam.* 7.132; 7. 217-47). Peraṇa may be the same as the preraṇa described by Abhinavagupta but it is hard to get a full picture of latter from his cryptic description, and hence it is difficult to be certain that the two were the same. It is likely that Abhinavagupta's preraṇa was not a dance proper but it may well have developed as a dance by the time when Pārśvadeva recorded it. Abhinavagupta quotes the cirantanas on a type of minor drama involving dance and music which was named preraṇa and which he describes as a farcical play, full of riddles. The peraṇa of Pārśvādeva calls for five components, which are nṛtta, kaivāra, gharghara, vāgaḍa and gīta. He describes nṛtta as consisting of lāsya and tāṇḍava, which are based on rhythm and tempo. This definition is different from previous definitions of nṛtta found in the *Nāṭyaśāstra* and in the *Viṣṇudharmottara Purāṇa.* Nevertheless, the basic idea of nṛtta does not seem to be different. Kaivāra is praising the king by praising his ancestors. Gharghara is stamping the ground with the feet in ankle bells to mark the rhythm. Vāgaḍa is the miming of farcical or ludicrous characters.[9] Finally, gīta, the last feature of peraṇa (the term gīta here is used as a technical feature peculiar to preraṇa, very likely a set musical

---

[8] *SSam.*7.126-92.

[9] This feature resembles preraṇa described in the *Abhinavabhāratī* (*NŚ.* Vol. I, p.181).

piece), denotes a song sung according to the rules of a pure or mixed rāga, complete with ālāpa (*SSam.* 7.217.-22). The details of the instrumental music to accompany are also given with the rhythm and time-beat specified(*SSam.* 7.223-25).

The other two dances, pekkhaṇa and guṇḍalī, are the most commonly described in all the texts dealing with deśī. They are described along with accompanying songs and instrumental music, rhythm and time-beat (*SSam.* 7.225-36). These songs can be of three types [10] and all of them can be applied to the two above mentioned dances.

No song is prescribed for the last deśīnṛtya described, called daṇḍarāsa, but the instrumental music along with the rhythm and tempo and the number of dancers dancing with sticks are mentioned (*SSam.* 7.240-47). The first three dance pieces described by Pārśvadeva call for abstract movements mixed with mimetic movements. Pekkhaṇa and gauṇḍalī are described with accompanying vocal and instrumental music. The fourth dance, daṇdarāsa, requires no miming but is likely to draw upon some Kṛṣṇa legend, as we gather from the later texts on dancing as well as from other literature. Daṇḍarāsa and its connection with the Kṛṣṇa story cycle has been discussed in a previous chapter while discussing the minor dramatic types that are described mainly in the works on poetics.[11] However, the *Saṇgītasamayasāra* is silent about daṇḍarāsa's connection with Kṛṣṇa. The association of Kṛṣṇa with daṇḍarāsa may have developed later when stories of Kṛṣṇa became popular in the western regions of India.

The *Saṅgītasamayasāra* adds a vital piece of information to the description of the deśī tradition when it lists what it calls the nineteen aṅgas or elements of deśī. These elements are not physical components but

---

[10] These are śuddha (pure), citra (varied) and sālaga (based on pure, chāyālaga>sālaga) *SSam.* 7.229-34.

[11] See pp. 187-88 *supra.*

modes of presentation particular to the deśī style. This emphasis upon the mode of presentation shows the basic difference between the writers on deśī and Bharata (and his immediate followers) in their respective approaches to dancing. Even though Bharata describes body movements in detail in the context of āṅgikābhinaya (that is, using the body in acting), he never discusses the manner of performing the movements. By contrast, the description of the deśī aṅgas in the *Saṅgītasamayasāra* shows the reader the qualities that characterize the movements.

The terms used by Pārśvadeva are mostly in the regional languages and not in Sanskrit. Most of them refer to delicate modes. These nineteen aṅgas of deśī, according to Pārśvadeva, are the following: mukharasa (facial appearance created by make-up, garlands and dress), sauṣṭhava (grace produced by proper and erect stance), lali (charm), bhāva (expression), tūkalī(swinging movement in rhythm), anumāna (miming while moving in specific gatis), pramāṇa (harmony), jhaṅkā (moving the body, which is raised to the left and to the right), revā (the head and the corners of the eyes moved in emotion), surekhatva (dancing without ludicrous movements), aṅga (performance of tāṇḍava), anaṅga (performance not dependant on tāṇḍava), ḍhāla (expressing emotion by a female dancer), dhillāyī(delicate and relaxed slow movement or a standing relaxed posture), namani[12] (bending down with ease even while performing difficult movements), kittu (moving the arms and the breasts delicately in rhythm), tarahara (quick movements of the breasts, the motion reaching upto the arms), ullāsa (the body moved upwards following the instrumental music) and finally sthāpana (the final stance producing beauty, grace and creating a symmetry of lines with difficult movements). Pārśvadeva remarks that both nāṭya and nṛtta depend entirely on sauṣṭhava, without which beauty cannot be created (*SSam.* 7. 199-200). He also states that delicate movements are dependent specially

[12] Tavaṇi in the Trivandrum edition of the *SSam*. 6. 208.

on two features, lali and bhāva, that is, charm and expression (*SSam.* 7. 208).

Bharata is not entirely silent on the manner of presentation but his treatment does not emphasize it as a technical requirement. When he uses the two terms, sauṣṭhava and pramāṇa (*NŚ.*10.94), he takes them as general qualities of presentation rather than as the technical aspects of a presentation. The closest successor to the *Nāṭyaśāstra* is the *Viṣṇudharmottara Purāṇa,* which does not mention qualities of presentation, nor does Someśvara. Pārśvadeva, however, brings them to the forefront when he calls them deśyaṅgas or features of deśī.

The same emphasis on presentation appears in the text that comes next, the *Saṅgītaratnākara* by Śārṅgadeva. It does not use the term deśyaṅga but describes ten deśī lāsyāṅgas, that is, features of deśī lāsya, namely, delicate modes of presentation, sometimes abstract and sometimes mimetic. These are different from the lāsyāṅgas of the Bharata tradition, regarding which Śārṅgadeva is silent. Lāsyāṅgas of the Bharata tradition, as we have mentioned earlier in chapter 4, are part of dramatic presentations and as such are not relevant in the context of dance.[13] These lāsyāṅgas of Bharata are quite different from the nineteen deśī aṅgas described in the *Saṅgītasamayasāra,* from the ten deśī lāsyāṅgas described in the *Saṅgītaratnākara,* and from the forty-six deśī lāsyas in the *Nṛttaratnāvalī.*

The diversity of the accounts of these movements shows that although the deśī tradition depended upon the body movements mentioned by Bharata and other early authors, in some cases the deśī tradition also added to the stock by considerably elaborating upon the basic movements described by Bharata. A case in point is the *Saṅgītasamayasāra*'s inclusion of five bhramarīs or revolving movements as a separate set of movements, which is a new addition to the dance tradition. Bharata's

---

[13] See pp. 145-46 *supra.*

tradition described a bhramarī merely as a variety of cārī, which is a revolving movement performed with one leg. It seems that from the time when *Saṅgītasamayasāra* recorded bhramarī as a separate set of movements, they gained major importance and became a common feature of the deśī tradition. However, the *Saṅgītasamayasāra* does not describe the five bhramarīs that its author mentions (*SSam.* 7.193-4). The *Saṅgītaratnākara* is the first text to describe the movements of bhramarīs in detail. It is apparent that in the styles from the south bhramarīs were important features, hence their being recorded in the *Saṅgītaratnākara,* in the *Nṛttaratnāvalī* and in the *Nartananirṇaya* [14] In today's Indian styles, however, the styles that have retained bhramarīs are those from the north, Kathak and Manipuri, although these styles delineate bhramarīs in two different ways. Kathak has spinning movements while Manipuri has slower, revolving movements which involves covering larger space.[15]

Śārṅgadeva's account, again, shows how the deśī tradition was being expanded, though on the groundwork of Bharata's tradition. Besides describing the bhramarīs and deśī lāsyāṅgas, Śārṅgadeva also distinguishes between two traditions of presentation, one consisting of what he calls the śuddhapaddhati or pure method, and the other consisting of two deśī forms named peraṇi and gauṇḍalī. By the time Śārṅgadeva wrote his text, these two dances seem to have been established in the traditions of deśī and they remained part of the deśī technique from the beginning of the history of deśī dancing till the eighteenth century, as evident in the literature of dancing.[16] Śārṅgadeva, like Someśvara and Pārśvadeva, describes the

---

14 *SR.* 7.775-82; *NR.*5. 83-99; *NN.* 47b.

15 Chakkars or spinning movements are vital to the kathak style (Kalyanpurkar, 1963, p. 24) and revolving movements are vital to cāli, the basic dance of the Manipuri style(Chatterjee, 1978, p. 226).

16 Guṇḍalī and peraṇī appear in all the texts, starting with the *Saṅgītasamayasāra* and ending with the *Saṅgītasārasaṁgraha.* Evidently, in Andhra Guru Vempati

movements of the parts of the body following Bharata. But he adds more varieties of deśī cārīs, sthānas and karaṇas to the existing lists in the two former writers on deśī. He records nine bhramarīs and includes them in his list of deśī karaṇas.

Apart from making these additions, Śārṅgadeva demonstrates a strong concern for the overall qualities of presentation, which is expressed by his interest in rekhā, defined by him in the following lines:

> शिरोनेत्रकरादीनामङ्गानां मेलने सति ।
> कायस्थितिर्मनोहारी रेखा प्रकीर्तिता ॥ (*SR.* 7. 1216)
> Rekhā is said to be the attractive position of the body [when there is a] the harmonious combination of the movements of parts of the body such as the head, the eyes and the hands.

According to Śārṅgadeva, then, rekhā is the composite image of the lines inscribed on the mind's eye by the movements of the body at any given moment.

In addition to his interest in rekhā he was also aware of the need for yet another intangible quality, one that was known as the sauṣṭhava of a presentation, about which he says:

> कटी जानुसमा यत्र कूर्परांसशिरः समम् ।
> उरः समुन्नतं सन्नं गात्रं तत्सौष्ठवं भवेत् ॥ (*SR.* 7. 1037)
> Where the waist, the knee are kept in straight [line], the elbows, the shoulders, the head are held straight, the chest is raised and the body rests in sanna [=resting in a natural position], that is sauṣṭhava.

Cinnasatyam of the Kuchipudi style is trying to revive peraṅi, which, according to him, never really died out.

It is clear from Śārṅgadeva's writing that by his time it was customary for theorists of dancing to speak of two separate traditions of dancing, for he speaks of the "pure" method of dancing and the deśī method. As we have seen, this distinction is also recognized by Dhanañjaya, Pārśvadeva and Śārṅgadeva's contemporary, Jāya Senāpati. The contrast between the two as he understands them is evident from his description of a dance in the pure mode and two in the deśī. The pure dance he describes is the same puṣpāñjali or flower offering that we find in Bharata. Like Bharata he starts with the arrangement of the stage and the description of the most important person among the spectators. However, unlike the puṣpāñjali Bharata describes, which is performed alternately by a single dancer and a group of dancers and which requires both nṛtta and abhinaya, Śārṅgadeva's puṣpāñjali involves only one dancer. The initial posture recommended for the dance by Śārṅgadeva is samapāda (vaiśākha sthāna in Bharata) which, incidentally, is the initial stance of the Bharatanāṭyam style today. Like Bharata, Śārṅgadeva does not offer any more details of the body movements required but says that all three kinds of nartanas (त्रिविधं नर्तनं. . . .) should be applied in this presentation (*SR*.7.1269). Śārṅgadeva is more interested in the technical details of the musical accompaniment, music being his chief interest, and he says that the accompaniment for puṣpāñjali follows the classical tradition (*ŚR*. 7. 1260-73).The musical composition that accompanies the presentation is described in full detail. The puṣpāñjali of Śārṅgadeva seems to have come from a tradition which may have evolved out of what Bharata had recorded in his *Nāṭyaśāstra* but is certainly different from it.

Of the two deśī styles that Śārṅgadeva places in a category distinct from the śuddhapaddhati or pure method, gauṇḍalī is described first. This dance seems to be a presentation involving the delicate lāsyāṅgas and is performed by a single dancer. Following the approach of his predecessors in the medieval period, Śārṅgadeva gives details of the accompanying vocal and instrumental music, complete with specific names of rāgas and tālas, but gives no details of the dance technique. He tells us that this dance can be performed in two different ways: either the dancer may dance to a song sung by a singer, or she may herself sing while dancing. This seems to be a graceful dance from the Karnataka region. The emphasis here is on the lāsyāṅgas and the accompanying vocal and instrumental music which is described in great detail. The use of the deśī lāsyāṅga named mana in sthāya tāla (*SR.* 7.1215; 1288)[17] is specifically recommended here. The presentation resembles the puṣpāñjali of the Bharata tradition in the alternate use of song and instrumental music but gauṇḍalī is danced by a single performer, not by a group. The performance ends with the playing of drums. It is suggested that the performer should stand still in a pose resembling a painting after ending the presentation with the concluding movement. The term for the concluding movement is kalāsa. This movement, which gained greater importance in the later texts,[18] first appears in this text. It is of major importance in the kathakali style of Kerala today, which uses this term to indicate the same movement. The presentation of this style of gauṇḍalī must have gained tremendous popularity at the time of Śārṅgadeva, because although he treats the entire subject of dance in a single concise chapter, only one of the seven that make up the text, he devotes as many as twenty-eight verses to gauṇḍalī. The rest of the text deals at length with music, that being his main interest (*ŚR.* 7.1273-1301).

The other deśī style described by Śārṅgadeva is Peraṇi. This is danced by a male performer as is apparent from the description of the performer's make-up. His head is shaven, with only a tuft of hair left at the top and he is supposed to smear ash over his body. The *Saṅgītasamayasāra,* where this dance appears for the first time, is silent

---

17 See pp. 147-48 *supra*. The description does not give us any idea about the movement apart from the fact that it is supposed to be a delicate movement.

18 *NRK*. 4.1. 37-85 ; *Nr.Adh*. 1566-1611

about the make-up. But the five features of the peraṇi dance are similar in both texts. However, some of the technical terms used for these features seem have been Sanskritized by Śārṅgadeva. The five features identified in the *Saṅgītaratnākara* are: gharghara (stamping the ground with the feet with ankle bells on) viṣama(karaṇas involving leaps; nṛtta in *SSam*), bhāvāśraya (imitation of comical things;[19] vāgaḍa in *SSam.*), kavicāra (description of the hero of high character; kaivāra in *SSam*), and gīta (refers to sālaga[20] songs suitable for gauṇḍalī) (*ŚR.* 7.1301-16). After describing the make-up for a dancer, the author describes the style of peraṇi dancing. One of the purposes of this dance, danced by a clean shaven male performer, seems to be to produce laughter, although the dancer's use of difficult dance steps and movements may suggest less comical intentions as well. As in describing the other two styles, Śārṅgadeva gives full details of the accompanying vocal and instrumental music, along with the rhythm and tempo in which they are to be performed.

The interesting point to note here is that although the style peraṇi seems to be a development of the preraṇa of Abhinavagupta, it is listed as a form of minor musical drama in the *Abhinavabhāratī*, whereas Pārśvadeva and Śārṅgadeva describe it in their chapters on dancing. Peraṇi is treated by these two authors as a mimetic dance (the word dance should be emphasized here) that uses a great deal of vocal and instrumental music of the deśī variety, and all the later texts follow in their footsteps in describing peraṇi, as they also do in describing gauṇḍalī. It is not surprising that considerable emphasis is laid on the accompanying music in describing the styles and that the authors give such full technical details of the music. Both Pārśvadeva and Śārṅgadeva are primarily interested in music, and dance is included in their discussion because the

---

19 This is where we find a trace of similarity between the peraṇi described in the later texts with preraṇa described in the *Abhinavabhāratī*.

20 Songs are supposed to be of three types: śuddha,citra and sālaga.

whole art of saṅgīta includes vocal and instrumental music as well as dance.

The next text to be considered,the *Nṛttaratnāvalī* by Jāya, is almost contemporaneous with Śārṅgadeva's *Saṅgītaratnākara.*[21] Since Jāya's work is entirely on dance and gives an elaborate description of both classical and regional styles, we get a fuller picture of the traditions in existence in that period. Jāya describes the entire tradition of Bharata following the *Nāṭyaśāstra,* which demonstrates the continuing interest in that tradition. However, Jāya's greater contribution lies in his elaborate description of the deśī tradition, which includes not only fifteen deśī nṛtyas but more movements of the feet, more cārīs, sthānas and karaṇas than in previous texts, as well as nine bhramarīs and forty-six lāsyas of the deśī variety. The fifteen deśīnṛtyas include goṇḍalī,preraṇī, preṅkhaṇa, rāsaka, carcarī, nāṭyarāsaka, daṇḍarāsaka, śivapriya, cindu, kanduka,[22] bhāṇḍika, ghaṭisaṇī, caraṇa, bahurūpa and kaullāṭa. Of these fifteen, preraṇa, rāsaka, carcarī, nāṭyarāsaka and daṇḍarāsaka are described in the earlier works as dance-dramas or minor dramas that involve music and dance. These are identified as dances by Jāya in *Nṛttaratnāvalī.*

The forty six deśī lāsyas listed by Jāya include, as we have noted in chapter 2 of the present study, the deśī aṅgas of Pārśvadeva and the deśī lāsyāṅgas of Śārṅgadeva.[23] The aṅgas and lāsyāṅgas of the deśī variety are styles of presentation rather than specific movements which may either be vigorous or delicate. Following are the deśī aṅgas described by Jāya.[24] Sauṣṭhava (grace, described in *SSam.*as a deśī aṅga and in the *Nāṭyaśāstra* and *Saṅgītaratnākara* as overall presentation technique),

---

21 See p. 60*supra.*

22 A dance item found in Mohiniattam of Kerala.

23 See p. 62 *supra.*

24 The terms are not literally translated here; rather, the actions denoted are briefly described.

sthāpanā (standing posture in a graceful line (=rekhā) with a pleasant expression), rekhā (moving the body along a graceful line), ḍāla (moving the body simulating a drop of water on the edge of a lotus leaf being moved by a slow breeze), cāli (a delicate, slow and simultaneous movement of the feet, hands, waist and the thighs)[25] calāvali (the same action done at front to a faster tempo), lali (oblique movement of the minor limbs done to rhythm and metre which is delicate and playful; it is also described as a beautiful movement generated from music and creating pleasure), ṭṛkani (moving the head following the rhythm and tempo with a pleasant expression of the face),[26] ullāsa (a quick movement in rhythm in slow and fast tempo while expressing emotion), sukalāsa (a harmonious blend of vocal and instrumental music with dance in between performed by an experienced dancer), uroṅgaṇa (a slow or quick and graceful movement of the shoulders and the breasts to the front, back, up and down, done in succession), bhāva (a dance danced to the song and instrumental music in rhythm and then the dancer stops quickly in a joyful manner), tharahara (the quick quivering and playful motion of the breasts, which flows up to the arms), kittu (the arms, the breasts and the waist are pulsated in rhythm with delicacy), deśīkāra (regional varieties of nṛtya which are not rustic), nijāpaṇa (an easy nṛtya which is performed with graceful body movements to please the audience and in it, glances follow the hand movements), ḍillāyī(same as dhillāyī of *SSam*; full of emotion, feminine charms such as helā, full of poise, relaxed and charming), lavaṇi (namani or navaṇi in the recent edition of *SSam.* and tavaṇi in the earlier edition of

---

[25] The term cāli is used in modern Manipuri style to indicate a similar movement which is one of the basic movements of that style.

[26] An important feature of the Bharatanatyam style.

SSam;[27] the easy bending of the body even in difficult positions), gītavādyatā (following in tempo the vocal and instrumental music),[28] abhinaya (miming with body movements the meaning of a song expressing emotions), laya (the tempo changes to two new ones and the female dancer quickly and beautifully whirls around), komalikā (the limbs are delicately moved round in vartanā with the play of tempo and an abundance of display of emotion is recommended), oyāra (the features of nṛtya are achieved and the beautiful movements of the female dancer grow faster in rhythm), anīkī (the dancer dances flawlessly in the rhythm and tempo of the song and instrumental music), aṅgahāra (delicate and amorous bending of both sides of the body in rhythm and tempo), manodharma (a dance that does not follow the prescribed rules, yet is attractive and captivating with movements of hands and other parts of the body), aṅga (a piece of nṛtta that uses lāsya movements), anaṅga (a dance danced in tāṇḍava), vivartana (karaṇas, bhramarīs, cārīs are performed following the instrumental music), jhaṅkā (with the body raised the dancer makes whirling movements to the sides and to the front), mukharasa (pleasant facial expression with make-up on), ṭhevā (emotion expressed through the outer corners of the eyes), vihasī (a smiling face like a lotus), dhasaka (graceful lowering of the breasts with tremulous dance movements from time to time following the instrumental music), tala (the dancer follows both easy and difficult pāṭas or syllables of the music), vitala (difficult cārīs, pāṭas etc are done delicately), rasavṛtti (sambhoga or union and vipralambha or separation are delineated by the female dancer through appropriate movements), masṛṇatā (erotic sentiment or rasa is expressed through nṛttahastas and snigdhā dṛṣṭi, that is, a gentle glance), anumāna (nṛtta is performed following the vocal and

---

27 *SSam*. 7. 196; 7. 211 (1977 ed.); *SSam*. 6. 208 (1920 ed.).

28 Rāghavan takes this as two separate aṅgas but this does not seem to be right (*NR*. p. 193 of the text).

instrumental music and the vacillating mind is expressed through the movement of one eyebrow), pramāṇa (the harmonious blend of dance, song and instrumental music), laṁghita (the movements follow the features of lāsya and they are characterized by small leaps with rest in between), aṁsagati (the dancer presents extracts of dance pieces through different exercises and other dance movements), susandhi (the dancer moves from one kind of rhythmic movement to another of kind of movement without the sense of disjunction), pādapāṭa (the pāṭākṣaras or the syllables of drumming is recited by the female dancer while marking the beat lightly with the feet), gatistha (the nṛtta is full of features from the mārga and deśī tradition done to the rhythm of drums and instrumental music), caṇḍana (an experienced dancer dances appropriately to the music with or without songs and stops, dancing in poise, and stays still like a picture). Of these, lali and bhāva seem in a general way to be important features of the overall presentation found both in the *Saṅgītasamayasāra* and in the *Nṛttaratnāvalī*. The importance of sauṣṭhava continues to be stressed in these texts as indeed in all the manuals since the time of the *Nāṭyaśāstra.*

Of the fifteen dance compositions described in the *Nṛttaratnāvalī* we have already discussed goṇḍalī or gauṇḍalī, preraṇi or peraṇī, preṅkhaṇa or pekkhaṇa, rāsaka, carcarī, nāṭyarāsaka and daṇḍarāsaka, all of which are viewed in the literature prior to the *Nṛttaratnāvalī* either as minor dramas or as dances.[29] The following eight dances are new, found for the first time in the *Nṛttaratnāvalī:* śivapriya, kanduka, cindu, bhāṇḍikā, ghaṭisani, cāraṇa, bahurūpa and kollāṭa. In his introduction to the *Nṛttaratnāvalī.* Raghavan has discussed all fifteen dances in full, comparing them with the dance descriptions in the *Saṅgītasamayasāra* and the *Saṅgītaratnākara.*[30] Here I shall briefly touch only upon the salient

---

[29] See pp. 165-66, 192-93 *supra.*

[30] Raghavan, 1965, Introduction, pp. 134-53

points in the descriptions of the eight new dance pieces, for the descriptions of the other seven add little to the accounts in the other texts, and although the *Nṛttaratnāvalī* does elaborate upon the musical accompaniment, it prescribes no specific movements.

As the name suggests, the deśī dance called śivapriya is a śaivaite dance. Drums, cymbals and musical instruments are played with this group- dance. The dancers smear their body with ashes and put on necklaces of the rudrākṣa beads favoured by Śiva. This dance calls for lāsyāṅgas which the dancers perform either by forming two lines facing each other, or in a circle (*NR*. 7. 108-12).

The next deśī dance described is cindu or cintu (*NR*. 7.113-16). This comes from the South and the accompanying song is in the Drāviḍa language. As Jāya points out, the main characteristics of this dance are swaying movements called kittu (*NR*. 7.115). This dance uses cārī and lāsyāṅgas and the author stresses the importance of sukalāsa or the harmonious blend of the music and dance for it (*NR*. 7.116). Raghavan points out that this dance was recorded in the *Saṅgītadarpaṇa* of Dāmodara and the *Saṅgītacintāmaṇi* of Vema. He also mentions that this continued to be a popular dance until at least 1935 when it was banned by legislation on account of what was considered to be its obscene character.[31] We also find it in the *Nartananirṇaya* of Puṇḍarīka Viṭṭhala, which describes several varieties of cinduṇṛtta.[32]

The dance named kanduka is still found in the repertoire of Mohiniattam of Kerala. This involves playing with a ball. As Raghavan points out, it is found in the *Svapnavāsavadattā* and in the *Daśakumāracarita.* He describes in detail the dance found in these texts.[33] Jāya describes it as a group dance in which the dancers form lotus-like

[31] *Ibid.*,.p.148

[32] *NN.* 49a-50b.

[33] Raghavan, 1965, Introduction, pp. 149-50.

figures, wavy lines, and other formations, all executed to rhythms played on instruments. A metal or wooden ball is used by a group of female dancers, who perform lāsyāṅgas and cārīs to begin this composition like a game but develop it into a dance (*NR.* 7.117-24).

Next comes the Bhāṇḍika nṛtta which is a dance of the clowns who imitate the sounds of animals and their gaits. They make funny sounds and they also simulate the movements of lame persons, dwarfs and children. It is supposed to provide comic relief to enliven dull moments (*NR.* 7.125-28).

The name of the next dance is not very clear, as Raghavan points out, since the text refers to ghaṭisanī and the colophon to ghaṭisiśrī. He also mentions that the accompanying drum ghaṭisa or ghaṭasa or ghaḍasa is a variety of huḍukkā.[34] This is described as a dance for female dancers but a male dancer sometime performs it. The dancer is a caṇḍālī who plays the drum, holding it on her shoulder while singing caryāpadas in a sweet voice. This also is a śaivite dance, dedicated to Śiva, the god of hunters, in the form of a kirāta. Other singers and players of musical instruments surround the dancer (*NR.* 7.129-33).

Cāraṇa nṛtta, the next dance described by Jāya, involves circular movements. Raghavan says that it is a style found mostly in Gujarat.[35] This is danced to a dohaka song and seems to be similar to the dohaka-nṛtta described by Mahārāṇā Kumbhā in his *Nṛttaratnakośa* [36] This dance uses both delicate and forceful movements with appropriate bhramarīs and hand-gestures (*NR.* 7.134-36).

The dance bahurūpa is described at great length (*NR.* 7.137-46). This dance is found in a number of later texts. Raghavan has made a note of the

---

[34] *Ibid.*, p.150.

[35] *Ibid.*, p.151. This is found in the folk dance named garbā in Gujarat. Similar revolving movements form part of the group dance of the Manipuri style.

[36] *NRK.* 4. 3. 120-22.

texts that describe this dance and commented that this is still found in certain parts of India. The texts that describe this dance are the *Saṅgītamakaranda* of Veda, the *Saṅgītasāra* of Vidyāraṇya, the *Saṅgītadāmodara* of Śubhaṅkara, the *Saṅgītanārāyaṇa* of Puruṣottama-miśra and the *Saṅgītakaumudī* as quoted in the *Saṅgītanārāyaṇa*.[37] This dance shows a variety of characters from different places (= loka) which makes it a popular presentation. Jāya refers to it as a nāṭya performed by a group of dancers where the main performer is versatile and capable of speaking different languages. This also includes some unbecoming actions and speeches towards the end of the performance. Rāghavan refers to similar performances found in the Andhra and Tamil regions.[38] In the eastern part of India, in Bihar, a similar presentation during daytime used to be very common till the late forties, in which one character would come and perform a mime imitating various characters and their speeches and voices. These modern presentations can hardly be described as dances but the bahurūpa of Jāya seems to have contained both dance and dramatic elements. The texts that originated in eastern India, such as the *Saṅgītadāmodara* and the *Saṅgītasārasaṁgraha,* call bahurūpa a variety of tāṇḍava dance without describing its characteristics.[39]

The last deśī dance described by Jāya is kollāṭa which is a pure acrobatic performance on a rope and involves swinging, wheeling round, etc. This is also performed on swords. This dance is full of leaping movements which are done to the accompaniment of drums, trumpets and cymbals(*NR.* 7.137-46). Śārṅgadeva's kohlāṭika seems to be similar to this dance (*SR.* 7.1330-1). Raghavan refers to some of the dances still

---

37 Raghavan,1965, Introduction, pp. 149-50; Text..p. .225.

38 *Ibid.*, Introduction, pp. 153.

39 *SDām.* p. 69; *SSār.* 63-69.

prevailing in the South that can be matched with this type of acrobatic performance.[40]

Two other works on saṅgīta from the early medieval period, the *Abhinayadarpaṇa* and the *Saṅgītamakaranda,* do not describe any complete dance but they do describe some movements. The *Abhinayadarpaṇa* describes seven bhramarīs and five leaping movements, calling them utplavanas (*ADar.* 282-98). It also adds a number of new hand-gestures, cārīs, maṇḍalas and gaits. The *Saṅgītamakaranda,* as we have noted in chapter 1, describes some movements employed in a debased tradition of deśī that appears in no other work. It does not describe any complete dance piece but describes eight bhramarīs (*SMak.* 2. 4.), of which only one has a name in common with bhramarīs in other texts but not the description. The names of the rest of the bhramarīs do not appear in any deśī tradition recorded in any other text.

The *Bharatārṇava* of Nandikeśvara (a controversial[41] and not satisfactorily identified figure) is in a way the most significant text of the medieval period, which not only offering another new deśī tradition but also being the only text to explain with the greatest possible detail the specific terms for movements needed for each dance-sequence along with its accompanying music and rhythm. The author takes the components of larger dance-units, which make up a total composition, and analyzes them systematically by giving their definitions, their divisions, the sthānas, cārīs and karaṇas they need, and finally the tāla required. He introduces a new set of aṅgahāras, nine in all: lalita, vikrama, kāruṇika, vicitra, vikala, bhīma, vikṛta, ugratara, śāntija. Each of these aṅgahāras have several sub-varieties: lalita can be of five kinds, vikrama of three, kāruṇika of four and vicitra, vikala, bhīma, vikṛta, ugratara and śāntija can all be of two kinds. The five varieties of lalita use different types of postures and

---

40 Raghavan, 1965, Introduction, pp. 153.

41 See chapter 2 *supra.*

three use a swaying movement termed sulū. Specific glances and hand-gestures are also prescribed. For vikrama aṅgahāras specific hand-gestures, glances, feet-movements and maṇḍalas are given. Different types of kāruṇika aṅgahāras are also described with specific hand-gestures, glances and feet movements. This aṅgahāra is characterized by the facial expression of karuṇā or compassion. The second type of this variety calls for sulū. Vicitra aṅgahāras are described with specific hand-gestures, glances and feet movements but nothing is said about facial expression. The other five aṅgahāras are also described in a manner similar to vicitra. As Nandikeśvara himself claims, aṅgahāras are defined, following Bharata, as combinations of karaṇas. But he also quotes another view which calls aṅgahāra a dance to be performed in the morning (*Bh.Ar.* 9. 583-85). These aṅgahāras do not appear in any other text. His descriptions of śṛṅganāṭya, another new category of sequence, also offers great detail. This dance-sequence is described by the author as a combination of two cārīs, one aṅgahāra and three sthānas. The cārīs are selected from both the groups of aerial (=ākāśa) and ground (=bhauma) cārīs. Śṛṅganāṭya can be of nine kinds; they are described but not named. In the first śṛṅganāṭya the movements are delineated in the following order: samaprekṣaṇacārī is performed, followed by lalita aṅgahāra and samapādā bhūmicārī. Samaprekṣaṇacārī is followed by āyatasthāna, lalita aṅgahāra by avahitthasthāna and samapāda bhūmicārī by aśvakrānta sthāna (*Bh. Ar.* 11. 643-45). The second śṛṅganāṭya begins with sārikā cārī followed by vikrama aṅgahāra and cāṣagati cārī. Sārikā cārī is followed by moṭita sthāna, vikrama aṅgahāra by vinivṛttasthāna and cāṣagaticārī by aindrasthāna (*Bh. Ar.* 11. 645-47). The third śṛṅganāṭya is constituted of agraplutācārī, kāruṇika aṅgahāra and sthitāvartācārī. Cāṇḍikasthāna follows agraplutācārī, vaiṣṇavasthāna follows kāruṇika aṅgahāra and samapādasthāna follows sthitāvartā bhūmicārī (*Bh. Ar.* 11. 648-49). The fourth śṛṅganāṭya starts with vidyullīlācārī followed by vicitra aṅgahāra and vicyavā bhūmicārī. Vaiśākhasthāna follows vidyudlīlācārī, maṇḍala sthāna follows vicitra aṅgahāra and ālīḍhasthāna follows vicyavā bhūmicārī (*Bh. Ar.*11. 650-52). The fifth śṛṅganāṭya is characterized by khaḍgabandhā cārī, vikala aṅgahāra and urudvṛttā bhūmicārī. The khaḍgabandhā cārī requires pratyālīḍha sthāna, samapādasthāna in vikala aṅgahāra and svastikasthāna in urudvṛttā cārī (*Bh. Ar.*11. 652-54). The sixth śṛṅganāṭya is constituted of rekhābandhā cārī, bhīma aṅgahāra and aḍḍitā bhūmicārī. Rekhābandhā cārī requires vardhamānasthāna, bhīma aṅgahāra requires nandīyasthāna and aḍḍitā cārī requires parṣṇipīḍasthāna (*Bh. Ar.*11. 655-56). The seventh śṛṅganāṭya is characterized by luṭhitollalitā cārī, vikṛta aṅgahāra and vakrabandhā bhūmicārī. Ekapārśvasthāna is done in luṭhitollalitā cārī, ekajānukasthāna is done in vikṛta aṅgahāra and parivṛttasthāna is done in vakrabandhā bhūmicārī(*Bh. Ar.*11. 657-59). The eighth śṛṅganāṭya is characterized by kuṇḍalāvartakā cārī, ugratara aṅgahāra and janitā bhūmicārī. Pṛṣṭhottānatala sthānaka follows kuṇḍalāvartakā cārī, ekapādasthāna follows ugra aṅgahāra and brāhmasthāna follows janitā cārī (*Bh. Ar.*11. 660-62). The ninth and the final śṛṅganāṭya requires vicitrā cārī, śāntaja aṅgahāra and utsanditā bhūmicārī. Vicitrā cārī is followed by vaiṣṇava sthāna, śāntaja aṅgahāra is followed by śaiva sthāna and utsanditā bhūmicārī is followed by gāruḍasthāna (*Bh. Ar.*11. 662-64). The names of the aṅgahāras do not come from Bharata's tradition.

In the next chapter of this text the author describes in detail the specific tālas required for these śṛṅganāṭyas as well as specific hand-gestures used in each particular sthāna. These are specifically meant for the sthānas to be used in the śṛṅganāṭya (*Bh. Ar.* 12). In the thirteenth chapter seven different lāsyas and seven different tāṅḍavas are described in detail. Some of the names of lāsyas are found in the *Saṅgītaratnākara* and the *Nṛttaratnāvalī* either as deśī lāsya or as deśī dance.[42] But the

[42]*Bh.Ar.* 13: 732-3*SR.* 7. 1206-1216; 7.1273-1302; 7.1303-1325; *NR.* 6. 117-173; 7.34-150 .

tāṇḍavas are not found in any other text. The seven pure tāṇḍavas are dakṣiṇabhramaṇa, vāmabhramaṇa, līlābhramaṇa, bhujaṅgabhramaṇa, vidyudbhramaṇa, latābhramaṇa and ūrdhvatāṇḍava. These form part of pure nāṭya and they use six different gatis which are mayūra, rājahaṁsa, kṛṣṇasāra, gaja, siṁha and śuka. In these tāṇḍavas karaṇas and cārīs are performed after the gatis. The author specifies the names of five cārīs appropriate for five specific karaṇas. The author claims that these follow Bharata's tradition (*Bh. Ar.* 13. 712-25).

The deśī tāṇḍava described in this text again has five different varieties, namely, nikuñcita, kuñcita, ākuñcita, pārśvakuñcita and ardhakuñcita, and they use five specific gatis, five specific cārīs and five specific karaṇas. The seven lāsyas are described next, the use of which are supposed to enhance the beauty of cārī. They can be both pure or deśī. They are named as śuddha, deśī, preraṇā (this is categorized as a variety of tāṇḍava in most texts), preṅkhaṇā, kuṇḍalī, daṇḍikā and kalaśa (*Bh. Ar.* 13. 732-33). We have already come across preraṇā (peraṇi or preraṇa in other texts), preṅkhaṇā (preṅkhaṇa or prekṣaṇa in other texts), kuṇḍalī (guṇḍalī, goṇḍalī or gauṇḍalī in other texts) and daṇḍikā (also described as daṇḍalāsya in the same text; daṇḍarāsa in other texts). The definitions given here match those in previous sources. Kalaśalāsya is the only new variety which is described along with karaṇa, cārī and the rhythm. The author then discusses the specific cārīs and karaṇas meant for these lāsyas and the gods ascribed to each of them. Specific gatis, cārīs, karaṇas and tālas applicable to the seven varieties of pure tāṇḍavas and five varieties of deśī tāṇḍavas are dealt with in the next chapter (*Bh.Ar.*14.770-870). At this point the author again takes up the lāsyas and describes the specific sthānas, cārīs, karaṇas and tālas applicable to them (*Bh.Ar.*14.871-93). Finally, in the whole of the last chapter the author describes the presentation of flower-offering, the puṣpāñjali (*Bh.Ar.*15.894-996). This is the only full composition that the author describes. He refers to two types of puṣpāñjali, one meant for the gods, which is termed daivika and one for human beings, which is known as mānuṣa. In the former type traditional dancing follows the puṣpāñjali and in the latter mukhacāli follows puṣpāñjali. The worshipping of different gods and semi-divine beings are prescribed for this presentation. He goes on to describe specific sthānas, specific flowers and specific karaṇas meant for each god, procedures of invoking gods, of offering flowers, of specific sides for offering flowers to each god. Then the main presentation follows. Caccatpuṭa or dhruva tāla is prescribed. The dance starts with the recitation of the syllables tā thai to nam, which is called alparīti when done fast. This is the most detailed description of a puṣpāñjali found in any of the texts studied here. Since parts of this text, as found and edited, are missing, we have no way of knowing whether the author had also described the Bharata tradition in the earlier part of his text. He mentions all the names of karaṇas from Bharata's tradition, which make up the dance sequences but does not describe the karaṇas. He is silent also about modes of presentation.

The *Saṅgītopaniṣatsāroddhāra* lists eight bhramarīs but gives no descriptions, nor does it mention any dance-piece. The author merely lists the movements required as in Bharata's tradition. He does not concern himself with the technique of presentation. The *Saṅgītacandra* of Vipradāsa follows the *Saṅgītaratnākara* by including the nine bhramarīs in its list of the deśī karaṇas and describing them after the *Saṅgītaratnākara*. The author's descriptions of pure and deśī styles of dancing (peraṅī and goṇḍalī) as well as is his concept of rekhā with reference to the aesthetics of presentation follow Śārṅgadeva's treatment of the subjects. Although his descriptions of the styles are quite elaborate, he does not contribute anything new to our knowledge.

The next saṅgīta text is the *Saṅgītadāmodara*, which includes dance as part of dramatic presentations. This text gives us a new class of movements, calling it viṣama alaga or leaping movement which are seven in number. The author describes nine lāsyāṅgas, most of which are found in Śārṅgadeva, but two of the names are from the lists of deśī aṅgas in Pārśvadeva and deśī lāsyas in Jāya (*SDām.* p. 74-5). He gives brief descriptions of four deśī dances, putting them under two categories: tāṇḍava and lāsya, each consisting of two dances. In the tāṇḍava category he includes peraṇi and bahurūpa and in the lāsya category he gives two new names: churita and yauvata. He treats guṇḍalī separately and in detail. Referring to it as a dance originating in the land of Karṇāṭa, he says that it is full of lāsyāṅgas and that delicate as well as forceful movements are performed by a single female dancer who sings the accompanying song herself and offers flowers on the stage. Basically, this description matches the previous descriptions of the dance found in the literature of this period(*SDām.* pp. 69;73).

The *Nṛtyādhyāya* of Aśokamalla is the earliest text to describe the deśī dance movement named kalāsa. The author also refers to śṛṅgābhinaya (*Nr.Adh.* 141; the only other text beside the *Bharatārṇava* and the *Nṛttaratnāvalī* to do so) and describes thirty-seven deśī lāsyāṅgas in detail, following the *Saṅgītaratnākara* as well as the *Nṛttaratnāvalī*. These lāsyāṅgas are, as we have already noted, considered to be modes of presentation. But the author does not describe full dance-compositions. We have already come across kalāsa in the *Saṅgītaratnākara* and, following it, in the *Saṅgītacandra*. Kalāsa was described merely as a concluding movement in those two texts. In the *Nṛtyādhyāya* we find that a whole class of movements named kalāsa, of several varieties, has developed by the time this text was written. Kalāsa, according to the author, has six varieties: vidyut, khaḍga, mṛga, baka, plava and haṁsa, each consisting of several sub-varieties which the author describes in forty-six verses (*Nṛ.Adh.* 1566-1611).

The *Nṛtyaratnakośa* of Mahārāṇā Kumbhā, which is the last representative text of the period, describes nine bhramarīs, including them in his list of fifty-one deśī karaṇas following the *Saṅgītaratnākara*' s lead. Kumbha describes an additional thirteen bhramarīs, following another text, the *Ānandasañjīvana* (*NRK*.Vol.II. pp 165-72). These thirteen bhramarīs are revolving movements that are found in no other text. The treatment of these movements is unusual here, for they involve leaps while they hardly ever do so in other accounts. Another important movement that this text elaborates upon is that called kalāsa. It seems that when the *Nṛtyādhyāya* and the *Nṛttaratnakośa* were written, kalāsa, or the concluding movement was considered an important feature of presentation and that its varieties were proliferating. Like the *Nṛtyādhyāya*, *Nṛttaratnakośa* describes six kalāsas and their twenty-two sub-varieties(*NRK*.Vol.II. pp.187-92). In discussing the deśī dances, the author devotes most of his attention to the peraṇi dance but his discussion does not yield any new information. This suggests that this particular dance had become so well established through the preceding three or four centuries that there was hardly any change in its structure (*NRK*.Vol.II, pp 195-98). The list of lāsyāṅgas includes the mārga as well as the deśī tradition. The author seems to have followed a tradition of mārga which adds two more lāsyāṅgas to the original ten. Except for a few,[43] his thirty-seven lāsyāṅgas of the deśī variety are the same as those found in the *Nṛtyādhyāya*, with minor changes in the terms caused perhaps by scribal errors or dialectal differences (*NRK*.Vol.II, pp. 202-9). The author describes six deśī dances, calling them nṛtyabhedas (a term used by writers on poetics to mean minor dramas employing dance and music),[44] as follows: śivapriya, rāsaka, nāṭyarāsaka, daṇḍarāsaka, carcarī and dohaka. All these varieties appear in other texts. Śivapriya and dohaka, already discussed above, are only described in this text and in the *Nṛttaratnāvalī*. The rest are common to most of the texts that contain material on deśī dance. The detailed descriptions of the dances do not give

---

43 Laṁghita and sruvā in *Nr.Adh.* 1546; 1558 are not found in *NRK*; vilaṁvitam in *NRK*. vol. II. p. 208 is not found in *Nr.Adh.*

44 See pp. 167-70 *supra*.

us any new information. The author refers to another opinion that prescribes the use of specific tālas for deśīnṛtyas, seven in number, namely, dhruva, maṇṭhaka, rūpaka, aḍḍatāla,yati, pratitāla and ekatālī and four features in a deśīnṛtya: śruti, gīta, kalāsa and tāla The author describes these seven deśī dances according to the use of different ālāpas and tālas. These dances are often described with specific hand-gestures and tempo(*NRK.* Vol.II. pp.212-13). In describing the deśīnṛtyavidhi, the author directs the dancer to move around the stage with feminine grace(=hāva), holding her veil with her left hand and placing both hands in patākā(*NRK.* 4.3.132). This is a distinctive feature of the Kuchipudi style of dancing of Andhra. Following the method of Śārṅgadeva, the author describes the pure style and the deśī style of gauṇḍalī at great length and the descriptions concentrate on the musical aspect of the presentation (*NRK.* Vol.II, pp. 225-28).

Our next period of study begins with the *Nartananirṇaya,* by Puṇḍarīka, which describes deśī dances at great length. From this time on, we find that the emphasis in the manuals falls rather on the particulars of the dances described than on the musical elements accompanying them. In *Nartananirṇaya* the first half of the discussion on dancing follows the *Nāṭyaśāstra* in describing the body movements and the *Saṅgītaratnākara* in describing specific lāsyāṅgas and modes of presentation. Perhaps the author's greatest contribution, fully examined in chapter 6, lies in the categorization of dancing into bandha and anibandha which he takes as, respectively, rule-bound and relatively free compositions.[45] If we analyze the descriptions, it becomes evident that the author is aware not only of the theoretical aspects of the art of dancing but the application of specific dance-movements as well. The dances in the bandha category are discussed in greater detail than those of the anibandha class. Since these dances have been already described elsewhere in detail by the present

45 See pp. 196-200 *supra*. For details, see Bose,1970, pp.149-61.

writer,[46] only a few will be described here to elucidate the degree to which the movements are defined in the text.

The bandhanṛttas can be of eleven kinds: mukhacāli, urūpa, dhuvāḍa, viḍulāgava, śabdacāli, śabdaprabandha, svaramaṇṭha, gītaprabandha, cindu, dharu and dhruvapada. Of these only cindu is described in the *Nṛttaratnāvalī* but none of its varieties. Mukhacāli is mentioned in the *Bharatārṇava* but no description is given there. Puṇḍarīka describes the invocatory dance, mukhacāli, involving puṣpāñjali, specifying in great detail the required hand-gestures, recakas, sthāna, gatis, cārīs, names of tālas and modes of movements. Although it is possible to reconstruct this dance following the description, surprisingly–unlike other authors of the early medieval period–Puṇḍarīka does not specify the tāla or any music for mukhacāli (*NN*.40a-43a). The definition of the bandhanṛtta named urūpa tells us that it is characterized by yati, tāla, laya, sthāna, cārī and hasta. It has twelve varieties which are also described in detail, with specific movements identified, including karaṇas(*NN*.43a-45b). One such variety called pure neri is described in the following way: this dance is danced in a slow tempo to rāsatāla where the dancer stands in caturasra. She performs rathacakrā with the appropriate gati and her hands are in patākā. Her movements are slow and to the left and to the right. This dance is featured with rekhā and sauṣṭhava. She performs bāhyabhramarī and concludes in caturasra (*NN*. 43a-b). Dhuvāḍas are described next. Twelve varieties of dhuvāḍas are characterized by bhramarīs at the beginning and at the end with lāgas (jumps) and bhujaṅgatrāsitā cārī is prescribed for the conclusion(*NN*.45b-46b). In viḍulāgavas, sixteen in number, lāgas are performed by revolving once or twice with sulūs (swaying movements) and jumps at the end(*NN*.46b-47b). Five bhramarīs are also described, which seems to be a required feature of this dance(*NN*. 47b). In śabdanṛtya the rhythm-keeper recites syllables and

---

[46] See Bose,1970 pp.150-64 for details.

the dancer performs with appropriate hand-gestures, feet movements, expressing emotion and keeping rhythm with the feet (*NN.*47b-48a). Svarābhinaya is the miming of the seven notes of the scale with appropriate hand-gestures, glances, sthānas, head-movements and karaṇas (*NN.* 48a-b). Besides specific movements, svaramaṇṭhanṛtya refers to music and rhythm (*NN.*48b-49a). Gītanṛtya refers to types of songs to which specific movements are performed to express the meaning of the songs (*NN.* 49b).

Next the author starts describing dances which he specifically mentions as originating from the south. The first of its kind is cindu, originating in the land of the Drāviḍa, which is of six kinds. Unlike the previous bandhanṛttas, in describing each variety of cindu the author concentrates on the accompanying music and rhythm rather than on specific movements. At the end, he names the specific cārīs, sthānas and modes of presentation used in all the cindus (*NN.* 49b). The pure style of cindu is described in the following way: the accompanying song of this dance is composed in the language of the Drāviḍas. The composition includes udgrāha and dhruvapada but does not contain melāpa and ābhoga (*NN.* 49b-50a). Another bandha dance from the south, dharu, is described in detail with its two varieties (*NN.* 50b-51a).[47] The dhruvapadanṛtya is the last in the list of the bandha dances in the *Nartananirṇaya.*(*NN.* 51b).[48]

The anibandha dances are described in two parts, the first consisting of twenty-one anibandha urūpas and the second of two anibandhanṛtyas. The descriptions mainly concern rhythm and tempo. As we have noted earlier,[49] this is not surprising since the emphasis in this style of dancing is on the overall presentation rather than on specific movements. In the list of anibandha dances the author includes nāmāvalī, yati, neri, sālaṅganeri,

---

[47] Dharu is still practised in Andhra. See p. 215 *supra*.

[48] See Bose, 1970, pp. 160-61 for details.

[49] See p. 203-10 *supra*.

saṁkīrṇaneri, bhāvaneri, naḍaneri, kaivartana, murū, raṭṭamurū, tālarūpa, guṇḍāla, kamala, maṇḍī, muḍupa, puraṇḍarī, kuḍupa, tiryakaraṇa, lāvaṅī and vaṭuka. The neri of the anibandha type is danced to āditāla and in slow tempo and a variety of gatis are delineated in it (*NN.* 52a). One of the two anibandhanṛtyas comes from Persia and the other is rāsa, which includes the form called daṇḍarāsa (*NN.* 53a-b).[50] Rāsa is the only dance recorded by Puṇḍarīka which seems to have continued over centuries and is found even today in at least two regions of India, Gujarat and Manipur.

The *Rasakaumudī* of Śrīkaṇṭha, the next text that describes deśī, mentions ten varieties of nāṭya, and calls the first nāṭya. Of the rest, gauṇḍalī and peraṇi are considered deśī by all the authors who write on deśī. Nṛtya, nṛtta, tāṇḍava, lāsya, viṣama, vikaṭa and laghu are named in other texts as varieties of the art of dance but not as deśī dances as in this text. The descriptions of peraṇi and gauṇḍalī offer us no new material. The author's concern for aesthetic qualities is noteworthy, particularly the concept of prāṇa or essence, which has already been discussed in chapter 2. The *Saṅgītadarpaṇa* of Dāmodara describes several deśī dance pieces following the *Nartananirṇaya.* The author also follows the categorization of bandha and anibandha offered by Puṇḍarīka. His list of dances is the same as found in the *Nartananirṇaya* but he adds some new dance pieces. His list includes mukhacāli, yatinṛtya, śabdacāli, uḍūpa, dhruvāḍa, lāganṛtya, śabdanṛtya, sūḍanṛtya, vivartananṛtya, camatkāranṛtya, gītanṛtya, svarmaṇṭhanṛtya, dhruvanṛta, maṇṭhanṛtya, rūpakanṛtya, tṛtīyanṛtya, aḍḍatālanṛtya and ekatālīnṛtya (*SDar.* 7.3-7; 8-234). He gives a separate list of the deśī dances, which includes cindu, vaipota, bandha, kalpanṛtya, jakkarī, deśīkaṭṭāri, peraṇi and gauṇḍalī (*SDar.* 7.235-82). The description of mukhacāli follows the pattern of the

---

50 The Persian dance jakkaḍī is described in the previous chapter, pp. 208-9. The description of rāsa offers no new material.

Nartananirṇaya's description with a few minor changes in detail (*SDar.* 7.8-52).[51] The following description of one dance named kalpanṛtya from the list of deśīnṛtyas will show the kind of directions given to the dancer for her performance: the dancer is asked to use appropriate karaṇas and sthānakas, the choice of which depends on the dancer. It is usually performed to kalpatāla (*SDar.* 7.265-67). Other dances are also described in a similar manner. In discussing the aesthetic element the author follows both Puṇḍarīka and Śrīkaṇṭha, the emphasis being on rekhā, pramāṇa and prāṇa.

The *Saṅgītanārāyaṇa* of Puruṣottama Miśra is another text that gives us some instances of deśī dances. The author follows the *Saṅgītadāmodara* extensively and his list and descriptions of tāṇḍava and lāsya with their respective varieties, peraṇi and bahurūpa, and sphurita and yauvata, are described after that text. He gives two sets of examples of twenty mārganāṭyas and sixteen deśīnāṭyas which include major and minor dramatic presentations, including musical plays and dance-dramas as cited by other authors. We have already mentioned in chapter 2 (pp. 95, 98) that the prakāranāṭya category to which the author refers is new. This is also described as deśīnṛtya and the type is briefly described. Of its five varieties, kāṣṭhā, jākaḍī, śāvara, kurañjī and mattāvalī, only jākaḍī (same as jakkaḍī) is found in other texts. The description of kāṣṭhānṛtya reminds us of daṇḍarāsa. In this dance, eight female dancers, described as gopanārīs, dance in circles of svastika with eight (imaginary) Kṛṣṇas. Jākaḍī, according to this text, is a dance in which the dancer gets intoxicated and dances to songs in the languages of Turaṣka with their hands holding peacock tails. In śāvaranṛtya the dancers dance while singing in their own language. A group of female dancers dressed as śāvarīs and adorned with clusters of guñjā dance to the songs sung in their own language in kurañjī. Mattāvalī is a dance of the Turaṣkas pretending

---

51 See Bose 1970, p.152. for details.

to be intoxicated (*SNār.* 3. 31-35). The author mentions that different dances originate in different regions and are performed to songs sung in the languages that the dancers prefer. He adds another new feature to his study of dance by describing six kalāsas with their thirty-two varieties, calling them karaṇas. This classification is similar to the divisions found in the *Nṛtyādhyāya* and the *Nṛtyaratnakośa* (*SNār.* 3. 793-96). But this text offers more sub varieties in number compared to the list of twenty-two kalāsas given in the *Nṛtyādhyāya* and the *Nṛtyaratnakośa* (*Nr.Adh.* 1566-1611; *NRK.* Vol. II.pp.187-192).

The approach of Vedasūri in his *Saṅgītamakaranda,* a text which was not available to me in full, takes yet another direction. This author describes gati in a different way, prescribing not only specific movements of sthāna, cārī, hasta, śira and dṛṣṭi but karaṇas as well, which is a new approach, as pointed out in chapter 2 (pp. 98-9). It is clear from this author's discussion that gatis were most definitely performed elaborately and for a long span of time to give a composite image of the gait of a particular bird, animal or human being. This text also describes in great detail an opening dance-sequence, mukhacāli, after the pattern described in the *Nartananirṇaya* and in the *Saṅgītadarpaṇa,* which follows the *Nartananirṇaya.* As we have shown with examples in the chapter 2, *Saṅgītamakaranda* describes some dances that are found in the *Nartananirṇaya* and in the *Saṅgītadarpaṇa,* but the author cites Kohala and the *Saṅgītadarpaṇa* as his sources (p.99). However, the descriptions are more elaborate in respect of the movements as well as the syllables recited to keep the rhythm in a dance performance.

The *Śivatattvaratnākara* of Bāsavarāja does not describe any dance but recognizes a class of dance termed deśīnṛtta. The author's selection of sixteen karaṇas as the most important ones in the traditional list of hundred and eight karaṇas may be influenced by the opinion of Puṇḍarīka who also gives a list of sixteen karaṇas required for the bandhanṛttas that he describes (*NN.* 32b; *STR.* 6.6.100). The last text of the period is the

Saṅgītasārasaṁgraha of Ghanaśyāmadāsa which originated in eastern India and records the dances which were prevalent there at his time and which seem to have continued since Śubhaṅkara wrote his *Saṅgītadāmodara.* The *Saṅgītasārasaṁgraha,* which has nothing original to offer, seems to have followed the *Saṅgītanārāyaṇa* closely in describing tāṇḍava with two of its varieties, peraṇi and bahurūpa, and lāsya with two of its varieties, sphurita and yauvata, which is a practice continuing from the *Saṅgītadāmodara* (*SDam.* p. 69;*SN.* 3.12-20; *SSār.Sam.* pp.63-69). The division of performances into mārganāṭyas, deśīnāṭyas and deśīnṛtyas comes from the *Saṅgītanārāyaṇa.* The list of five deśī dances, kāṣṭhā, jākaḍī, śabda, karañjī and mattāvalī is again from the *Saṅgītanārāyaṇa* except for śabda. The *Saṅgītanārāyaṇa* has śavara instead and the two dances are different (*SN.* 3.31-36; *SSār.Sam.* pp.63-69).

The reason why our study of the deśī dances begins in the early medieval period is that no work on deśī is available from an earlier period. Our survey of the texts reveals that there were several approaches to the subject by authors, which varied according to their primary concerns. Beginning with Abhinavagupta, Dhanañjaya, Bhoja, Rāmacandra and Guṇacandra, Sāgaranandin, Śāradātanaya and Viśvanātha, most of the writers who wrote on poetics and dramaturgy and who included the regional varieties of performances treated dance as a part of dramatic presentation. The earlier writers on poetics before Abhinavagupta, such as Daṇḍin or Bhāmaha, also refer to dramatic performances. While they were not interested in dealing with modes of presentations they mention certain types of performances which are categorized as mimes (by Bhāmaha) and as visual presentations (by Daṇḍin).

To be distinguished from these writers was another group of writers who were primarily interested in music, most of whom belonged to the early medieval period. They emphasized in their descriptions of individual dance-pieces the accompanying music and rhythm but prescribed hardly any specific movement. A new concern also developed in this period, a concern for modes of presentation and the aesthetics of presentation. Most important among these writers are Pārśvadeva, Śārṅgadeva and Jāya. Towards the end of the early medieval period and in the late medieval period the approach to describing the dances changed. The descriptions began to include specific dance-movements and the interest in describing the accompanying music waned. So specific are some of these texts that they may be taken as manuals of dancing. The best examples are the *Abhinayadarpaṇa,* the *Bharatārṇava* and the *Saṅgītamakaranda* of Vedasūri, but many others contain precise directions to be followed by practising dancers. One complete dance sequence, mukhacāli, is described in the *Nartananirṇaya* in such detail that the description may be taken as practical instruction.

This emphasis on the details of composition is thus a distinctive feature of the later texts. The details are so full that these texts may be followed as guides in reconstructing to a large extent the dances they describe. That these dances for the most part belong to the deśī tradition shows how, through time, the emphasis shifted to that tradition from the older tradition of Bharata. By the time of Puṇḍarīka Viṭṭhala not only had the dances considered peripheral by Bharata gained enough recognition in dance literature to coalesce into a distinct tradition but that tradition had replaced Bharata's as the dominant one. The technical and structural features of the dances in this later tradition form the immediate bases of the dances of India today as noted in chapter 6. It is by taking note of these features that we may establish the links in the evolution of the dance from Bharata's time to our own, a process that was sustained, according to the evidence of the dance literature, by the deposition of one tradition by another.

Chapter 8

CONCLUSION

The recorded history of the dance in India began at a time when the dance was viewed as a developed art with an already established body of technique rationalized by aesthetic principles and hallowed by a legendary origin. In the *Nāṭyaśāstra* Bharata presented a tradition so fully formed that it was followed faithfully by the early writers on dancing who also accepted Bharata's selection of a particular dance style as the core of the tradition. However, in the scholarly conception of the art there was some uncertainty with regard to the place of dancing in the framework of the performing arts. Bharata considered dancing to be exclusively the art of body movements pleasing to the senses. But from fairly early times we find the recognition that there was more to dance than the beauty of form and that it could also be an art that had mimetic action for its content. This recognition was to lead to substantial changes in the understanding of the dance and to an enhancement of Bharata's conception of the art.

In Bharata's view, dancing, for which he uses the term nṛtta, is a non-representational art. In its relationship to drama it is seen as a subsidiary art, a decorative aid that lends formal beauty, not referential meaning, to a dramatic performance. But in the later texts dancing emerges as a more complex art-form, one of whose branches is representational and known as nṛtya; in this sense dance is a parallel to drama, not a subsidiary to it. This shift in the understanding of dancing shows that the separate techniques of nṛtta and abhinaya, or acting, came to be regarded as complementing one another within the framework of nṛtya. This development suggests that as dance evolved, it was nṛtya that developed the more vigorously. Thus, from the dance manuals we discover how the concept of dance widened to include–and indeed emphasize–the variety of mimetic purposes to which dance was put.

In addition, the view of the dance tradition handed down by Bharata also widened owing to the need for accommodating stylistic variations. Our survey of the literature of dance indicates that Bharata's account represented only a small part of the total body of dance styles of the time. When, therefore, these styles became prominent enough after Bharata, particularly in medieval times, that is, from about the eleventh century onwards, they had to be included in descriptions of dancing. Such a widening of frontiers meant a great increment of technical description in the texts. In contrast with the *Nāṭyaśāstra,* the later texts offer fuller details even while they fit these details within the framework established by Bharata.

However, the distinction between the *Nāṭyaśāstra* and the later texts is not merely one of detail. Of greater significance is the fact that unlike the *Nāṭyaśāstra,* the later texts recognize a different tradition composed of the styles beyond the pale of Bharata's account. They differentiate the two by according Bharata's tradition the distinction of being the main path or mārga tradition of dancing. But this idealization of Bharata's tradition cannot obscure the fact that the later texts concern themselves more and more with other styles, whose technique and structural principles are sufficiently different from the style described by Bharata–as discussed in chapters 3 to 6–to be placed in a tradition different from Bharata's. The evidence of the texts shows that through the ages the emphasis of the discourse on dancing shifted away from Bharata's mārga tradition to the tradition that later grew up on the basis of styles known generically as deśī. Eventually, through this shift the later tradition gradually replaced the older.

The augmentation of the technique of dancing was not the only significant sign of the evolution of dancing. Equally–if not more–important were changes in the concept of the aesthetic purposes to which bodily motion was to be put, and of the role of the dancer in the creative process of dancing. In contrast with the bare descriptions of body movements given in early texts such as the *Nāṭyaśāstra* and the *Viṣṇudharmottara Purāṇa,* medieval texts such as the *Saṅgītasamayasāra,* the *Saṅgītaratnākara* and the *Nṛttaratnāvalī,* emphasize the purpose of achieving certain imaginative effects through bodily motion, such as that of simulating the quiver of a drop of water on a lotus leaf, or the trembling of a flame. This emphasis on the communication objectives of dance movements was a major step in the evolution of dance concepts.

At the same time there began the tradition of allowing the dancer considerable latitude–indeed encouraging the dancer–in employing body movements to create compositions that best achieve the mimetic and aesthetic ends of the performance. Again, this was a major departure from the tradition of requiring the dancer rigorously to follow the prescriptions for set compositions. This development was marked by the emergence of the categories of bandha and anibandha, that is, rule-bound and flexible regimens of dancing. The opportunities that this approach provided for artistic innovation within a secure technical framework undoubtedly contributed to the continuing vitality of the dance and was responsible for its increasing popularity through the period, as attested by the proliferation of works on dancing.

The works studied here thus show how dancing in India evolved through a process of accretion and assimilation. The *Nāṭyaśāstra* sets out the principles and describes the technique of the established dance style of its time, but while it does acknowledge the existence of regional and popular dance forms, it does not describe them, presumably because they were not developed enough or sophisticated enough to be regarded as distinct styles. Whether this neglect was general or limited to Bharata cannot be ascertained, for no relevant work by other early authors, such as Kohala, Dattila or Mataṅga is extant. But the fact that no description, however brief, of regional and popular forms appears in any literary source suggests that they could not have been of any great importance in this early period.

In the medieval period, however, regional and popular forms became part of the general discourse on dancing. It was at that stage that a clear distinction between the older tradition described by Bharata and the newly emerging styles began to be made, a distinction marked by the use of the term mārga for the old style and deśī for the new. It was in this period that rapid developments took place in dancing, as evidenced by the wealth of material on new styles recorded in dance treatises of the time. The first record of the deśī style appears in the *Mānasollāsa* of Someśvara who describes a few deśī karaṇas. Soon after, Pārśvadeva records some deśī dances in his *Saṅgītasamayasāra.* But the first full as well as systematic account of deśī dancing appears in the thirteenth century in the *Saṅgītaratnākara* of Śārṅgadeva, which was almost immediately followed by a similar but more elaborate treatment of the subject in the *Nṛttaratnāvalī* of Jāya Senāpati. Later, in the sixteenth century, Puṇḍarīka Viṭṭhala in his *Nartananirṇaya* records the emergence of still newer styles, many of which are very close in their technique to dance styles now practised in India. This text marks a watershed in the dance literature of India; for with it the inclusion of the deśī dance sequences becomes a standard feature of dance manuals. Instead of merely reiterating Bharata's description, as the early texts do, the later texts record the dances of their own time. For instance, the *Nartananirṇaya,* which was from the late Mughal period, describes a style which it says was practised by Persian dancers; from its description we can identify this style as the present day kathak, and from other historic sources we know that this style was indeed imported to India by Persian court dancers in the Mughal era. Styles such as this were not part of the tradition derived from Bharata. The heightened emphasis on these styles shows the very considerable expansion that the dance in India underwent from about the eleventh century to the seventeenth, absorbing within its fold new styles.

The emergence of such styles as subjects of serious study in works such as the *Mānasollāsa,* the *Saṅgītaratnākara,* and the *Nartananirṇaya* suggests that by this time the newer dances had assumed an importance that was equal to if not greater than that of the dance described by Bharata.

But we must also bear in mind that the importance of the *Nāṭyaśāstra* remains unparalleled, not only because it set the pattern of the entire discourse on the performing arts but because it recorded the basic range of the body movements that constitute dancing. Even though the later styles varied considerably from the older in the composition of dance figures and choreography, they tended to utilize most of the basic movements found in Bharata. Through all the diversity and proliferation of dance forms the continuity of the art was thus clearly maintained.

The collation of the techniques of dancing found in textual sources demonstrates how the dance in India evolved through the continuation of old styles and the rise of new styles. Our study of technique also shows that present day classical dancing in India is grounded more directly in the tradition recorded in the later dance manuals, especially the *Nartananirṇaya,* than in the older tradition of the *Nāṭyaśāstra.* This suggests that those styles which had a marginal existence in Bharata's time not only came to be admitted into the mainstream of dancing but eventually became the dominant current. The evolutionary process is therefore one of dynamic growth rather than a static survival. The milestones of that process, it is hoped, have been marked by the comparative analysis of the concepts and techniques of dancing attempted in the present study.

GLOSSARY OF SELECTED TECHNICAL TERMS

A

aṅkura	pantomiming through gestures
aṅga	major limb, feature; a feature of deśīlāsya (q.v.)
aṅgahāra	sequence of dance units; a feature of deśīlāsya (q.v.)
agratalasañcara	a foot movement
agraplutā	a deśī (q.v.) cārī (q.v.)
añcita	a neck movement; an arm movement; a foot movement; a karaṇa (q.v.); an utplutikarañа (q.v.)
añcitabhramarī	a whirling movement
añjana	a hand gesture
aḍḍa	a tāla (q.v.)
aḍḍitā	a bhūmicārī (q.v.)
aḍḍatālanṛtya	a bandha (q.v.) dance
adrutālanṛtya	same as above
anaṅga	a feature of deśīlāsya (q.v.)
anibaddha	loosely constructed in comparison to nibaddha (q.v.)(as applied to a song)
anibandha	freer composition in comparison to rigidly structured (as applied to a dance)
anibandhanṛtta	a pure dance with scope for improvisation
anibandhanṛtya	a mimetic dance with scope for improvisation
anīkī	a feature of deśīlāsya (q.v.)
anumāna	a feature of deśīlāsya (q.v.)
antarālaga	an utplutikaraṇa (q.v.)
apasāra	exit; dance interludes in a play

abhinaya	acting, miming; a feature of deśīlāsya (q.v.)
ardhakuñcita	a deśītāṇḍava (q.v.)
ardhanikuṭṭaka	a karaṇa or dance unit
ardhacandra	a single-hand gesture
ardhasūcī	a karaṇa or dance unit
alaṁkāraśāstra	the manual on poetics
alapallava	a single-hand gesture
alapadma	a single-hand gesture
avamarśasandhi	a technical feature of drama
avahittha	a margasthāna or a standing posture of traditional variety
aśvakrānta	a margasthāna or a standing posture of traditional variety
alaga	a leaping movement
alāta	a maṇḍala (q.v.); a mārga (q.v.) karaṇa (q.v.); a deśīkaraṇa (q.v.)
alātā	a cārī (q.v.)
aṁśagati	a feature of deśīlāsya (q.v.)

Ā

ākāśacārī	a cārī (q.v.) performed in the air
ākuñcita	a deśītāṇḍava (q.v.)
ākṣiptaka	a karaṇa or dance unit
āṅgika	related to body
ācārya	a teacher who is conversant with both theory and practice
āṭṭam	a Tamil word for drama
āditāla	a deśī (q.v.) tāla (q.v.)
ābhoga	part of a musical composition
āyatasthāna	a deśī(q.v.) sthāna (q.v.)

ārabhaṭī	a vigorous style of presentation
ālāpa	exposition
ālāpacārī	the opening dance in the deśī (q.v.) tradition
ālipallava	a karaṇa or dance-unit
ālīḍha	a margasthāna or a standing posture of traditional variety
āvarta	a karaṇa or dance unit
āsīna	a feature of lāsya (q.v.) (in the Bharata tradition)
āhaṅga	a musical element (?)
āhārya	dress, make-up and stage accessories

U

uktapratyukta	a feature of lāsya (q.v.) (in the Bharata tradition)
ugra	a deśī (q.v.) aṅgahāra (q.v.)
ugratara	same as above
uḍupa	a class of deśī (q.v.) dance(of the bandha (q.v.) variety), same as urūpa (q.v.)
uttamottaka	a feature of lāsya (q.v.) (in the Bharata tradition)
utplavana	leaping movements
utplutikaraṇa	a deśī (q.v.) karaṇa (q.v.)
utsāhavatī	a mārganāṭya (q.v.) (of the deśī (q.v.) variety)
utsanditā	a cārī (q.v.)
utsṛṣṭāṅka	a major dramatic type
udgrāha	part of a musical composition
uddhata	forceful
uddhatamiśritmasṃanṛtta	a delicate dance mixed with forceful movements
uparūpaka	minor drama
upāṅga	minor limb
upādhyāya	a teacher

urudvṛttā	a bhūmicārī (q.v.)
urupa	same as uḍupa (q.v.)
urūpa	same as uḍupa (q.v.)
uroṅgaṇa	a feature of deśīlāsya (q.v.)
uromaṇḍala	a karaṇa or dance unit
ulmukī	a deśīnṛtta (q.v.), same as bhillukī (q.v.)
ullāpyaka	a minor dramatic type
ullāsa	a feature of deśīlāsya (q.v.)
ullopyaka	a minor dramatic type

Ū

ūrdhvajānu	a karaṇa or dance unit
ūrdhvatāṇḍava	a śuddha or pure (non-representational) tāṇḍava (q.v.)

E

ekajānuka	a deśīsthāna (q.v.)
ekatālīnṛtya	a bandha (q.v.) dance
ekapāda	a deśīsthāna (q.v.)
ekapārśva	a deśīsthāna (q.v.)
eṇapluta	an utplutikaraṇa (q.v.)

AI

aindra	a deśīsthāna (q.v.)

O

oyāraka	a feature of deśīlāsya (q.v.)

Odissi	a classical dance style from Orissa

KA

kakubha	a rāga (q.v.)
kaṭicchinna	a karaṇa or dance-unit; a deśī (q.v.) dance,
kaṭṭari	a deśī (q.v.) dance
Kathak	a classical dance style from North India
Kathakali	a classical dance style from Kerala
kanduka	a deśī (q.v.) dance; a similar dance item is found in Mohiniattam of Kerala
kamala	an anibandha (q.v.) dance
kartarīmukha	a single-hand gesture
karañjī	a deśī (q.v.) dance
karaḍā	a drum
karaṇa (nṛtta)	a basic dance-unit (coordinated movement of the hands and feet)
karaṇa (hasta)	a special movement of the hand
karaṇaneri	a bandhanṛtta (q.v.)
karuṇa	rasa, a tāla
karṇa	a minor drama
karṇāṭagolaka	a musical mode
karma (pāda)	a special movement of the leg
karma (hasta)	a special movement of the hand
kalaśa	a deśīlāsya (q.v.)
kalāsa	a concluding movement
kalāsakaraṇa	a class of karaṇa (q.v.)
kalāsalāsya	a deśī lāsya (q.v.)
kalpa	a deśī (q.v.) tāla; a deśī (q.v.) dance
kalpanṛtya	a bandha (q.v.) dance
kalpavallī	a minor drama

kalla	a musical element(?)
kavicāra	a feature of peraṇī (q.v.) dance, same as kaivāra (q.v.)
kāruṇika	a deśī (q.v.) aṅgahāra (q.v.)
kāvya	a poetic composition; a deśī (q.v.) dance of prakāranāṭya (q.v.) variety; a minor drama
kāṣṭhā	a deśī (q.v.) dance of prakāranāṭya (q.v.) variety
kāhala	a drum
kiṅkiṇī	ankle bell
kittu	a feature of deśīlāsya (q.v.)
Kuchipudi	a classical dance style from Andhra
kuñcita	a deśītāṇḍava (q.v.), a karaṇa or dance-unit
kuḍupa	an anibandha (q.v.) dance
kuṇḍalāvartakā	a deśī (q.v.) cārī (q.v.)
kuṇḍalī	a deśīlāsya (q.v.); same as guṇḍalī (q.v.)
kutapa	musical ensemble
kurañjī	a deśī (q.v.) dance (of prakāranāṭya (q.v.) variety)
kuvāḍa	a deśī (q.v.) dance
kṛṣṇasāragati	a gait simulating the gait of a deer
kaiśikīvṛtti	a graceful style of presentation
kaivrtana	an anibandha (q.v.) dance
kaivāra	a feature of peraṇi (q.v.), same as kavicāra (q.v.)
kaivāla	a double-hand gesture
komalikā	a feature of deśīlāsya
kollāṭa	a deśī (q.v.) dance
kolkāṭika	an acrobatic dancer
kollāṭika	same as above
kolhāṭika	same as above
kaulāṭa	same as kollāṭa
krīḍārāsaka	a variety of rāsaka (q.v.)
kriyā	keeping the time with hands

KṢA

kṣetra (hasta)	position of the hand

KHA

khaḍga	a kalāsa (q.v.)
khaḍgabandhā	a deśī (q.v.) cārī (q.v.)
khaṇḍasūcī	a foot movememt
kharjurikā	a pattern of rhythm

GA

gaṅgāvataraṇa	a karaṇa or dance-unit
gajagati	a gait simulating the gait of an elephant
gajara	a musical element (?)
gati	gait
gatistha	a feature of deśīlāsya (q.v.)
gandharvarañjaka	an entertaining performer
garbhasandhi	a technical feature of drama
garvā	a folk dance from Gujarat
garuḍa	a mārgasthāna (q.v.)
garuḍapluta	a karaṇa or dance-unit
gāna	a song sung in regional style
gāndharva	(a song) in the classical mode
gīta	vocal music
gītakādyabhinayonmukhanṛtta	a dance that mimes the meaning of a song
gītanṛtya	a bandha (q.v.) dance
gītaprabandha	a bandha (q.v.) dance

gītavādyatā	a feature of deśīlāsya (q.v.)
gīyamānarūpaka	musical play
guṇḍalī	a deśī (q.v.) dance
guṇḍāla	a variety of anibandha (q.v.) dance
gulma	a group dance, a variety piṇḍībandha (q.v.); a variety of nṛtyabheda (q.v.),
goṭipua	a boy dancer of Orissa
goṇḍalī	same as guṇḍalī (q.v.)
goṣṭhī	a deśīnāṭya (q.v.); a minor drama
gopucchikā	a pattern of rhythm
gauṇḍalī	same as guṇḍalī (q.v.)
geya	(a play) to be sung
geyapada	a feature of lāsya (q.v.) (in the Bharata tradition)
geyarūpaka	a play to be sung
geyalāsyā	a lāsya (q.v.) to be peformed to a song
graha	a feature of music, the note on which the music begins
grāma	a group of tones

GHA

ghaṭasa	a drum
ghaṭisa	same as above
ghaḍasa	same as above
ghaṭisanī	a deśī (q.v.) dance
ghaṭisiśrī	same as above
gharghara	to stamp on the ground marking the rhythm with anklebells
ghargharī	same as above

CA

cañcu	a drum
cakkar	a spinning movement, (a feature of Kathak)
cakramaṇḍala	a karaṇa or dance-unit
cakrabhramarī	a spinning movement
caccatpuṭa	a tāla of the older tradition
caṇḍana	a feature of deśī lāsya
caturasra	a kind of measure; a double-hand gesture; a standing posture
caturaśra	same as above
caturasrapada	a quartet
candraka	a hand-gesture
candrāvarta	a karaṇa or dance-unit
camatkāranṛtta	a bandha (q.v.) dance
carcarī	a song; a tāla or rhythm; a deśī (q.v.) dance; a deśī (q.v.) dance
calāvali	a feature of deśīlāsya (q.v.)
calli	a dance by a female performer playing a drum called huḍukkā (q.v.)
cāṇḍikasthāna	a deśī (q.v.) sthāna (q.v.)
cāraṇa	a wandering performer; a musician; an expert in the music of ankle bells; a deśī (q.v.) dance
cārī	the movement of one leg
cālaka	a movement of the arms
cāli	a feature of deśīlāsya (q.v.); the basic dance of the Manipuri style
cālivaḍa	a feature of deśīlāsya (q.v.)
cāṣagati	a cārī
ciṇṭu	a deśī (q.v.) dance

cindu	a bandha (q.v.) dance originating in the land of Drāviḍa
citra	varied; a deśī dance
citrā	a mārganāṭya or mimetic dance of the regional variety
citrakalāsa	concluding movement of a special type
citrakāvya	a minor dramatic type
citrābhinaya	a special mode of presentation
cilli	same as calli (q.v.)
ceṣṭākṛta	movements of the entire body
caukā	the basic standing pose of the Odissi style, a square posture

CHA

chalika	a song, a mimetic dance
chalita	same as above
chāyānāṭa	a musical mode
chāyālaga	music based on pure form, same as sālaga
chālikya	same as chalika (q.v.)
churita	a variety of lāsya (q.v.); a deśī (q.v.) dance
chau	a regional dance from the eastern part of India

JA

jakkaḍī	a Persian dance categorized as anibandha (q.v.) dance, a prakāranāṭya (q.v.)
jakkarī	same as above
janāntika	an aside
janitā	a cārī (q.v.)
jayadarpa	a deśī (q.v.) karaṇa (q.v.)

jayanta	a hand-jesture
jākaḍī	same as jakkaḍī (q.v.)
jāti	a melodic type
jugupsitā	a mārganāṭya (q.v.)

JHA

jhaṅkā	a feature of deśīlāsya (q.v.)
jhampātāla	a deśī tāla or regional rhythm

ṬA

ṭakka	a rāga (q.v.)

ṬHA

ṭhevā	a feature of deśīlāsya (q.v.)

ḌA

ḍāla	a feature of deśīlāsya (q.v.)
ḍima	a major dramatic type
ḍimikā	a mārganāṭya (q.v.)
ḍillāyī	a feature of deśīlāsya (q.v.); same as dhillāyī (q.v.)
ḍomikā	a deśīnṛtta (q.v.)
ḍombalikā	a minor drama, a dance-drama
ḍombikā	same as above
ḍombī	same as above
ḍolapāda	a karaṇa or dance-unit; same as dolapāda (q.v.)

ḌHA

ḍhāla	a feature of deśīlāsya (q.v.)

TA

tatkār	movements of ankle bells (a feature of Kathak)
tarahara	a feature of deśīlāsya (q.v.), same as tharahara (q.v.)
tala	a feature of deśīlāsya (q.v.)
talapuṣpapuṭa	a karaṇa or dance unit
talavilāsita	a karaṇa or dance unit
tavaṇi	a feature of deśīlāsya (q.v.); same as navaṇi, lavaṇi or namani
tāṇḍava	nṛtta or dance in the Bharata tradition; later taken to mean a vigorous dance
tāla	rhythmic system or cycle
tālarūpaka	an anibandhanṛtta (q.v.)
tirapabhramarī	a revolving movement
tiryakaraṇa	an anibandhanṛtta (q.v.)
tivaṭī	a technical feature of music
tūkali	a feature of deśīlāsya (q.v.)
tumbikā	a deśīnṛtta (q.v.)
tṛtīyanṛtya	a bandha (q.v.) dance
tṛkani	a feature of deśīlāsya (q.v.)
toṭaka	a minor drama; same as troṭaka (q.v.)
trigūḍhaka	a feature of lāsya (q.v.) (in the Bharata tradition), same as trimūḍhaka (q.v.)
tripatākā	a single-hand gesture
tribhaṅgī	a standing posture in the Odissi style, breaking the line of the body into three
trimūḍhaka	same as trigūḍhaka (q.v.)

triśūla	a hand gesture
toṭaka	a minor drama; a deśīnāṭya (q.v.), same as toṭaka (q.v.)

THA

tharahara	a feature of deśīlāsya (q.v.); same as tarahara (q.v.)

DA

dakṣiṇabhramaṇa	a śuddha or pure (non-representational) variety of tāṇḍava (q.v.)
daṇḍapakṣa	a karaṇa or dance-unit
daṇḍarāsa	a deśīnṛtta (q.v.)
daṇḍalāsya	a deśīlāsya (q.v.)
daṇḍikā	same as above
daṇḍinī	a deśīnṛtya (q.v.)
dāsīāṭṭam	the dance of the devadāsīs of Tāmilnāḍu
durmallī	a minor dramatic type of deśī (q.v.) variety; a deśīnṛtta (q.v.)
durmilitā	a minor dramatic type
durmallikā	same as above
deśī	regional
deśīkaṭṭari	a deśī (q.v.) dance
deśīkāra	a feature of deśīlāsya (q.v.)
deśīnāṭya	a dramatic presentation of the regional variety
deśīnṛtta	an abstract dance of the regional variety
deśīnṛtya	a mimetic dance of the regional variety
deśīlāsya	graceful dance of regional variety
deśyaṅga	a feature of deśī (q.v.) dance
dvigūḍhaka	a feature of lāsya (in the Bharata tradition)

dvimūḍhaka	same as above
dvipadī	a metre; a song consisting of two verses; a mimetic dance
dṛśyakāvya	a poetic composition to be seen
dolapāda	a karaṇa or dance-unit; same as ḍolapāda (q.v.)
dohaka	a deśī(q.v.) dance

DHA

dhammilla	a special way of braiding hair
Dharu	a bandhanṛtta (q.v.) from Andhra region
dhasaka	a feature of deśīlāsya (q.v.)
dhātu	a musical element
dhillāyī	a feature of deśīlāsya (q.v.); same as ḍillāyī (q.v.)
dhūvāḍa	a śuddha (non-mimetic) dance; a bandhanṛtta (q.v.)
dhyānaśloka	pictorial verses presenting anthropomorphic images of the musical modes
dhruva	a feature of music; a tāla (q.v.); a song-piece
dhruvagītanṛtya	a pure(non-mimetic) nṛtta (q.v.) danced to a dhruva (q.v.) song
dhruvapadanṛtta	a bandhanṛtta (q.v) danced to a dhruvapada song
dhruvā	a rāga (q.v.)
dhruvāḍa	same as dhūvāḍa (q.v.)

NA

naṭa	an actor
naṭana	dancing
naṭasūtra	guidelines for actors
naṭībhāva	emotional expression appropriate for women
naḍaneri	an anibandha (q.v) dance

natajānuka	an anibandhanṛtta (q.v.)
nandī	a sthāna (q.v.)
nandimālī	a variety of bhāṇaka (q.v.)
namani	a feature of deśīlāsya (q.v.); same as navaṇi, lavaṇi or tavaṇi
nartaka	a male dancer
nartakabhāṣā	the special language of dancers
nartakī	a female dancer
nartana	dancing
nartanaka	a minor drama
navaṇi	a feature of deśīlāsya (q.v.), same as namani, lavaṇi or tavaṇi
nāṭa	a rāga (q.v)
nāṭaka	a major dramatic type
nāṭikā	a minor drama; a mārganāṭya (q.v.)
nāṭī	same as above
nāṭya	drama (often used as nṛtya (q.v.) in the manuals)
nāṭyanṛtya	an expressive dance
nāṭyadharmī	stylized (movement)
nāṭyarāsaka	a deśī (q.v.) dance; a minor drama; a deśī nāṭya (q.v.)
nāndī	an opening verse
nāda	sound
nāmāvalī	an anibandha (q.v.) dance
nikuñcita	a deśītāṇḍava (q.v.)
nijāpaṇa	a feature of deśīlāsya (q.v.)
nitamba	a karaṇa or dance-unit
nibaddha	rigorously constructed (applied to music)
niśumbhita	a karaṇa or dance-unit
nīrājitapadma	a cālaka or a special movement of the hand
neri	an anibandhanṛtta (q.v.)
nṛtta	a non-representational dance

nṛttakāvya	dance-drama
nṛttacāra	a form of drama
nṛttapradhānarāgakāvya	musical play with dance as its main feature
nṛttavāra	same nṛttacāra
nṛttahasta	hand gesture for dance
nṛttātmakaprabandha	dance-drama
nṛtya	a mimetic dance
nṛtyakāvya	dance drama
nṛtyabhāva	a special expression used by dancers
nṛtyabheda	dance-drama
nyāya	rules

PA

patākā	a single-hand gesture
padārthābhinaya	miming the meaning of words
paryastaka	an aṅgahāra (q.v.); a non-representational dance-sequence
parivṛtta	a deśīsthāna (q.v.)
pāṭa	syllables uttered with drumming or dancing to keep the rhythm
pāṭamaṇi	striking the ground with the feet
pāṭākṣara	syllables of drumming
pāda	footwork
pādapāṭa	a feature of deśīlāsya (q.v.)
pārśvakuñcita	a deśītāṇḍava (q.v.)
pārśvajānu	a karaṇa or dance-unit
pārṣṇipīḍa	a deśīsthāna (q.v.)
pārijātaka	a minor dramatic type
pārijātalatā	same as above

pāla	the movement of one leg, generally known as cārī (q.v.)
piṇḍī	a group dance in a cluster
piṇḍībandha	group dances that form auspicious figures on the stage
pipīlikā	a pattern of rhythm
puraṇḍarī	an anibandha (q.v.) dance
puṣpagaṇḍikā	a feature of lāsya (q.v.) (in the Bharata tradition)
puṣpāñjali	a flower-offering to the gods with dance and music
pūrvaraṅga	the preliminaries to a play
pṛṣṭhottānatala	a sthāna (q.v.)
pekkhaṇa	a deśī (q.v.) dance
peraṇa	a deśī (q.v.) dance; also a variety of tāṇḍava (q.v.)
peraṇi	same as above
prakaraṇa	a major dramatic form
prakaraṇikā	a minor dramatic type; a mārganāṭya (q.v.)
prakaraṇī	same as above
prakāranāṭya	a deśīnṛtya (q.v.)
prakīrṇa	miscellaneous; performance practice (Nienhuis,1977, p.38).
pracāra (hasta)	a movement of the hand
pracchedaka	a feature of lāsya (q.v.) (in the Bharata tradition)
pratitāla	a tāla (q.v.)
pratimukha	progression
pratyaṅga	minor limb
pratyālīḍha	a mārgasthāna or a standing posture of the tradtional variety
prabandha	a musical composition
pramāṇa	harmony; a feature of deśīlāsya (q.v.)
pravṛtti	the means of application
prastāvanā	introduction

prasthāna	a deśī (q.v.) dance; a minor drama
prahasana	a major dramatic type
prekṣaṇa	a minor drama; same as pekkhaṇa (q.v.), a deśī (q.v.) dance
prekṣaṇaka	same as above
prekṣyaprabandha	a composition to be seen
preṅkhaṇa	a deśī (q.v.) dance, same as pekkhaṇa and prekṣaṇa; a deśīlāsya (q.v.)
preraṇa	a deśī (q.v.) dance; a minor drama
preraṇā	a deśīlāsya (q.v.)
plava	a kalāsa (q.v.)

BA

baka	a kalāsa (q.v.)
baṭunṛtta	an anibandhanṛtta (q.v.); a dance item of Odissi style
baddha	structured, same as nibaddha (q.v.)
bandhanṛtta	a set, structured and abstract dance in the deśī (q.v.) tradition
bandhanṛtya	a set, structured and mimetic dance in the deśī (q.v.) tradition; a dance-piece called bandhanṛtya (q.v.)
bahurūpa	a deśī.(q.v.) dance
bāhyabhramarī	a revolving movement
bindu	a structural division in a play; a point marking the sudden development of secondary incidents

BHA

Bharatanatyam	a classical dance style from Tamilnad
bhadrāsana	a group dance forming an auspicious figure
bhāṇa	a major dramatic type

bhāṇaka	a minor dramatic type
bhāṇikā	a minor dramatic type
bhāṇī	same as above
bhāṇḍikā	a deśī (q.v.) dance
bhāva	emotion; a feature of deśyaṅga (q.v.)
bhāvaneri	an anibandha (q.v.) dance
bhāvāśraya	dependant on emotional expression, a feature of peraṇi (q.v.) dance; same as bāgaḍa (q.v.)
bhitra	a deśī (q.v.) dance
bhillukī	a deśīnṛtta (q.v.); same as ulmukī (q.v.)
bhīma	a deśī (q.v.) aṅgahāra (q.v.)
bhujaṅgatrasta	a karaṇa or dance-unit
bhujaṅgatrāsitā	a cārī (q.v.)
bhujaṅgabhramaṇa	a śuddha or non-representational tāṇḍava (q.v.)
bhūmicārī	a cārī (q.v.) performed touching the ground
bhedyaka	a group dance (a variety of piṇḍībandha) (q.v.)
bhramarī	a pirouette; a spinning, revolving or whirling movement

MA

maṭṭanṛtya	a bandha (q.v.) dance
maṇikulyā	a mystery story
Manipuri	a classical dance style from Manipur
maṇṭhanṛtya	a bandha (q.v.) dance
maṇṭhaka	a tāla (q.v.)
maṇḍala	the combination of cārī (q.v.) movements
maṇḍalasthāna	a mārgasthāna or a standing posture of traditional variety
maṇḍalarāsaka	a variety of rāsa (q.v.) dance
maṇḍī	an anibandhanṛtta (q.v.); a variety of deśī (q.v.) dance

mattāvalī	a prakāranāṭya (q.v.); a deśīnāṭya (q.v.)
madhupacārī	a deśī (q.v.) cārī (q.v.) described by Kohala who is quoted by Kallinātha in the commentary on the *Saṅgītaratnākara*
madhyama	a musical mode
mana	a feature of deśīlāsya (q.v.)
manodharma	same as mana (q.v.)
mayūragati	a gait simulating the gait of a peacock
mallikā	a minor drama
masṛṇatā	a feature of deśīlāsya (q.v.)
masṛṇamiśroddhata	a vigorous dance mixed with delicate movements
mahācārī	a forceful cārī (q.v.) movement
mahodvṛtta	a karaṇa or dance-unit
māṇḍalī	a deśī (q.v.) dance; same as guṇḍalī (q.v.)
mātrā	a musical measure
mārga	classical or traditional
mārganāṭya	a traditional dramatic presentation; a regional variety of dance found in the *Saṅgītanārāyaṇa* and the *Saṅgītasārasaṁgraha*
mārganṛtta	an abstract classical dance
mārganṛtya	a mimetic dance of the classical variety that generates rasa (q.v.)
mukula	a hand gesture
mukha	exposition
mukhacāli	the opening dance
mukhaja	pertaining to facial expression and movement
mukharasa	a feature of deśīlāsya (q.v.)
mukharāga	colouring of the face according to the character and the mood
muḍupa	an anibandhanṛtta (q.v.); a variety of deśī (q.v.) dance

muḍupacārī	same as madhupacārī (q.v.) but quoted by Kumbhā as muḍupacārī (q.v.)
mudrā	natural grace; hand gesture for religious ritual
muraṇḍarī	an anibandhanṛtta (q.v.), a variety of deśī (q.v.) dance
murū	an anibandhanṛtta (q.v.), a variety of deśī (q.v.) dance
muṣṭi	a hand gesture
mūrchanā	the ascent and descent of svara (q.v.)
mṛga	a kalāsa (q.v.)
mṛgīgati	a gait like a deer
mṛdaṅgī	a pattern of rhythm
melāpaka	part of a musical composition
moṭita	a mārgasthāna or standing posture of classical variety

YA

yakṣagāna	a folk-dance from Andhra
yati	a pattern of rhythm; a tāla (q.v.); an anibandha (q.v.) dance
yatinṛtya	an mimetic dance of the deśī (q.v.) variety
yantra	an auspicious diagram (?); mechanical device
yoni	an auspicious diagram from by a group of dancers
yauvata	a variety of deśīlāsya (q.v.) dance

RA

raṭṭamurū	an anibandha dance
rathacakrā	a cārī
rasa	aesthetic affect
rasadṛṣṭi	a glance generating rasa (q.v.)
rasavṛtti	a feature of deśīlāsya (q.v.)

rahasyamudrā	a mystical hand gesture
rāga	musical mode; melodic pattern
rāgakāvya	musical play
rāgadarśanīya	musical play to be seen
rājavilāsinī	women of royal court
rājahaṁsagati	a gait simulating the gait of a swan
rāmākrīḍa	a minor drama
rāsa	a deśī (q.v.) dance; a minor (dance) drama; an anibandhanṛtta (q.v.)
rāsaka	same as above
rāsakāṅka	a play about Kṛṣṇa and Rādhā in a regional language
rāsikā	a deśīnṛtta (q.v.)
rūpaka	major drama; a bandha (q.v.) dance
rekhā	the imaginary lines described by the body in motion ; a feature of deśīlāsya (q.v.)
rekhābandhā	a deśī(q.v.) cārī (q.v.)
recaka	a movement that involve streching
revā	a feature of deśīlāsya (q.v.)

LA

laghu	a dance using minor karaṇas (q.v.); a nāṭya (q.v.)
laṅghita	a feature of deśīlāsya (q.v.)
laḍhi	a feature of deśīlāsya (q.v.)
latā	a group dance (a variety of piṇḍībandha) (q.v.)
latābhramaṇa	a pure (non-representational) tāṇḍava (q.v.)
latāvṛścika	a karaṇa or dance-unit
laya	tempo; a feature of deśīlāsya (q.v.)
lalāṭatilaka	a karaṇa or dance-unit
lali	a feature of deśīlāsya (q.v.)
lalita	delicate; a deśī (q.v.) aṅgahāra (q.v.)

lalitoddhata	a mixture of graceful and vigorous movements
lavaṇi	a feature of deśīlāsya (q.v.); same as navaṇi, namani or tavaṇi
laharīcakra	a cālaka (q.v.)
lāga	leaping movements
lāganṛtya	a bandhanṛtya (q.v.)
lāghava	dancing with delicate movements
lāvaṇī	an anibandhanṛtta (q.v.), a variety of deśī (q.v.) dance
lāsikā	a minor drama; a deśīnāṭya (q.v.); a deśīnṛtta (q.v.)
lāsya	originally a dramatic art, later treated as a delicate dance style
lāsyāṅga	a feature of lāsya (q.v.)
līna	a karaṇa or dance-unit
līlābhramaṇa	a pure (non-representational) tāṇḍava (q.v.)
lokadharmī	the realistic convention of performance
luṭhitollalitā	a deśī (q.v.) cārī (q.v.)

VA

vakrabandhā	a bhūmicārī (q.v.)
vakṣas	movement of the chest
varṇam	an item in Bharatanāṭyam which is a combination of mimetic and non-mimetic movements
vartanā	movement of the arms
vardhamāna	a deśī (q.v.) sthāna (q.v.)
vastu	subject matter
vākyārthābhinaya	miming the meaning of an entire sentence
vāggeyakāra	a composer musician
vāgaḍa	a feature of peraṇi (q.v.) dance; same as bhāvāśraya
vācika	verbal
vāmabhramaṇa	a pure (non-representational) tāṇḍava (q.v.)

vāra	a minor dramatic type
vikaṭa	comic dance
vikala	a deśī (q.v.) aṅgahāra (q.v.)
vikṛta	a deśī (q.v.) aṅgahāra (q.v.)
vikrama	a deśī (q.v.)aṅgahāra (q.v.)
vicitra	a deśī (q.v.) aṅgahāra (q.v.)
vicitrā	a mārganāṭya (q.v.)
vicitrābhinaya	various ways of acting
vicyavā	a cārī (q.v.)
viḍulāgava	a variety of bandhanṛtta (q.v.)
vitala	a feature of deśīlāsya (q.v.)
vidagdhā	a deśīnṛtta (q.v.)
vidyut	a kalāsa (q.v.)
vidyudbhramaṇa	a pure (non-representational) tāṇḍava (q.v.)
vidyudbhrānta	a karaṇa or dance-unit
vidyullīlā	a deśī (q.v.) cārī (q.v.)
vinivṛtta	a karaṇa (q.v.); a deśī (q.v.) sthāna (q.v.)
viyoginī	a mārganāṭya (q.v.)
vilambitam	a feature of deśīlāsya (q.v.)
vilasamanda	a karaṇa or dance-unit
vilāsikā	a minor drama
vivartana	a feature of deśīlāsya (q.v.); a bandhanṛtya (q.v.)
vivṛtta	a karaṇa or dance-unit
viṣama	an acrobatic dance
viṣamatāṇḍava	a difficult tāṇḍava (q.v.) dance
viṣamālaga	difficult dance movements involving jumps
vihasī	a feature of deśīlāsya (q.v.)
vīṇā	a stringed instrument
vṛtti	style
vṛnda	vocal ensemble
vṛndaka	a deśīnāṭya (q.v.)

vṛścika	a karaṇa or dance-unit
vṛścikakuṭṭita	a karaṇa or dance-unit
vaitālika	a bard; a general entertainer, a critic who is knowledgeable in music
vaipota	a deśīnṛtya (q.v.) of the bandha (q.v.) variety
vaiśākha	a mārgasthāna or standing posture of traditional variety
vaiśākharecita	a karaṇa or dance-unit
vaiṣṇava	a mārgasthāna or standing posture of traditional variety
vyañjanā	rhetorical expression
vyābhicārībhāva	transitory mood
vākyārthābhinaya	miming the meaning of a sentence
vyāyāma	excercise
vyāyoga	a major dramatic type

ŚA

śabda	a deśī (q.v.) dance
śabdacāli	a bandhanṛtta of the deśī tradition accompanied by the utterance of musical syllables
śabdanṛtta	same as above
śabdanṛtya	a mimetic deśī (q.v.) dance to the utterance of syllables or notes; a bandhanṛtya (q.v.)
śabdaprabandha	a mimetic bandha (q.v.) dance of deśī (q.v.) variety
śamyā	a time beat; a mimetic group dance where dancers dance with sticks in hands; a dramatic presentation
śākhā	body movement expressing meaning
śāṭaka	a minor dramatic type; same as saṭṭaka (q.v.)
śāntija	a deśī (q.v.) aṅgahāra (q.v.)

śārīra	the use of body movements; one of the three components of āṅgikābhinaya (q.v.)
śāvara	a prakāraṇāṭya (q.v.); a variety of deśī (q.v.) dance
śikhara	a hand gesture
śiṅgaka	a minor dramatic type, same as ṣidgaka
śilpaka	a minor drama; a deśīnāṭya (q.v.)
śilpinī	a deśīnṛtta (q.v.)
śivapriya	a deśī (q.v.) dance
śukagati	a gait simulating the gait of a parrot
śuddhapaddhati	presentation of a pure (traditional) technique
śṛṅkhalā	a group dance, a variety of piṇḍībandha (q.v.)
śṛṅkhalikā	same as above
śṛṅga	in the context of dance refers to erotic movement
śṛṅganāṭya	an erotic dramatic presentation of a regional variety
śṛṅgābhinaya	a mimetic movement containing erotic elements
śṛṅgāra	erotic
śravyakāvya	poetic compositon to be heard
śrī	a musical mode
śrīgadita	a minor drama, a deśīnāṭya (q.v.)

ṢA

ṣidgaka	a minor drama, same as śiṅgaka

SA

saṅkīrṇa	mixed
saṅkīrṇaneri	an anibandha (q. v.) dance
saṅgīta	vocal and instrumental music and dance
saṅgītaka	a mimetic dance

saṭṭaka	an uparūpaka or minor drama; a deśī (q.v.) nāṭya (q. v.); same as śāṭaka (q.v.)
sattva	expression (in the context of dance)
sandaṁśa	a hand gesture
sandhi	the juncture of a play (structural element of a play)
samagaika	a double hand gesture
samapāda	a foot movement; a mārgasthāna or standing posture of traditional variety
samapādā	a deśī (q.v.) bhūmicārī (q.v.)
samā	a pattern of rhythm
saṁprekṣaṇacārī	a deśī (q.v.) cārī (q.v.)
saṁlāpaka	an uparūpaka or minor drama; a deśīnāṭya (q.v.)
sallāpaka	same as above
sāttvika	expressive
sādhanā	methods of practice
sāmānyābhinaya	natural expression
sārikā	a cārī (q.v.)
sālaga	music based on pure form, same as chāyālaga
sālaṅganeri	an anibandha (q.v.) dance
siṁhagati	a gait simulating the gait of a lion
sukalāsa	a feature of deśīlāsya (q.v.)
sukumāra	delicate
sukumāraprayoga	the graceful application of dance movements
surekhatva	a feature of deśīlāsya (q.v.)
susandhi	a feature of deśīlāsya (q.v.)
sūka	a feature of deśīlāsya (q.v.)
sūḍanṛtya	a bandha (q.v.) dance
sūcī	a foot movement
sūlu	movement simulating a flame
saindhava	a feature of lāsya (q.v.) (in the Bharata tradition)
sauṣṭhava	grace; skill; an erect stance; a deśīlāsya (q.v.)

skandhaka	a metre; a mimetic presentation
sthāya	a tāla
sthāna	posture
sthānaka	same as above; posture meant for men
sthāpanā	a feature of deśīlāsya (q.v.)
sthāyībhāva	permanent mood
sthitapāṭhya	a feature of lāsya (q.v.) (in the Bharata tradition)
sthitāvartā	a cārī (q.v.)
sthirahasta	an aṅgahāra (q.v.)
snigdhādṛṣṭi	a soft glance
sphurita	a pattern of rhythm; a deśīlāsya (q.v.)
sruvā	a feature of deśīlāsya (q.v.)
srotogatā	a pattern of rhythm
svara	a musical note
svaramaṇṭhanṛtya	a bandha dance in which musical notes are mimed
svarābhinaya	a mimetic bandhanṛtta (q.v.) of the deśī (q.v.) variety
svastika	a double-hand gesture, a sthāna (q.v.)

HA

hallīśa	a deśī (q.v.) nāṭya (q.v.); a deśī dance; a minor drama
hallīsaka	same as above
hasta	hand-gesture
hastaneri	a deśī (q.v.) dance
hastinī	a deśī (q.v.) nṛtta (q.v.)
haṁsa	a kalāsa or concluding movement
hāva	feminine movements
hāsikā	a mārganāṭya (q.v.) (described as part of the deśī (q.v.) repertoire)
helā	feminine movements
huḍukkā	a drum

BIBLIOGRAPHY

Manuscripts

Dāmodara. *Saṅgītadarpaṇa,* Bodleian Library, Oxford, MS. No. Mill, 47d.

Puṇḍarīka Viṭṭhala. *Nartananirṇaya,* India Office Library, London, MS. No. 5197.***

Puṇḍarīka Viṭṭhala. *Nartananirṇaya,* Asiatic Society Library, Calcutta, MS. No. III.D. 5.

Puṇḍarīka Viṭṭhala. *Nartananirṇaya,* Jaipur Khas Mahal Library, Jaipur, MS. No. 6885.

Texts

Agnipurāṇa, ed. Hari Narayan Apte, Anandashrama Sanskrit Series, No. 41 (Poona, 1900).

Ajñātakartṛkaḥ, *Nṛttasaṁgraha,* ed. Priyabala Shah, Rajasthan Oriental Research Institute, No. 17 (Jaipur, 1956)

Amarasiṁha. *Cosha, or, Dictionary of the Sanskrit Language,* with an interpretation and annotations, ed. H. T. Colebrooke, 2nd ed. (1825).

Aśokamalla. *Nṛtyādhyāya, A Work on Indian Dancing by Aśokamalla,* ed. Priyabala Shah, Gaekwad Oriental Series, 141 (Baroda, 1963).

Bāsavarāja. *Śivatattvaratnākara,* ed. S. Narayanasvami Shastri, Vol. I, Oriental Research Institute (Mysore, 1964).

Bodhāyana. *Bhagavadajjukīyam, A Prahasana,* ed. P. Anujan Achan, Jayantamangalam (Trichur, 1925).

Bharatamuni. *Nāṭyaśāstra of Bharatamuni with the Commentary Abhinavabhāratī by Abhinavaguptācārya,* ed. Manavalli Ramakrishna Kavi, Gaekwad Oriental Series, I-IV (Baroda, 1934-1964).*

Bharatamuni. *Nāṭyaśāstra,*. ed. Madhusudan Shastri, Vols. I, II (Varanasi, 1971, 1975).

Bharatamuni. *Nāṭyaśāstra,* ed. Batuk Nath Sharma and Baldev Upadhyaya, Kashi Sanskrit Series, 60 (Varanasi, 1929).

Bharatamuni. *The Nāṭyaśāstra of Bharatamuni,* ed. Pandit Shivdatta and Kashinath Pandurang Parab, Kavyamala, 42 (Bombay, 1894).

Bharatamuni. *The Nāṭyaśāstra of Bharatamuni,* with an introduction and various readings with translations, ed. Manomohan Ghosh, Vols. I-II (Calcutta, 1950).

Bhavabhuti. *Mālatīmādhavam,*, ed. Ramakrishna Gopala Bhandarkar, Bombay Sanskrit Series, XV (Bombay, 1876).

Bhāmaha. *Kāvyālaṅkāra,* ed. Batuk Nath Sharma and Baldev Upadhyaya, Kashi Sanskrit Series, No. 61 (Benaras, 1928).

Bhoja. *Maharana Bhoja's Shringara Prakasa,* ed. G. R. Joysa, Vols. I-IV (Mysore, 1955, 1963, 1969, 1975).

Bhoja. *Sarasvatīkaṇṭhābharaṇam,* ed. Anandaram Barooah (Gauhati, repr. 1979).

Catura Dāmodara. *Saṅgīta Darpaṇam,* ed. K. Vasudeva Sastri, Saraswathi Mahal Series, No. 34 (Tanjore 1952)

Caturbhāṇī, ed. Moticandra and Vasudevasaran Agarwal, Hindi Grantha Ratnakar (Bombay, 1959)

Daṇḍin. *Kāvyādarśa.,* ed. Ramacandra Misra, Chowkhamba Vidyabhavan (Varanasi, 1972).

Daṇḍin. *The Kāvyādarśa of Daṇḍin,* with the commentary of Taruṇavācaspati and also with an anonymous commentary known as Hṛdayaṁgamā, ed. Raṅgācārya (Madras, 1910).

Dattila. *Dattilam, Dattilamuni praṇītam,* ed. K. Sāmbaśiva Śāstrī, Trivandrum Sanskrit Series, No. 102 (Trivandrum, 1930).

Dāmodaragupta. *Kuṭṭanīmatam,* ed. Pandit Durgaprasad and Kashinath Pandurang Parab, Kavyamala, Part. iii (Bombay, 1887).

Dhanañjaya. *Daśarūpaka,* ed. F. E. Hall (Calcutta, 1865).

Dhanañjaya. *Daśarūpaka,* ed. G .C. O. Haas (New York, 1912).

Dhanañjaya. *The Daśarūpaka,* with the commentary Avaloka by Dhanika and the sub-commentary Laghuṭīkā by Bhaṭṭanṛsiṁha, ed. T. Venkatacharya, Adyar Library Series, No. 97 (Madras, 1969).

Gajapati Nārāyaṇadeva. *Gajapati Nārāyaṇadevaviracitaḥ Saṅgītanārāyaṇa* (Bhuvaneśvar, 1966).

Ghanaśyāmadāsa. *Saṅgītasāra Saṁgraha of Ghanaśyāmadasa,* ed. Svami Prajnanananda (Calcutta, 1956).

Harivaṁśa with Bhārata Bhāvadvīpa by Nīlakaṇṭha, ed. Ramachandra Sastri Kinjawadekar, Citrasala Press edition (Poona, 1933).

Hemacandra. *Kāvyānuśāsana* with alaṁkāracūḍāmaṇi and viveka by Ācārya Hemacandra, ed. R. C. Parikh, Shri Mahavir Jaina Vidyalaya, i-ii (Bombay, 1938).

Hemacandra. *The Kāvyānuśāsana of Hemacandra,* ed. Paṇḍit Shivadatta and Kashinath Pandurang Parab, Kavyamala, 71 (Bombay, 1901).

Jayantabhaṭṭa. *Āgamaḍambara,* ed. V. Raghavan and Anantalal Thakur, Mithilā Vidyāpiṭh (Darbhanga, 1964).

Jāya Senāpati. *Nṛtyaratnāvalī,* ed. V. Raghavan, Government Oriental Manuscripts Library (Madras, 1965).

Kālidāsa. *Abhijñānaśakuntalā of Kālidāsa,* with a commentary styled Arthadyotanikā of Rāghavabhaṭṭa, ed. M. R. Kale (Bombay, 1902).

Kālidāsa. *Mālavikāgnimitram* with commentary of Kāṭayavema, ed. Kashinath Pandurang Parab (Bombay, 1912).

Kālidāsa. *Mālavikāgnimitra of Kālidāsa,* ed. R. D. Karmakar, Bhandarkar Oriental Research Institute (Poona, 1950).

Kālidāsa. *Vikramorvaśīyam,* ed. H. D. Velankar (New Delhi, 1961).

Kauṭilya. *Arthaśāstra,* ed. R. Sharma Shastri, Government Oriental Library Series, No. 37 (Mysore, 1909).

Kumārilabhaṭṭa. *Tantravārtika* with Nyāyasudhā of Someśvara, Chowkhamba Sanskrit Series (Varanasi, 1909).

Mataṅga. *Bṛhaddeśī*, ed. K. S. Shastri, Trivandrum Sanskrit Series, No. 94 (Trivandrum, 1928).

Manusmṛti, ed. J. Jolly, Trübner Oriental Series (London, 1887).

Mahārāṇā Kumbhā. *Nṛtyaratnakośa*, ed. R. C. Parikh, Vol. I,No. 24, Rajasthan Oriental Research Institute (Jaipur, 1957).

Mahārāṇā Kumbhā. *Nṛtyaratnakośa*, ed. R. C. Parikh, Vol. II, No. 25, Rajasthan Oriental Research Institute (Jodhpur, 1968).

Mīmāṁsākośa, ed. Kevalānandasaraswatī, part. iii, Prajñāpāṭhaśālāmaṇḍalagranthamālā (Gangapuri, 1954).

Nandīkeśvara. *Abhinayadarpaṇa*, ed. and tr. by M. Ghosh, 3rd. ed. (Calcutta, 1975).

Nandīkeśvara. *Bharatārṇava*, ed. Vachaspati Gairola, Chowkhamba Amarabharati Prakashan (Varanasi, 1978).

Nārada. *Saṅgītamakaranda of Nārada*, ed. M. R. Telang, Gaekwad Oriental Series, No. 16 (Baroda, 1920).

Nārada. *Saṅgītamakaranda*, ed. Laksminarayan Garg, Sangeet Karyalaya (Hathras, 1978).

Pāṇini. *Aṣṭādhyāyī*, ed. Virajananda Daivakarani, Ārṣakanyā Gurukula Narelā (Delhi, 1977).

Pārśvadeva. *Saṅgītasamayasāra*, ed. Acharya Vrihaspati, Kundakundabhārati (Delhi, 1977).

Puṇḍarīka Viṭṭhala. *Die Śighrabodhini Nāmamāla Des Puṇḍarīka Viṭṭhala*, ed. A. Schmitt-Rouselle, Indica et Tibetica 7, (Bonn, 1985).

Rājaśekhara. *Karpūramañjarī*, ed. M. M. Ghosh (Calcutta, 1939).

Rājaśekhara. *Karpūramañjarī*, ed. Sten Konow, Harvard Oriental Series (Boston, 1901).

Rājaśekhara. *Kāvyamīmāṁsā*, ed. C. D. Dalal and R. A. Shastri, Gaekwad Oriental Series, No. 1, 3rd ed. (Baroda, 1934).

Rājānaka Ratnākara. *Haravijayam*, ed. Goparaju Rama, Ganganath Kendriya Sanskrit Vidyapith, Vols. I-II, No. 17 (Allahabad, 1983).

Rāmacandra and Guṇacandra. *Nāṭyadarpaṇa of Rāmacandra and Guṇacandra* with their own commentary, ed. G. K. Shrigodekar and L. B. Gandhi, Gaekwad Oriental Series, No. 48 (Baroda, 1929).

Śārṅgadeva. *Saṅgitaratnākara*, ed. S. S. Shastri, Adyar Library , Vols. I-IV (Madras, 1943-1953).**

Śārṅgadeva. *Saṅgitaratnākara*, tr. Kunjunni Raja and Radha Burnier, Adyar Library, Vol. IV (Madras, 1976).

Śārṅgadeva. *Saṅgitaratnākara of Śārṅgadeva*, text and tr. ed. R. K. Shringy and Premlata Sharma, Vol. I (New Delhi, 1978).

Śubhaṅkara. *Saṅgītadāmodara*, ed. G. Shastri and G. G. Mukhopadhyaya, Sanskrit College Series, No. 11 (Calcutta, 1960).

Śubhaṅkara. *The Hastamuktāvalī*, ed. Mahesvar Neog, Journal of the Music Academy (Madras, 1952-59), 23-30.

Śūdraka. *The Mṛcchakaṭika of Śūdraka*, ed. Hiranand Mularaj Sharma Shastri and Kashinath Pandurang Parab (Bombay, 1910).

Śrīharṣadeva. *Ratnāvalī*, ed. Ramnarayan Shastri (Pudukkotai, 1978).

Śrīharṣadeva. *The Ratnāvalī of Śrīharśadeva*, ed. N. B. Godbole and Kashinath Pandurang Parab (Bombay, 1890).

Śrīkaṇṭha. *Rasakaumudī of Śrīkaṇṭha, A Work on Music by Śrīkaṇṭha*, ed. A. N. Jani, Gaekwad Oriental Series, No.143 (Baroda, 1963).

Sāgaranandin. *The Nāṭakalakṣaṇaratnakośa*, ed. Myles Dillon, Vol. I (1937).

Sāgaranandin. *Nāṭakalakṣaṇaratnakośa*, Tr. Myles Dillon, Murray Fowler and V. Raghavan (Philadelphia, 1960).

Sāradātanaya. *Bhāvaprakāśanam of Sāradātanaya*, ed. Y. Y. Svami of Melkote and K. S. Ramasvami Shastri Shiromani, Gaekwad Oriental Series, No. 45 (Baroda, 1968).

Sudhākalaśa. *Saṅgītopaniṣatsāroddhāra*, a work on music and dancing by Vācanācārya Sudhākalaśa, ed. U. P. Shah, Gaekwad Oriental Series, No. 133 (Baroda, 1961).

Suttāgame, ed. Pupphabhikkhu, part ii (Gurgaon, 1954), pp. 55-56.

Somadeva. *Kathāsaritsāgara,* ed Pandit Durgaprasad and Kashinath - - Pandurang Parab (Bombay, 1930).

Someśvara. *Mānasollāsa,* ed. G. K. Shrigondekar, Gaekwad Oriental Series, No. 138 (Baroda, 1961).

Udyotana. *Kuvalayamālā,* ed. A. N. Upadhyaye (Bombay, 1959).

Vararuci. *Ubhayābhisārikā,* ed. T. Venkatacharya and A. K. Warder (Madras, 1967).

Vāgbhaṭa. *The Kāvyānuśāsana,* ed. Pandit Shivadatta and Kashināth Pandurang Parab, Kavyamala, 43 (Bombay,1894).

Vātsyāyana. *Kāmasūtra,* ed. Mahesh Pal, revised 2nd ed., Tridivnath Roy (Calcutta, 1980).

Vedasūri. *Saṅgītamakaranda,* ed. K. V. Vasudeva Shastri, Journal of the Tanjore SaraswathiMahal Library (Tanjore, 1955-58).

Vipradāsa. *Saṅgītacandra,* ed, P. Sri Ramacandrudu (Hyderabad, 1982).

Viśvanātha. *Sāhityadarpaṇa,* ed, P. V. Kane (Bombay, 1923).

Viṣṇudharmottarapurāṇa, ed. Dr. Priyabala Shah, Gaekwad Oriental Series, Vols. I and III (Baroda, 1958, 1961).

*All references to the *Nāṭyaśāstra* are to the G. O. S edition of the *Nāṭyaśāstra* unless otherwise stated.

**All references to the *Saṅgītaratnākara* are to the Adyar Library edition of the *Saṅgītaratnākara* unless otherwise stated.

***All references to the *Nartananirṇaya* are to the India Office Library Ms. unless otherwise stated.

General Works

Ambrose, Kay. *Classical Dances and Costumes of India* (London, 1950).

Aufrecht, Theodore. *Catalogi Codicum Manuscriptorum Bibliothecae Bodleianae pars octava, Codices Sanscriticoes Complectens* (Oxford, 1864).

Bhatt, G. K. *Bharata Nāṭya Mañjarī*, Bhandarkar Oriental Research Institute, No. 12 (Poona, 1975).

Bhatt, G. K. *Theatric Aspects of Sanskrit Drama*, Bhandarkar Oriental Research Institute, No. 18 (Poona, 1983).

Bhārati, Shivaji. *The Art of Mohiniyattam* (New Delhi, 1986).

Bose, Mandakranta. *Classical Indian Dancing* (Calcutta, 1970).

-- A Critical and Comparative Study of Sanskrit Texts Dealing with Dancing, Ms. B.Litt. Thesis, D1008, Oxford University, 1964.

Bowers, Faubion. *The Dance in India* (New York, 1953).

Burrow, Thomas and M. B. Emeneau. *A Dravidian Etymological Dictionary* (Oxford, 1961).

Byrski, M. Christopher. *Concept of Indian Theatre* (New Delhi, 1974).

Chattopadhyaya,Gayatri. *Bharater Nrityakala* (Calcutta, 1978).

Chattopadhyaya, Siddheswar. *Nāṭkalakṣaṇaratnakośa in the Perspective of Ancient Drama and Dramaturgy* (Calcutta, 1974).

Classical and Folk Dances of India (Bombay, 1953).

Coomarswamy, Ananda. *The Dance of Śiva*, Essays on Indian Art and Culture (New York, 1985).

Coomarswamy, Ananda and Gopala Kristnayya Duggirila. *The Mirror of Gesture*, Being the Abhinaya Darpaṇa of Nandikeśvara, 2nd ed. (New Delhi, 1970).

Dasgupta, S. N. and S. K. De, *A History of Sanskrit Literature*, Vols. I.-II (Calcutta, 1961).

Devi, Ragini, *Dance Dialects of India* (Delhi, 1972).

De Zoete, Beryl. *The Other Mind* (London, 1953).

Gerow, Edwin. "Indian Poetics," *A History of Indian Literature*, No. 5 (Wiesbaden, 1977).

Ghosh, M. M. *Contributions to the History of Hindu Drama* (Calcutta, 1958).

Gupta, Manjul. *A Study of Abhinavabhāratī on Bharata's Nāṭyaśāstra and Avaloka on Dhanajaya's Daśarūpaka* (Delhi, 1987).

Iyer, K. Bharata, *Kathakali: The Sacred Dance-drama of Malabar* (London, 1955).

Jacob, Colonel G. A. *Laukikanyāñjaliḥ, A Handful of Popular Maxims in Sanskrit Literature* (Bombay, 1900).

Janaki, S. S. A Critical Study of the Caturbhāṇī and An Account of Bhāṇas in Sanskrit Literature, Ms. D. Phil. Thesis, D5219, Oxford University (1971).

Kavi, Ramakrishna. *Bharatakośa* (Tirupati, 1951).

Kane, P.V. *History of Sanskrit Poetics* (Delhi, 1961).

Katz, Jonathan. The Musical Portions of the Saṅgītanārāyaṇa: a critical edition and commentary, Ms. D. Phil. Thesis, C6899-6900, Oxford University, (1987).

Keith, A. B. *The Sanskrit Drama* (Oxford, 1924).

Kendadamath, G. C. *Indian Music and Dance, A Select Bibliography* (Varanasi, 1986).

Khokar, Mohan. *Traditions of Indian Classical Dance* (Delhi, 1979).

Krishnamachariar, M. *History of Classical Sanskrit Literature,* 3rd ed. (Delhi,1974).

Lath, Mukund, *A Study of Dattilam, A Treatise on the Sacred Music of Ancient India* (New Delhi, 1978).

Levi, Sylvain. *Le Theatre Indian* (Paris, 1890).

Mankad, D. R. *The Types of Sanskrit Drama* (Karachi, 1936).

Monier-Williams, Monier. *A Sanskrit English Dictionary* (Oxford, 1899, repr. 1960).

Naidu, V. Narayanasvami, Naidu, P. Srinivasulu and Pantulu, V. Rangayya. *Tāṇḍava Lakṣaṇam* (Madras, 1936).

Nijenhuis, Emmie Te. "Musicological Literature," *A History of Indian Literature,* No. 6 (Wiesbaden, 1977).

Patnaik, Dhirendranath. *Odissi Dance* (Bhuvanesvar, 1971).

Poddar, Ram Prakash. *An Introduction to Karpūramañjarī,* with text and Hindi tr., Prakrit Jain Institute Research Publications, No. 11 (Vaishali, 1974).

Prajñānānanda, Swamī. *Saṅgīt o Saṁskṛti,* Bhāratīya Saṅgīter Itihās, Vol. I (Calcutta, 1953).

-- *Historical Development of Indian Music: A Critical Study* (Calcutta, 1960).

Rāghavan,V. *Bhoja's Śṛṅgāra Prakāśa* (Madras, 1963).

-- *Abhinavagupta and His Works.* Chowkhamba Oriental Research Studies, No. 20 (Varanasi, 1980).

Rocher, Ludo. "The Purāṇas," *A History of Indian Literature,* No. 26 (Wiesbaden, 1986).

Scharfe, Hartmut. "Grammatical Literature," *A History of Indian Literature,* No. 5 (Wiesbaden, 1977).

Shastri, Ajay Mitra. *India As Seen in the Kuṭṭanīmatam of Dāmodaragupta* (Delhi, 1975).

Shastri, Surendranath. *The Laws and Practice of Sanskrit Drama,* Chowkhamba Sanskrit Series, No, 14 (Varanasi, 1961).

Shekhar, I. *Sanskrit Drama: Its Origin and Decline,* 2nd ed. (Delhi, 1977).

Smith, David James. *Ratnākara's Haravijayam, An Introduction to the Sanskrit Court Epic* (Delhi, 1985).

Srinivasan, Srinivasa Ayya. *On the Composition of the Nāṭyaśāstra,* Studien Zur Indologie Und Iranistik, No. 1 (Reinbek, 1980).

Subrahmanyam, Padma. *Bharatha's Art: Then and Now,* Bhulabhai Memorial Institute, Bombay, and Nrithyodaya, Madras (1979).

Sushma Rani, *Āgamaḍambara Nāṭaka: eka adhyana* (Delhi, 1987).

Tarlekar, G. H. *Studies in the Nāṭyaśāstra,* with special reference to the Sanskrit drama in performance (Delhi, 1975).

Varma, K. M. *Nāṭya, Nṛtta and Nṛtya: Their Meaning and Relation* (Calcutta, 1957).

Vatsyayan, Kapila. *Dance Sculpture in Sarangapani Temple* (Madras, 1982).

-- *Dance in Indian Painting* (New Delhi, 1982).

-- *Indian Classical Dance* (New Delhi,1974).

-- *Classical Indian Dance in Literature and the Arts* (New Delhi, 1968).

Vogel, Claus. "Indian Lexicography," *A History of Indian Literature*, No. 5 (Wiesbaden, 1974).

Warder, A. K. *Indian Kavya Literature*, vols. I-IV (New Delhi, 1972-83).

Articles

Agarwala, V. S. "The Śiva Tāṇḍava Stotra of Rāvaṇa," *Journal of the Oriental Institute*, M. S. University of Baroda, no. x (Baroda, 1960), 18-21.

Benesh, Rudolph, Joan Benesh and Mariane Balchin. "Notating Indian Dance," *Sangeet Natak*, no. 9 (New Delhi, 1968), 5-24.

Bhattacharya, Ashutosh, "Mask Dances of Bengal," *Sangeet Natak*, no. 7 (1968), 5-12.

Bose, Mandakranta. "*Nartananirṇaya:* A Neglected Source of Classical Indian Dancing," *South Asian Horizons*, vol. I (1984), 52-58.

-- "Śāstra and Prayoga: The Use of *Abhinayadarpaṇa*," paper read at the American Oriental Society's Conference, Chicago, 1988; in press: *The Samskrita Ranga*,.felicitation volume for S.S. Janaki, (Madras, 1991).

-- "The Textual Source of Odissi," unpublished paper read at the American Oriental Society's Conference, Chicago, 1987.

Byrski, Christopher. "Is Kudiyattam a Museum piece?" *Sangeet Natak*, no. 5 (New Delhi, 1967), 45-54.

Chattopadhyaya, Aparna. "The Institution of 'Devadasis' according to the Kathāsaritsāgara," *Journal of the Oriental Institute,* M. S. University of Baroda, no. xvi (Baroda, 1967), 216-22.

Gode, P. K. "Notes on Indian Chronology," *The Poona Orientalist* (Poona, 1936-37), 26-29, 33-42, 55-64, 47-49.

Iyer, E. K. "Bhagavata Mela Dance Drama of Bharatanatya," *Sangeet Natak,* no. 13 (New Delhi, 1964), 46-56.

Kalyanpurkar, M. S. "The Technique of Kathak: Nritta," in *Classical and Folk Dances of India,* part iii (Bombay, 1963).

Katz, Jonathan. "Indian Musicological Literature and its context," *Purussartha* , no. 7 (Paris, 1983), 57-75.

Khokar, Mohan. "Technique and Repertory," in *Classical and Folk Dances of India,* part iii (Bombay, 1963), 28-31.

-- "Natya: Bhagavata Mela and Kuchipudi," in *Classical and Folk Dances of India,* part i (Bombay, 1963), 27-36.

-- "The Tradition: A Brief Historical Survey," in *Classical and Folk Dances of India,* part ii (Bombay, 1963).

-- "Dance and Ritual in Manipur," *Sangeet Natak,* no. 10 (New Delhi, 1968), 35-53.

Krishna Chaitanya. "The Aesthetics of Kathakali," *Sangeet Natak,* no. 8 (New Delhi, 1968), 5-10.

Kothari, Sunil. "Bhārater Śāstrīya Nṛtyakalā," *Desh* Vinodan issue (Calcutta, 1987), 58-65.

-- "Sabdaswarapata Dance," *Sangeet Natak,* no. 18 (New Delhi, 1970), 31-38.

-- "Gotipua Dancers of Orissa," *Sangeet Natak*, no. 8 (New Delhi, 1968), 31-43.

Menon, Devaki, "The 'Kuttu' of the Kerala Theatre," *Journal of the Music Academy*, no. xxv (Madras,1954), 122-29.

Misra, Minati. "A Glimpse Into Odissi Dance," *Dances of India* (Madras, 1981), 87-92.

Patnaik, D. N. "History and Technique of Odissi Dance," *Sangeet Natak*, no. 5 (New Delhi, 1967), 55-56.

Pancal, Govardhan. "Sanskrit Drama of Kerala," *Sangeet Natak*, no. 8 (New Delhi, 1968), 17-30.

"Kuṭiyāṭṭam and its links with Classical Sanskrit Theatre," *Journal of the Oriental Institute*, M. S. University of Baroda, no. xxvi (Baroda, 1977).

Pani, Jiwan. "A Comparative Study of Saraikela and Mayurbhanj Forms," *Sangeet Natak*, no. 13 (New Delhi, 1969), 33-45.

Pollock, S. "The Theory of Practice and the Practice of Theory in Indian Intellectual History," *Journal of the American Oriental Society*, no. 105, iii (New Haven, 1985).

Raghavan, V. "Writers Quoted in the Abhinavabhāratī," *Journal of Oriental Research* (Madras, 1932).

-- "Nāṭyadharmī and Lokadharmī," *Journal of Oriental Research*, .no. xxv (Madras, 1933), 359-375.

-- "A Note on the name Daśarūpaka," *Journal of Oriental Research* (Madras, 1933).

-- "The Hastamuktāvalī of Śubhaṅkara: A Brief Note," *Journal of the Music Academy*, no. iv (Madras, 1933), 16- 24, 50-84.

-- "Bhagavata Mela Nāṭaka," *Journal of the Indian Society of Oriental Art* (Calcutta, 1937), 167-70.

-- "Sabdas," *Journal of the Music Academy*, no. xx (Madras, 1949), 160-62.

-- "Uparūpakas and Nṛtyaprabandhas," *The Samskrita Ranga Annual*, no. xxi (Madras, 1950), 37.

-- "Some Corrections and Emendations to the Text of the Abhinavabhāratī," *Adyar Library Bulletin*, no. 18 (Madras, 1954), 196-209.

-- "Some Names in Early Sangita Literature," *Bulletin of the Sangit Natak Academy*, no. 5 (New Delhi, 1956), 19-28; no. 6 (New Delhi, 1957), 23-30.

-- "Later Sangita Literature," *Bulletin of the Sangit Natak Academy*, no. 17 (New Delhi, 1960), 1-24; no. 18 (New Delhi, 1961), 1-18.

-- "Veethi Bhagavatam of Andhra," *Sangeet Natak*, no. 10 (New Delhi, 1969), 33-36.

Ragini Devi. "Indian Dance," *Journal of the Music Academy*, no. iv (Madras, 1933), 153-54.

Raja, Kunjunni. "Kṛṣṇaāṭṭam," *Journal of the Music Academy*, no. xxix (Madras, 1958), 121-29.

Rajagopalan, L. S. "Damayanti in Nalacharitam," *Sangeet Natak*, no. 14 (New Delhi, 1969), 30-39.

Ramachandran, K. V. "The Grace Notes of Dance," *Journal of the Music Academy*, no. xxv (Madras, 1933), 93-100.

-- "Music and Dance in Kālidāsa," *Journal of Oriental Research,*, no. xviii (Madras, 1948), 116-35.

Rao, Maya. "The Hastas in Kathak," in *Classical and Folk Dances of India*, part iii (Bombay, 1963), 44-47.

Raphy, Sabeena. "Chavittu-Nāṭaka – Dramatic Opera of Kerala," *Sangeet Natak*, no. 12 (New Delhi, 1969).

Rele, Kanak. "Mohiniaattam," *Dances of India* (Madras, 1981), 67-71.

Rocher, Ludo. "The Textual Tradition of the Bhāratīyanāṭyaśāstra: A Philological Assessment," Wiener Zeitschrift Fur Die Kunde Sudasiens und Archiv Fur Indische Philosophie, Sonderdruck Aus Band, xxv (Wien, 1981), 107-130.

Sandesara, B. J. "Cultural Data of Vasudeva Hindi," *Journal of the Oriental Institute*, M. S. University of Baroda, no. x (Baroda, 1960), 7-17.

Sharma, V. Venkatarama. "Bharata Nāṭya," *Journal of the Music Academy* (Madras, 1930), 32-37.

Shastri, K. V. "Literature and Other Sources in Indian Classical Dances," *Journal of the Tanjore Saraswathi Mahal Library*, no. xii (Tanjore, 1958), 1-12.

Singh, E. Nilkanta, "Classical Tradition of Naṭa Movements," *Sangeet Natak*, no. 10 (New Delhi, 1968), 26-34.

Upadhyaya, K. S. "Yaksagana Bayalata," *Sangeet Natak*, no. 11 (New Delhi, 1969), 37-51.

Varadapande, M. L. "Performing Arts and Kautilya's Arthaśāstra," *Sangeet Natak*, no. 41 (New Delhi, 1976), 45-54.

-- "Theatrical Arts in Jataka Tales," *Sangeet Natak*, no. 38 (New Delhi, 1975),29-34.

Vatsyayan, Kapila. "Kathak," *Journal of the Music Academy,* no. xxvii (Madras, 1956), 74-88.

-- "Sanskrit Drama in Performance," *Dance or Movement Techniques of Sanskrit Theatre* (Honolulu, 1972).

-- "Is there an Indian Modern Drama?" *Sangeet Natak,* no. 7 (New Delhi, 1968), 85-91.

-- "The 108 Karaṇas," *Sangeet Natak,* no. 3 (New Delhi, 1966), 51-62.

-- "Classical Indian Sculpture and Dancing," *Journal of the Oriental Institute,* no. xi (Baroda, 1962), 247-59.

INDEX

A

Ū

E

AI

O

KA

GHA

CA

ḌHA

TA

DA

PA

BA

BHA

MA

YA

RA

LA

VA

Śa

ṢA

SA

HA